The Eleme
Literacy

Julie Lindquist
Michigan State University

David Seitz
Wright State University

Longman

New York   San Francisco   Boston
London   Toronto   Sydney   Tokyo   Singapore   Madrid
Mexico City   Munich   Paris   Cape Town   Hong Kong   Montreal

Executive Editor: Lynn M. Huddon
Senior Marketing Manager: Sandra McGuire
Production Manager: Stacey Kulig
Project Coordination, Text Design, and Electronic Page Makeup:
    S4Carlisle Publishing Services
Cover Designer/Manager: John Callahan
Senior Manufacturing Buyer: Roy Pickering
Printer and Binder: Courier Corporation
Cover Printer: Phoenix Color Corporation

For permission to use copyrighted material, grateful acknowledgment is made to the copyright holders on p. 245, which are hereby made part of this copyright page.

Library of Congress Cataloging-in-Publication Data

Lindquist, Julie.
    The elements of literacy / Julie Lindquist, David Seitz.
        p. cm. — (The elements of composition series)
    Includes bibliographical references and index.
    ISBN-13: 978-0-321-32891-5
    ISBN-10: 0-321-32891-4
    1. Literacy.   2. Language arts.   I. Seitz, David.   II. Title.

LC149.L44 2008
302.2'244—dc22   2008045135

1 2 3 4 5 6 7 8 9 10—CRW—11 10 09 08

Longman
is an imprint of

www.ablongman.com

ISBN 13: 978-0-321-32891-5
ISBN 10:   0-321-32891-4

Contents

Preface for Teachers

To Our Colleagues:

If there's one thing we've learned in our lives as teachers and researchers, it's how vast and contested the conceptual landscape of literacy really is. Everyone—politicians to policymakers to academics to parents—claims to know what literacy is, what it's good for, and how we should use it. As teachers and researchers of literacy, we know that "literacy" names a varied set of assumptions, histories, practices, and research topics. And we know how much its uses differ widely across publics and discourse communities.

Furthermore, any critical discussion of literacy invariably leads to the recognition of multiple ways of communicating, whether these involve alphabetic print or multimedia forms. When we teach about literacy, we see how difficult it is to draw stable boundaries around the human activities (and interdisciplinary inquiries) the term encompasses. We also see how important it is to situate research on literacy culturally and historically within scenes of everyday social practice.

This book aims to map out and identify the questions and issues central to literacy studies over the past 30 years. To draw this map, we have concentrated on five sites of literacy research and practice:

- **Mind:** cognitive studies and theories of literacy and orality
- **Culture:** ethnographic research on literacy
- **Class:** effects of social class on literacy practices, education, and opportunity
- **Work:** workplace literacies in the information economy
- **Technology:** social uses and effects of digital and multimodal literacies

Obviously (as we explain in Chapter One), there are other equally important sites we could have emphasized—race and history, for example.

Nevertheless, we believe these five sites very much overlap with these other contexts that we have not featured.

We intend this map of five sites as a conceptual introduction to broad but foundational questions and issues related to literacy as a field of study and as a domain of practice. It introduces questions for writers, future teachers, and beginning researchers: What is literacy? In what ways is literacy talked about in and out of educational institutions? How do we know what we know about literacy, and how can we find out more? In whose interests are its terms and uses defined? How do literacy practices vary in space and over time?

We imagine that this book will be most useful for

- undergraduate students interested in learning more about the connections between reading/writing/composing and culture,

- students in English education programs preparing to teach English Language Arts, and

- advanced undergraduates or beginning graduates preparing to move into fields (such as Education and Composition and Rhetoric) that will require qualitative research on literacy.

We have conceived this book as an introductory pedagogy, designed to introduce concepts by asking students to theorize about literacy practices from their experiences with schooling, community life, work, and technology. The sequence of the five "sites" in the book is organized so that each chapter elaborates upon and complicates the lessons of the prior chapter. While the chapters can be approached as independent units, we think the book will be most effective read from beginning to end, so that what is learned in working through each chapter can be used as set of resources for the next. This conceptual scaffolding makes *Elements of Literacy* less modular than many texts, but we believe that its subject matter—complex and wide-ranging as it is—warrants an approach that works from a carefully planned pedagogical infrastructure. This is why we've organized the book into "sites" of literacy—to enable well-grounded inquiries into literacy as cultural practice while supporting the conceptual complexity involved in such conversations.

In each chapter we have framed the discussion of literacy research for that particular site around popular scenes that represent literacy values and practices—films, TV shows, and news parodies, for instance. These popular scenes provide relevant stories to help students understand key concepts and research approaches. Some of these popular references are very recent, and some less so. In each case, however, we have chosen scenes from popular culture that help illuminate the historical contexts that helped shape the assumptions about literacy for a particular site. In the case of those with which students may be less familiar, we encourage you to invite your students to find their own connections to the narratives they know from their own popular culture(s).

To help readers, the text contains three different kinds of "signposting" mechanisms.

- *Definition* boxes call attention to key terms and concepts.
- *Activity* boxes suggest activities to explore particular questions or concepts.
- *Focus point* boxes invite students to pause and reflect on complex ideas.

Each chapter also includes a brief "For Further Reading" list of sources to support students' learning and ongoing research projects.

Unlike most textbooks in English studies, we have provided fully detailed Projects and Activities for students that draw from a variety of disciplinary perspectives and genres. We developed these projects with our own students' motivations in mind, building on their knowledge and their creativity. Activities and projects appear in three places: (1) at relevant moments within chapters, (2) at the end of each chapter, and (3) in the appendix at the end of the book. These can be adapted for use as long-term projects, shorter heuristic activities, or in-class activities.

We have intentionally provided detailed steps for each project and activity, which should particularly help teachers new to literacy studies. These steps can be shortened and used to direct discussion or to structure shorter, in-class activities. For teachers and students who want greater guidance with research methods and approaches, the Project Appendix explains the steps involved in various ways of approaching research and writing on literacy (such as analysis/critique, ethnographic interviews, field study, dialogues, and manifestos).

We hope you and your students find *Elements of Literacy* to be both inviting and thought-provoking.

Julie Lindquist and David Seitz

Acknowledgments

Thanks to Bill Covino for his faith in our work and his ongoing support of the project, and to Eben Ludlow, who helped to launch the project. We are exceedingly grateful for the wisdom of the following reviewers, who read our manuscript with great care and deep intelligence, and who offered suggestions that have made this a much better book: Irene Clark, California State University, Northridge; James Countryman, University of Minnesota; Gwen Gorzelsky, Wayne State University; Patricia Jenkins, University of Alaska; Elizabeth Chiseri-Strater, University of North Carolina at Greensboro; and Seth Kahn, West Chester University of Pennsylvania. We thank our colleagues on WPA-L, who have so often come to our aid in locating just the right examples of popular media for our purposes. And, of course, many thanks to Ginny Blandford, who stepped in at a critical moment and saw the project through to its conclusion.

Julie wishes to thank the support and intellectual companionship of her colleagues at Michigan State University—especially Laura Julier, Malea Powell, and Leonora Smith, who have read outlines and drafts of this work and have always pointed directly to the thing that needed doing. Their intelligence, expert advice, and fine editorial skills show up all over this work. Both Danielle DeVoss and Jeff Grabill offered expert advice on sources in technology and workplace issues. David thanks his dear colleagues Nancy Mack and Peggy Lindsey for their suggestions and shoulders throughout the project. He also appreciates the advice of pop connoisseurs and former graduate students Rob Boley and Bill Bicknell.

Finally, we would like to thank our families. For Julie: My husband, Richard Hallstein; my son Jonas; and my mother, Doris Lindquist. For David: His soulmate Daniele, and his sons Eli and Josh, who helped him learn about gaming literacies. All have made our commitment to this project, just as they make all our work, possible.

1

Introduction

Journal Sentinel/Stuart Carlson

"If you teach a child how to read, they will pass a reading test."
—President George W. Bush

> *"Although literacy is a problem of pressing national concern,*
> *we have yet to discover or set its boundaries"*
> —*Scribner and Cole, "Metaphors," paraphrasing*
> *George McGovern in 1978*

In 2004, the following story ("Nonhuman Factors") appeared in the *Dayton Daily News*:

When the Dayton school board asked principals in a November meeting to share their workplace concerns, the room boiled over with frustration. The No. 1 topic—testing.

Boxes had arrived at each of the city's elementary schools filled with something new. The state of Ohio would now require teachers in kindergarten through second grade to give new diagnostic tests.

These tests are long and complex. For the youngest children, teachers needed more than an hour of one-on-one time with each child to administer it.

Kemp Elementary School Principal Burt Thompson, a 37-year educator and principal for 14 years, had seen enough.

"Teachers had a concern they were not going to be able to meet their goals for instructional time," he said. "Some teachers got three binders full of test material."

The federal No Child Left Behind Act has sparked an explosion of new tests. The 2002 law requires states to test all students in grades three through eight each year in reading and math and to develop a high school exam by the 2005–06 school year.

With new tests have come problems. Ohio ultimately was forced to back off its plans to test all students in kindergarten through second grade, agreeing in late November to shelve those tests for a year in the face of a near mutiny by teachers and principals across the state who, like those in Dayton, were fed up.

A study for Congress by the General Accounting Office last year estimated states will need to create more than 433 tests to satisfy what the No Child Left Behind law requires.

Dayton Daily News (Ohio), May 23, 2004, Sunday City Edition

BYLINE: Scott Elliott and Mark Fisher

We live in a world (or at least, a country) of high-stakes testing. In the current political climate, testing—its uses, its benefits, its hazards, and its conduct—dominates public conversation about schooling and "achievement." The news story just excerpted goes on to describe the effects of the new explosion of standardized testing requirements brought about by

No Child Left Behind (NCLB): increased reliance on the few testing companies responsible for creating standardized tests, pressure on teachers to prepare students for tests at the expense of other lessons and curricula, an enormous increase in the numbers of administrative personnel needed to manage the tests, and a high-stakes atmosphere in which errors of test design or accounting have serious consequences for students' futures. The practice of building educational policy around standardized testing has various stakes and stakeholders: it affects the lives of students, parents, teachers, and communities.

Why begin a book about literacy with a discussion of testing? Most people would agree that tests are a measure of literacy—that they index whether or not a person can read and write across subject areas and in general. But what if, as the news story seems to suggest, tests are "about" literacy in other ways? What if tests, as one example of how views of literacy are enacted in policy, help us to see how definitions of literacy matter in the "real world"?

Considering the various stakeholders involved in high-stakes testing, and, in particular, the No Child Left Behind Act signed in January of 2002, brings us to the important questions about literacy—what it is, what it does, and what its "effects" are—that structure our discussions in chapters to follow:

- What does "literacy" mean—and for whom?

- How do perspectives on literacy change when viewed from different (cultural, social, institutional) locations?

- When (in response to what social and historical forces) do definitions and uses of literacy seem to change?

- Who is affected by which definitions of literacy?

A closer look at the No Child Left Behind Act is instructive for what it stands to teach us about the importance of questions of definition, use, and effect when it comes to thinking about literacy. According to the *Dayton Daily News* piece, the explosion of testing is a direct result of recent changes in national educational policy. The No Child Left Behind Act has a very special definition of literacy behind it: Literacy is a technical skill that can be easily identified, quantified, and measured—and claims for the democratizing potential of NCLB have to be evaluated in light of this fundamental view of what literacy is and how it works. Proponents of NCLB describe the policy as an investment by the federal government in public education. On its website (*http://www.ed.gov/nclb/ overview/intro/4pillars.html*), the Department of Education describes the primary features, or "four pillars," of NCLB as follows:

Stronger Accountability for Results

Under No Child Left Behind, states are working to close the achievement gap and make sure all students, including those who are disadvantaged, achieve academic proficiency. Annual state and school district report cards inform parents and communities about state and school progress. Schools that do not make progress must provide supplemental services, such as free tutoring or after-school assistance; take corrective actions; and, if still not making adequate yearly progress after five years, make dramatic changes to the way the school is run.

More Freedom for States and Communities

Under No Child Left Behind, states and school districts have unprecedented flexibility in how they use federal education funds. For example, it is possible for most school districts to transfer up to 50 percent of the federal formula grant funds they receive under the Improving Teacher Quality State Grants, Educational Technology, Innovative Programs, and Safe and Drug-Free Schools programs to any one of these programs, or to their Title I program, without separate approval. This allows districts to use funds for their particular needs, such as hiring new teachers, increasing teacher pay, and improving teacher training and professional development.

Proven Education Methods

No Child Left Behind puts emphasis on determining which educational programs and practices have been proven effective through rigorous scientific research. Federal funding is targeted to support these programs and teaching methods that work to improve student learning and achievement. In reading, for example, No Child Left Behind supports scientifically-based instruction programs in the early grades under the Reading First program and in preschool under the Early Reading First program.

More Choices for Parents

Parents of children in low-performing schools have new options under No Child Left Behind. In schools that do not meet state standards for at least two consecutive years, parents may transfer their children to a better-performing public school, including a public charter school, within their district. The district must provide transportation, using Title I funds if necessary. Students from low-income families in schools that fail to meet state standards for at least three years are eligible to receive supplemental educational services, including tutoring, after-school services, and summer school. Also, students who attend a persistently dangerous school or are the victim of a violent crime while in their school have the option to attend a safe school within their district.

Even though these central features of the policy, taken together, appear to suggest increased flexibility and freedom for students and parents, the major operating principle of NCLB is *accountability*—the practice of measuring performed knowledge and using these measurements to distribute rewards and punishments to institutions. Through NCLB, money is directed according to results—that is, schools whose students perform well on annual standardized tests are rewarded with money; funds are withheld from those that don't measure up. The NCLB Executive Summary emphasizes the policy's commitment to the practice of distributing monetary rewards to schools on the basis of measured performance:

INCREASED ACCOUNTABILITY

The NCLB Act will strengthen Title I accountability by requiring States to implement statewide accountability systems covering all public schools and students. These systems must be based on challenging State standards in reading and mathematics, annual testing for all students in grades 3–8, and annual statewide progress objectives ensuring that all groups of students reach proficiency within 12 years. Assessment results and State progress objectives must be broken out by poverty, race, ethnicity, disability, and limited English proficiency to ensure that no group is left behind. School districts and schools that fail to make adequate yearly progress (AYP) toward statewide proficiency goals will, over time, be subject to improvement, corrective action, and restructuring measures aimed at getting them back on course to meet State standards. Schools that meet or exceed AYP objectives or close achievement gaps will be eligible for State Academic Achievement Awards.

As the language of "corrective action" suggests, there are clear consequences for schools that don't meet annual yearly progress targets. If a school doesn't meet AYP for a third year, it has to pay for tutoring for students (or contract these services) and it must continue to allow students to transfer to other schools. After 4 years, "corrective actions" become more serious—appointing outside advisors, mandating longer school days or years, and dismissing teachers alleged to be responsible for the failure. After 5 years, school staff will be purged, and the school will either become a charter program or will be handed to a private management firm.

When we look closely at the effects of policies like NCLB, it becomes clear how the practice of testing expresses beliefs about what literacy is and how it works. Consider President George W. Bush's remarks in a 2004 National Institutes of Health speech about Reading First, a competitive grant program under NCLB created to help states and districts to implement "scientific, research-based" reading programs for children in elementary school:

> **THE PRESIDENT:** You know, people are going to say, well, that sounds good. How do you know it works? And, as you know, I'm a how-do-you-know-it-works kind of guy. Reid mentioned there is a debate. Governors are very familiar with the reading curriculum debate and there are some very strong opinions about what might work, what might not work. I'm the kind of fellow that says, you ought to be able to figure it out pretty clearly.
>
> Why are you so certain that your attitude is the right attitude?
>
> **THE PRESIDENT:** Good. This is based upon science, is what I'm telling you. And if you've got something that works, then it makes sense to spread the news. So that's what we're talking about here: How do we make sure the research that has been done here in Washington is shared around the country?
>
> *(http://www.whitehouse.gov/news/releases/2004/05/20040512-8.html)*

In taking up the matter of how literacy teachers should be properly educated, President Bush emphasizes the need to correct defects in current teacher education programs, remarking that "one of the things we have to address is why teacher colleges aren't teaching reading teachers how to teach in the first place, so you don't need to retrain."

In keeping with the accountability principles of NCLB, President Bush's remarks suggest that literacy is a simple matter, something that anybody "ought to be able to figure . . . out pretty clearly," and that answers to what literacy *is* can be reliably found through science (elsewhere in the speech, in fact, President Bush corrects what he sees as false notions about literacy, declaring that "reading is more of a science than people think"). If literacy is seen as a stable, easily quantifiable, measurable piece of technical knowledge, then policies and programs will enact these beliefs—and these enactments will have consequences for schools, students, parents, and communities. As the *Dayton Daily News* piece suggests, though sitting down to take a test may seem like a simple act, such an act of literacy is anything but simple. One very important question is this: Who wins and who loses when particular definitions of literacy are enacted?

What Does Literacy Mean?

It depends on who "we" are, and on what defining literacy in one way or another lets us get done or make happen. The definition of literacy is an especially difficult thing to pin down: what does "an act of literacy" entail, exactly? While it's possible to say, for example, "Jane loved her dog," you can't say "Jane literacied her students." As our friend and colleague Seth Kahn has pointed out, literacy is an abstract noun with no corresponding verb to tell us what range of actions might possibly be associated with it. An act of literacy can entail everything from finding a book to decoding print on the page to instant messaging a friend about a writing project. And yet, while it's common for people to be as evangelical about the importance and benefits of literacy as they are vague about its actual meaning, the examples of educational policies we've introduced here indicate that definitions of literacy do not remain abstractions of exclusive interest to educational philosophers, but instead have very real effects in real-world domains (as in, for example, schools—but also, as we will see, in other places, such as communities and workplaces). Although most people talk very much as if "literacy" has a meaning that is both stable and transparent (e.g., confident assertions like "lack of literacy keeps people from getting jobs" or "video gaming is making kids these days illiterate" or "when it comes to political decision making, the voting public is illiterate"), if you pause for a moment and consider these claims, you'll notice that very different assumptions about what literacy "is" are at work even in these three commonly expressed propositions: that literacy is a quantifiable workplace skill; that literacy refers to practiced engagement with print texts; that literacy has to do with higher-order information processing and reasoning skills. In President Bush's words noted earlier, we can see the following definitions of literacy at work: literacy teaching and learning is a scientific endeavor ("this is based on science"), is easily quantifiable and measurable as a skill ("you've got to measure"), is transparent ("you ought to be able to figure it out"), and is a finite body of knowledge with easily identifiable boundaries (teachers who know "how to teach in the first place" don't need to "retrain").

If you type "what is literacy?" into a Google search box, you'll wind up with something like 2600 hits. (This isn't as many as you'll get for "what is love," to take an example of another notoriously difficult-to-define word—that comes in at 14,900—but it's still quite a lot.) Yet *literacy* is one of those words, like *love*, that people use commonly and confidently, as if its meaning were transparent and stable. Regardless, there are implicit meanings at work in uses of either of these words (consider, by analogy, the consequences of very different ideas of what *love* means for a married couple, one of whom assumes love means "coexisting in comfortable silence," while the other thinks it means "intimacy through frequent conversation"). In looking at the educational practices of NCLB testing mandates, we can see how powerful definitions of literacy can be, even when—and perhaps especially when—they are implicit.

The current fascination with standardized testing as realized through the No Child Left Behind Act is a fair illustration of just how deeply definitions of literacy are rooted in historical, political, and cultural contingencies. These definitions not only underwrite public discussions of literacy, but also drive the policies that affect people's lives: at

---

Focus Point

Consider the following posting from a political website covering the election of President George W. Bush to a second term in office:

> Sure, you can get all upset about a nation of illiterate redneck
> cultists electing the anti-christ to a second term, or you can just
> warm up to the idea of an even better season of "The Daily Show."
> We're tending towards the latter.
> *http://www.evil.com/archives/2004/200411/20041117.htm*

What, in your view, does the author of this posting mean by "illiterate"? What more general definition of literacy does this particular usage imply?

one end of the conversation there is an abstract definition; at the other end, there's somebody sitting in a room with a Scantron form whose future hangs in the balance. Still, the relationship between the two is neither simple nor direct—it's not a mere matter of

> Scribner's three metaphors for literacy:
> - As adaptation
> - As power
> - As a state of grace

cause and effect (defining literacy *this way* immediately and predictably makes *these things* happen). In her essay entitled "Literacy in Three Metaphors," psychologist Sylvia Scribner (with whose words we began this section) writes about these matters of definitional difficulty and consequence, identifying three dominant metaphors for literacy: literacy as *adaptation*, as *power*, and as a *state of grace*.

Scribner writes that "each of these three metaphors is rooted in certain assumptions about the social motivations for literacy in this country, the nature of existing literacy practices, and judgments about which practices are critical for individual and social enhancement." These metaphors are not, she points out, mere language play—rather, they direct practices that ultimately affect people's lives. "Each," explains Scribner, "has differing implications for educational policies and goals" (1984, p. 73).

Literacy as Adaptation

The common view that literacy is necessary for social and economic well-being (even survival) is what Scribner calls *literacy as adaptation*. Scribner points out that thinking about literacy in this way strongly appeals to our common sense—*of course* people "need" literacy to get by! How else would they decipher signs, documents, policies, products? And yet, how do we know what level or kind or form of literacy is necessary? Some argue that you need only know how to decode basic written information to be literate enough. Others, like literary critic Robert Pattison (1984), insist that you need to be fluent in complex and sophisticated uses of language to be sufficiently literate in modern society. Similarly, when George Bush says, as he did in his speech to the NIH quoted earlier, that "if you cannot read in the 21st century, you don't have a chance to succeed," he is suggesting that literacy is a way of adapting to social and economic mechanisms. And once you make the claim that people "need" literacy to get by, then a parade of questions follows: What kind of literacy? For whom? Under what circumstances? To what ends?

Literacy as Power

Another common metaphor Scribner identifies is *literacy as power*. To equate literacy with power is, as with the literacy-adaptation equation, to make a claim for the social benefits of literacy. The difference in this case is that literacy here is perceived to advance community or group interests. Literacy, in other words, is an essential precondition for social change. In this view, writes Scribner, "not to be literate is a state of victimization" (1984, p. 75). Here again the questions proliferate: What is the relationship between literacy and socioeconomics? How much do social inequalities follow from unequal distributions of literacy? Interestingly, *literacy as power* is a metaphor central to both conservative and radical views of education. Marxist educator Pauolo Freire, for example, sees in literacy the potential for "critical consciousness" and revolutionary action, while American critic E. D. Hirsch believes that "cultural literacy" can ensure upward social mobility for the educationally underprivileged.

Literacy as a State of Grace

The third metaphor Scribner sees as commonly operative in discussions of literacy is *literacy as a state of grace*, which Scribner uses to describe a view of reading and writing that seeks to "endow the literate person with special virtues" (1984, p. 76)—a perspective that has ancient origins but is nonetheless still powerfully present today. In this view, literacy is not necessarily or directly linked to political or economic processes, but rather names a deep, humanistic understanding or creative knowledge. Though the idea of "state of grace" is religious in connotation, this view of literacy is not linked to religion in any direct sense except that it assumes that a state of spiritual and emotional well-being comes uniquely through intellectual engagement with the written word. If you're literate, the thinking behind this metaphor goes, then you're smarter, more civilized, more ethical, more humane.

Literacy Then, Literacy Now: Changing Meanings of Literacy

But where do ideas about the nature of literacy come from? Why do some ways of conceiving literacy seem to be more popular, more powerful, more viable than others? A historical perspective quickly reveals that definitions of literacy are not fixed or stable: they are, like any other social value, products of historical moments, and particular ways of conceiving and valuing literacy emerge, reemerge and fade, morph and shift over time. But what, really, makes a particular way of defining literacy emerge and take hold? What's happening in the national and global political scene, and how these politics determine economic states, predicts, and explains what literacy is perceived to "be" at a given time.

According to literacy historian Deborah Brandt, definitions of literacy emerge and change in response to socioeconomic conditions. Brandt has spent decades studying patterns and trends of literacy in American life and culture, doing archival research and collecting oral histories from everyday people to learn about what literacy "does" for people and how these uses change over time. In her essay (2004) about shifting meanings of literacy around the time of World War II, Brandt gives us one example of how definitions of literacy are not arbitrary or stable over time, but rather depend on the historical moment. Brandt explains that the economic changes brought by World War II also brought changes in the reasons for promoting mass literacy in the United States—specifically, that the rationale for literacy shifted from an emphasis on morality (Scribner's *state of grace*) to an emphasis on production (Scribner's *adaptation*). During the war, the United States stepped up production of goods to meet wartime needs, giving rise to new ideas about literacy as a necessary condition for productivity. Up until World War II, explains Brandt, literacy was believed to be a cultural good, an essential human (and humanizing) value. But under the pressure of increased wartime production, the speed and efficiency of learning became a pressing issue, and perceptions of a "crisis" in literacy intensified as the demand for production outstripped existing literacy resources. Led by the U.S. Army, the federal government launched "one of the largest programs of adult basic education in human history" (p. 487).

Interestingly, Brandt sees the relationship between literacy and the sociopolitical environment in the mid-20th century and the 21st century as having a great deal in common. She writes: "There is the atmosphere of high anxiety around literacy, rapidly changing standards, an imposition of those standards onto more and more people, a search (largely futile) for reliable testing, a context of quick technological development, a heightened concern for world dominance, and a linking of literacy with national security, productivity, and total quality control" (2004, p. 499). NCLB would seem to be one example of how such concerns are currently expressed in policy.

What Brandt's analysis indicates is that even in 21st-century America, literacy is not "neutral," but rather carries the social values of our time. In Brandt's analysis, "literacy remains a cultural mandate, taught and learned as a general good," despite the increasing emphasis on literacy as the productive engine of the knowledge economy—as evidenced by the messages our public institutions and media consistently send out reinforcing the idea that literacy is not just a productive instrument, but also a cultural value. These messages insist that, in Brandt's words, "Good children read to get ahead in school and in life. Good parents read to children," and that "illiteracy is . . . the road to crime." Brandt suggests, however, that the *terms* of the morality of literacy are different from what they once were: As much as literacy may still count as a moral pursuit, it is no longer assumed (as it once was) to *create* morality. Its real value lies in its relationship to productivity and economic well-being. In the America of the 21st-century, living without literacy makes you morally unfit not because you are socially inappropriate as much as because you're not perceived to be an asset to the economy, because you don't "pull your weight" as a productive participant in the workforce.

As natural and common-sense as current views of literacy seem to us now, they weren't always the prevailing views, and their development can be explained with a look into historical events and processes. Understanding historical contexts of literacy, then, helps us come to two understandings:

- that definitions and perceived uses of literacy are linked to historical moments and change over time; and
- what literacy "is" today is best understood with a broader historical perspective.

Thinking of literacy as an historical development is helpful in understanding the emergence and power of particular definitions of literacy—like the ones we see at work in No Child Left Behind.

Sites of Literacy: How This Book Is Organized

If one thing *is* very clear about literacy, it is that it is a conceptually sprawling and ever-shifting subject. For this reason, it can be difficult to take in the broader theoretical and functional landscape of literacy. The necessity of perceiving the vast dynamism of literacy study at the same time as we keep an eye on concrete practices and effects is what motivated us to organize this book into locations, or "sites," of literacy study. It is because literacy is a matter of attaching definitions to real-world causes and effects—that is, because it is *rhetorical*—that we have organized our book into "sites" of literacy. Because the multiple and shifting definitions of literacy can be difficult to pin down, we think it's important to assess the motives that are at work when people talk about literacy. We want to acknowledge that conversations about and uses of literacy always operate from particular *definitions* of literacy, but also that these definitions are situated—that is, they're given shape and meaning by their economic, historical, intellectual, political, and cultural contexts. In this way, understanding what literacy "is" is a matter of understanding it as it is situated in a time and place. As a way to "pin down" literacy at the same time as we acknowledge its concreteness and specifity, we have organized our discussion of literacy into chapters representing five sites of literacy research and practice: mind, culture, class, work, and technology. This organization assumes that what you see and understand about literacy—what literacy is and what literacy does—is, in large part, a matter of where you look for it.

Or, to put it another way, literacy travels. To understand its full range of possibility as a subject for research and as a social practice, you have to follow it around into the places where it lives—in people's heads, in communities, in workplaces, in virtual and digital spaces. You have to ask: What does it mean to locate literacy in the mind, in culture, in socioeconomic space, in machines? To *put* literacy somewhere is to stabilize it long enough to take in its complexity by foregrounding particular aspects of literacy as a human accomplishment, an activity, and a social predicament. So we approach literacy in this way rather than purely philosophically (as a more abstract conversation about definitions or concepts) because we think *placing* literacy allows for richer and more focused discussions of literacy in its conceptual *and* practical dimensions. Locating literacy, even metaphorically, helps us organize terms, issues, and debates.

While it is not within the scope of this book to conduct an exhaustive survey of research and scholarship, we can indicate where some axes of inquiry and points of tension lie. Because research on literacy is both diverse and specialized—many people claim to work on "literacy" as a special area of research expertise, but the kinds of research they do involves years of training and immersion in the literature—it can appear to be chaotic and incomprehensible to nonspecialists. The definitional complexity of literacy means that it invites inquiry and analysis from researchers and scholars across the humanities and social sciences: research on literacy happens in education, psychology, anthropology, sociology, and history. At the same time, most people are deeply concerned with literacy as an issue that affects their lives—their cultural identities, social possibilities, job prospects—and so they naturally have passionate opinions about it. While academics approach literacy as a rich area of scholarly activity, other people experience it not as an abstraction, but as something that happens in the here and now. Add to this a dynamic political arena in which politicians and groups advance their interests by tuning in to people's fears, passions, and dreams, and you've got a situation in which there can be a good deal of tension between literacy as an area of academic inquiry and literacy as a subject in the popular imagination and of everyday conversations. (You can see this in President Bush's words, which are clearly set against academic understandings of literacy as a complex set of issues: "they should be able to figure it out.") The "experts" in literacy can appear to be playing games with something that people take very seriously indeed. (For those inclined to suspect as much, no doubt this very discussion will serve as evidence of more of the same.) The challenge is to think in useful ways about what literacy can be and how it operates without losing touch with people's real and immediate experiences with the processes and artifacts of literacy—with, for example, tests. It doesn't help to tell someone whose future hangs in the balance over test scores that literacy is multiplex and unstable, and that the ordeal they are preparing to undergo is really an instantiation of historical exigency and ideology.

On the other hand—as we have seen in the case of current educational policy—we ignore the theoretical complexities of literacy at our peril. Definitions undergird policies and practices that directly affect people's lives. Though for our purposes the literacy sites we propose are largely heuristic—they give us a useful way to organize discussion of a conceptually complicated set of issues—there are very real consequences that come with understanding literacy as located in one place or another. If you locate literacy *only* in the mind, for example, then you're missing the cultural importance of literacy practices. If you locate it *only* within bounded cultural groups, then you won't see economic causes and effects. In inviting you to think of literacy in terms of various sites of theory and practice, we ask you to consider these questions: What are the stakes of locating literacy in various places? What are the stakes for learning how literacy works, and what are the stakes for the people for whom—or to whom—literacy happens? What is it possible to see, and not see, about literacy by locating it in, for example, "mind"? What does that location reveal and obscure? What forms of research does that location enable, and what are the benefits and limitations of those forms of research? What are the consequences of putting literacy in each place, and for whom? Any issue of literacy can be located in this way, but if we return to the example of high-stakes testing, for example, we can see what each of the sites reveals and obscures:

Mind

If, as the creators of No Child Left Behind policies believe, literacy is something that happens solely in the minds of individuals, then several assumptions follow: that individuals are responsible for the reading and writing capacities they have or don't have; that literacy is something that can be easily measured as a cognitive skill; that social, economic, and cultural factors are largely irrelevant to literacy acquisition; that all children are equally well-equipped to learn the kind of literacy behaviors and practices valued and rewarded by mainstream institutions, regardless of cultural background or economic circumstance.

Culture

If we look to culture to find literacy, then the literacy any given person "has" is a product of his or cultural traditions, values, habits, and assumptions. Standardized testing, for example, is an *act* of literacy in that it enacts the values of middle-class institutions: values of rationality and individual achievement (so we see that it may be the case that the tendency to see literacy as located "in the mind" is itself the expression of a cultural value). Moreover—if we assume that literacy is a cultural thing—then tests, in measuring children's literacies, are really evaluating their cultural practices and values as much or more than they are assessing their individual "abilities." Any educational policy that treated literacy as a practice located in culture would have to recognize cultural ways of knowing as relevant to reading and writing instruction—how, for example, people read, for what purposes, in what situations, in relation to what kinds of nonreading events, and so on—and make such questions relevant to literacy learning. Locating literacy in *culture* rather than *mind* challenges policies oriented to individual achievement, scientific measurement, and quantifiable accountability.

Class

If we put literacy in scenes of social class, several possibilities come into view. One is that how people identify themselves in social space (as working-, middle-, or upper-class) matters when it comes to literacy learning (whom do they wish to be or become through their reading and writing practice?—or, on the other hand, whom do they wish to avoid being or becoming?). Also, we see how literacy is related to economic circumstances and inequalities as well as to traditional cultural practices: Who has access to resources for literacy (good schools, libraries, computers, etc.), and who can afford to maintain access to these? Standardized testing makes inequalities of access even more high-stakes: those who already have cultural and economic access can afford to hire help for children to prepare for the very tests on which school success and upward mobility may well depend. In the case of No Child Left Behind legislation, we can also see how understanding literacy only as a matter of mind (of individual ability) or even of culture (as a set of diverse practices) can put underfunded schools that serve poorer children in a double-bind. According to NCLB, "underperforming" schools—schools that may not have the economic resources to perform well in the first place—are held accountable (punished) by a withdrawal of funding. To locate literacy in the domain of social class is to make yet more visible the dimensions of identity, economic power, and access that are at work in scenes of reading and writing.

Work

Locating literacy in contexts of labor and professional activity makes apparent several things that might otherwise remain invisible: One, that acts of reading and writing happen in relation not only to economic situations, but also to dynamic economic trends and forces. And two, that the nature of these marketplaces is changing as new technologies and new forms of labor emerge. Now, in the "information economy," reading and writing perform social and economic functions, and carry cultural values, different from those in pre- or even postindustrial economies of work. Following literacy into workplaces helps us further understand the dynamics of the relationship between literacy and social class. It lets us ask: What is the relationship between particular reading and writing practices and economic participation? Just what can literacy "buy" you, and who stands to profit? In an age of standardized testing, the question becomes: Are the literacies we measure commensurate with those that are actually viable in workplace and professional scenes? As we will see, in the information economy, there is increasing emphasis on distributed knowledge (collaboration, networking, teamwork)—that is, on new cultural practices of literacy. So when we measure literacy through standardized tests—which assume that knowledge resides within the minds of individuals—are we measuring literacy practices that carry economic power?

Technology

Situating conversations about literacy in scenes of technology helps us, first, to see how cultural practices and social values associated with literacy are changing. For one thing, understanding literacy *as* a technology makes visible the historical cycles of cultural and social change literacy brings. Thinking about how reading and writing practices are changing with the introduction of new information and digital technologies helps bring into focus patterns of continuity and change in uses and effects of literacy. In what ways do new technologies make new literacies possible, and in what ways do these technologies allow old cultural practices to surface and to circulate differently? When we think of standardized testing in relation to this literacy site, we begin to see just how socially dynamic literacy practices are, and that there may be gaps between the literacies schools teach and reward and those "in the wild" in people's everyday lives. What happens when children's understandings of literacy (as practices of networking, for example, or gaming, or design) outstrip literacies taught in schools? What happens when students' literacy practices happen in environments not acknowledged or measured by tests? Or, on the other hand, what happens when students who don't have access to new technologies of literacy are held accountable for those? What are the cultural and socioeconomic consequences of these "gaps"?

There are many other questions we could raise in relation to each of these sites—and as you can see, some of the questions overlap across domains. We recognize that our organizational plan isn't comprehensive, and that there are important issues that this scheme treats implicitly or indirectly. We could, for instance, have titled a chapter "literacy and race," since literacy has been both a cause and effect of racial oppression. On the other hand, this is also something that cuts across all other categories (locating literacy in the mind, for example, is one way to avoid responsibility for social inequality and cultural exclusion). It's not until you locate literacy in class, culture, and work that you begin to understand the relationship of literacy and race. We also don't have a chapter called "literacy and history"—though again, this is a theme that runs through all other locations. Each of these spatial "locations" can also be understood as having a temporal dimension—though "time" works differently in each of these cases.

ACTIVITIES AND PROJECTS

1. **Diary study: documenting everyday literacy.** Keep track of your own literacy practices for 2 or 3 days. Every time you read or write something, make a note of it in your diary. Document every reading and writing activity, noting not only the nature and duration of the activity, but also where, when, and with whom it happens.

   After you complete your diary activity, look carefully at your data and reflect on what you've found. How would you describe the literacies you see from the data you have? Compare your findings with others in your group or class.

   Keep your literacy diary to use as a data set to help you test and situate concepts in the chapters to follow.

2. **Collaborative report: popular definitions of literacy.** So far, we have suggested that *literacy* is a term that circulates widely in popular conversations about education, work, and citizenship. Test this claim: with others in your group, collect examples of how the word *literacy* is used in popular media (TV news, magazines, social service ads, etc.). Pool and analyze your data. What are the most common definitions of literacy in the examples you've found? Are there patterns? Is it possible to arrive at any general conclusions? Summarize your findings in a brief (two to three pages) report, including representative examples of the common definitions you found.

3. **Website/document analysis**

   Option 1: The study of "English," traditionally associated with literature, is also associated with the acquisition of a particular kind of (or orientation to) literacy. The English Department website at Michigan State University, for example, describes its mission as follows: "to help students develop their analytical and critical skills; to enhance their ability to explore, organize, and articulate their ideas through writing; and to deepen their understanding of literature and language as significant cultural phenomena that are shaped by particular historical and cultural contexts." What assumptions about literacy—what it is, why it's important, who should have it—seem to you to underlie this description?

Now find the mission statement in the website for the English department at your own institution, and ask these same questions about literacy and citizenship. Then compare what you find to English websites from

- different kinds of institutions of higher education—community college, state, regional; vocational, liberal arts, religious, private, elite/Ivy League. (Some websites don't have missions at all, so be prepared to do some looking around); AND/OR
- other programs and/or other departments in communications and humanities fields at your college or university.

What conclusions can you draw about attitudes toward and assumptions about literacy in higher education—what it looks like, how it's used, and who claims to have it—from what you have found?

Option 2: Find documentation about the first-year writing program at your college or university: mission statements, program descriptions, outcomes statements, curriculum guides. From these, speculate on which definition of literacy your writing program implicitly assumes: what kinds of reading and writing capabilities are students expected to learn? What should they be able to do after finishing the first-year writing program? Why are students required to take first-year writing courses? Compose a short (two to three pages) argument essay in which you posit a definition of literacy and then give as evidence "data" from the documents you've found.

4. **Literacy metaphors collage.** Find visual representations—images and photos—that communicate each of Scribner's three metaphors of literacy. From these, compose a literacy collage that demonstrates popular conceptions of literacy. Narrate your collage to the class: how do you think each visual example expresses a literacy metaphor? Does your collage "add up" to a larger argument about literacy?

FOR FURTHER READING

Barton, David. (2006). *Literacy: An introduction to the ecology of written language.* London: Blackwell.

Brandt, Deborah. (2004, May). Drafting U.S. literacy. *College English, 66*(5).

Cushman, Ellen, Rose, Mike, Kroll, Barry, & Kintgen, Eugene. (2001). *Literacy: A critical sourcebook.* Boston: Bedford-St. Martin's.

Darling-Hammond, Linda. (2007, May 21). Evaluating No Child Left Behind. *The Nation.*

Freire, Paulo, & Macedo, Donaldo. (1987). *Literacy: Reading and word and the world.* New York: Bergin and Garvey.

Hirsch, E. D. (1988). *Cultural literacy: What every American needs to know.* New York: Vintage.

Luna, Catherine, Solsken, Judith, & Kutz, Eleanor. (2001, Sept. 1). Defining literacy: Lessons from high-stakes teacher testing. *Journal of Teacher Education, 51*(4), 276.

Pattison, Robert. (1984). *On literacy: The politics of the word from Homer to the Age of Rock.* New York: Oxford.

Scribner, Sylvia. (1984, Nov.). Literacy in three metaphors. *American Journal of Education, 93*(1), 6–21.

2

Literacy and Mind

"They're harmless as long as you don't sign anything."

© *The New Yorker Collection 2005 Tom Cheney from cartoonbank.com*

Before You Read. Describe your own literacy in terms of the kinds of reading and writing you do: for school, personal uses, work; print and digital; on- and offline. Then consider: is this literacy a *possession* or a *practice* (is it something you *have* or something you *do*)? Can you think of examples of ways you think and behave "like a literate person"? Now imagine yourself as a person unable to read or write at all. How do you imagine that your ways of seeing and thinking about the world would be different from what they are now? From this "thought experiment," what can you conclude about what cognitive/intellectual capacities a person gains in becoming literate—and what a person *loses*?

Kids These Days: Literacy and the End of Dialogue

Imagine, if you will, the following scene:

Athens, Greece. 360 BCE. A venerable philosopher sits under a sycamore tree on a fine Mediterranean day with his young and eager student. Relaxing in the shade, they talk of many things: life, love, language, the nature of the soul and of divine truth. For the philosopher and his student, who live in a world unmediated by print and information technologies, these things belong in the same conversation.

The philosopher, Socrates, leads his student, Phaedrus, through a philosophical exploration of the nature of love and the motives of lovers, the soul, and the path to knowledge. As Socrates asks Phaedrus to consider the relationship between language and truth, the conversation turns to the uses and nature of writing. After challenging the idea that writing serves as an aid to memory, Socrates assures his young student that anyone who believes writing to be superior to knowledge that lives in conversation or memory is mistaken:

Soc. At the Egyptian city of Naucratis, there was a famous old god, whose name was Theuth; the bird which is called the Ibis is sacred to him, and he was the inventor of many arts, such as arithmetic and calculation and geometry and astronomy and draughts and dice, but his great discovery was the use of letters. Now in those days the god Thamus was the

> "This discovery of yours will create forgetfulness in the learners' souls, because they will not use their memories; they will trust to the external written characters and not remember of themselves. They appear to be omniscient and will generally know nothing."

king of the whole country of Egypt; and he dwelt in that great city of Upper Egypt which the Hellenes call Egyptian Thebes, and the god himself is called by them Ammon. To him came Theuth and showed his inventions, desiring that the other Egyptians might be allowed to have the benefit of them he enumerated them, and Thamus enquired about their several uses, and praised some of them and censured others, as he approved or disapproved of them. It would take a long time to repeat all that Thamus said to Theuth in praise or blame of the various arts. But when they came to letters, This, said Theuth, will make the Egyptians wiser and give them better memories; it is a specific both for the memory and for the wit. Thamus replied: O most ingenious Theuth, the parent or inventor of an art is not always the best judge of the utility or inutility of his own inventions to the users of them.

Panel from Understanding Comics by Scott McCloud © 1993, 1994 Scott McCloud. Reprinted by Permission of HarperCollins Publishers

And in this instance, you who are the father of letters, from a paternal love of your own children have been led to attribute to them a quality which they cannot have; for this discovery of yours will create forgetfulness in the learners' souls, because they will not use their memories; they will trust to the external written characters and not remember of themselves. The specific which you have discovered is an aid not to memory, but to reminiscence, and you give your disciples not truth, but only the semblance of truth; they will be hearers of many things and will have learned nothing; they will appear to be omniscient and will generally know nothing; they will be tiresome company, having the show of wisdom without the reality.

After ruminating on the noble origins of philosophy, Socrates goes on to argue that writing is a philosophically impotent, morally questionable form of communication:

> **Soc.** He would be a very simple person, and quite a stranger to the oracles of Thamus or Ammon, who should leave in writing or receive in writing any art under the idea that the written word would be intelligible or certain; or who deemed that writing was at all better than knowledge and recollection of the same matters?
>
> **Phaedr.** That is most true.
>
> **Soc.** I cannot help feeling, Phaedrus,

Panels from Reinventing Comics by Scott McCloud © 2000 Scott McCloud. Reprinted by Permission of HarperCollins Publishers

that writing is unfortunately like painting; for the creations of the painter have the attitude of life, and yet if you ask them a question they preserve a solemn silence. And the same may be said of speeches. You would imagine that they had intelligence, but if you want to know anything and put a question to one of them, the speaker always gives one unvarying answer. And when they have been once written down they are tumbled about anywhere among those who may or may not understand them, and know not to whom they should reply, to whom not: and, if they are maltreated or abused, they have no parent to protect them; and they cannot protect or defend themselves.

Phaedr. That again is most true.

Soc. Is there not another kind of word or speech far better than this, and having far greater power—a son of the same family, but lawfully begotten?

Phaedr. Whom do you mean, and what is his origin?

Soc. I mean an intelligent word graven in the soul of the learner, which can defend itself, and knows when to speak and when to be silent.

Phaedr. You mean the living word of knowledge which has a soul, and of which written word is properly no more than an image?

> "I cannot help feeling Phaedrus, that writing is unfortunately like painting; for the creations of the painter have the attitude of life, and yet if you ask them a question they preserve a solemn silence."

Soc. Yes, of course that is what I mean.

Socrates goes on to explain that writing is a thin imitation of spoken dialogue, and asks Phaedrus to consider the consequences of writing in the wrong hands and motivated by unethical purposes:

Soc. And now may I be allowed to ask you a question: Would a husbandman, who is a man of sense, take the seeds, which he values and which he wishes to bear fruit, and in sober seriousness plant them during the heat of summer, in some garden of Adonis, that he may rejoice when he sees them in eight days appearing in beauty? At least he would do so, if at all, only for the sake of amusement and pastime. But when he is in earnest he sows in fitting soil, and practises husbandry, and is satisfied if in eight months the seeds which he has sown arrive at perfection?

Phaedr. Yes, Socrates, that will be his way when he is in earnest; he will do the other, as you say, only in play.

Soc. And can we suppose that he who knows the just and good and honourable has less understanding, than the husbandman, about his own seeds?

Phaedr. Certainly not.

Soc. Then he will not seriously incline to "write" his thoughts "in water" with pen and ink, sowing words which can neither speak for themselves nor teach the truth adequately to others?

Phaedr. No, that is not likely.

Soc. No, that is not likely—in the garden of letters he will sow and plant, but only for the sake of recreation and amusement; he will write them down as memorials to be treasured against the forgetfulness of old age, by himself, or by any other old man who is treading the same path. He will rejoice in beholding their tender growth; and while others are refreshing their souls with banqueting and the like, this will be the pastime in which his days are spent.

Phaedr. A pastime, Socrates, as noble as the other is ignoble, the pastime of a man who can be amused by serious talk, and can discourse merrily about justice and the like.

Soc. True, Phaedrus. But nobler far is the serious pursuit of the dialectician, who, finding a congenial soul, by the help of science sows and plants therein words which are able to help them-

Action Philosophers!, © 2005 Fred Van Lente and Ryan Dunlavey

selves and him who planted them, and are not unfruitful, but have in them a seed which others brought up in different soils render immortal, making the possessors of it happy to the utmost extent of human happiness. (trans. Benjamin Jowett; *http://www.fordham.edu/halsall/ancient/plato-phaedrus.txt*)

In Plato's characterization, Socrates, who believes that truth can be made available through philosophical dialectic—through the careful positing and challenging of ideas through spoken conversation—is skeptical of the knowledge-making power or ethical basis of the written word. Socrates, who himself wrote nothing down, sees writing as an inferior, limited rhetorical practice. Socrates' charge against writing is that it stabilizes ideas, so that writing falsely represents ideas as frozen in time, ripped from the living, human situations in which they naturally move (writing is "a copy of a copy"). How, Socrates wonders, can the written word participate in the process of moving toward truth and justice through philosophical questioning and engagement? Of written texts, Socrates complains that "if you ask them a question they preserve a solemn silence."

In this chapter, we introduce you to conversations about the "consequences"—for cognition, in particular, and by extension, for civilization more generally—that have been claimed by philosophers and historians for writing as a technology. Specifically, we'll set out some well-established and foundational questions about

- Characteristics of "orality" versus "literacy" as modes of communication
- How oral and written forms of communication may have different "affordances"—that is, how they may make different kinds of things possible for their users
- How literacy is related to thinking—that is, ideas about what the cognitive "effects" of writing and reading might be
- How cognitive changes brought about by literacy may initiate broader social changes
- How cognitive habits might be specifically connected to particular uses of reading and writing
- How studies of literacy practices in cultural contexts may complicate broader claims about the relationship of literacy to cognition and civilization.

Socrates: Literacy Ruins Memory, Gets in the Way of Thinking

Nowadays most people see literacy as a virtue, but Socrates insisted that written texts are not only unresponsive to human needs, but also *dangerous*. Not only can written texts not "answer" for themselves,

Definition

Plato was a Greek philosopher who lived in the 4th century BCE. Plato was a student of *Socrates,* and among his many writings on rhetoric, philosophy, and ethics are several *dialogues* featuring Socrates as a character. As far as we know, Socrates himself never wrote anything down.

but they are always in danger of falling, helpless, into the hands of those who would misread and misuse them: Once ideas are written down, points out Socrates, "they are tumbled about anywhere among those who may or may not understand them, and know not to whom they should reply, to whom not: and, if they are maltreated or abused, they have no parent to protect them; and they cannot protect or defend themselves." At Socrates' suggestion that there is another form of communication that is superior to this, Phaedrus offers, "You mean the living word of knowledge which has a soul, and of which written word is properly no more than an image?" Socrates assures Phaedrus that that is exactly what he means. The philosopher works through spoken language, a medium that must be engaged by human contact to have meaning and address the most vital questions of ethics, truth, and beauty: the philosopher works like a farmer who plants "seeds" (words) that can "help themselves and him who planted them, and are not unfruitful, but have in them a seed which others brought up in different soils render immortal, making the possessors of it happy to the utmost extent of human happiness."

But what about the more modest claim for writing's usefulness—that it can serve as an aid to memory? Even this idea Socrates contests, claiming that writing weakens the mind's faculties because it serves as a weak substitute for memory and divests it of any power. Socrates predicts that writing "will create forgetfulness in the learners' souls, because they will not use their memories; they will trust to the external written characters and not remember of themselves. The specific which you have discovered is an aid not to memory, but to reminiscence." Without living memory, contends Socrates, acquired knowledge will have no foundation: students "will be hearers of many things and will have learned nothing; they will appear to be omniscient and will generally know nothing." Since Socrates believed in a transcendent reality (or a world of ideal "forms") beyond the physical

> **Focus Point**
>
> Plato's Socrates believed that literacy—specifically, writing—was bad for people: written communication stood to make them unethical and forgetful. Explore this idea through reflections on your own observations and experiences. What examples can you come up with of writing as unethical or dangerous? What is it about *writing* that ensures these qualities?

world, he thought of writing as doubly mediated, twice removed from the origins of Truth. Memory, for Socrates, was an important feature of learning and a necessary instrument for attaining wisdom—and writing, which allows people to document things they might otherwise have committed to memory, interferes with thinking and learning. Socrates worried that this property of writing itself would have consequences for relations between people—who would no longer need to keep shared memories "alive" in dialogue—and therefore, for human knowledge and experience. Writing theorist Louise Wetherbee Phelps writes that Plato and others in the Platonic tradition equated speech with "the real, the concrete, with the flow and change of life itself, with process, event, and a sense of belonging and participation in the culture." In contrast, this tradition characterizes writing as "abstract, static, unresponsive to questioning, and empty of life and passion" (2001, p. 62). In Socrates' view, explains Phelps, writing is a dangerous technology, one that represents "the absence of the vital, dialogic qualities found in face-to-face speech" (62). Written words become disembodied ideas, cut off from their human lifeworlds. Socrates was probably not the first intellectual to worry about what changes in how people communicate were doing to the kids—and he certainly wasn't the last.

Letters, Thought, and Civilization

Nowadays, it's easy to find examples of a common story about literacy—a story with a lesson very different from one Plato's Socrates wanted his students to take home. The story goes like this: if you learn to read and write, your life will change. You'll be more humane, more productive, civilized—even cleaner. This is a story that plays out again and again in popular culture, such as in films.

Reading at the Movies: Stanley and Billie Dawn Get Literacy Makeovers

The films *Stanley and Iris* and *Born Yesterday* offer classic case examples. Both films are conventional Hollywood love stories, but in each the conflict emerges from the main character's struggle with illiteracy or inability to read well. Both films can be seen as products of their own historical moments and as expressions of prevailing cultural sentiments about education and citizenship; in both cases, the main character finds freedom and enlightenment through literacy.

I live in silence, afraid to speak
of my life of darkness because I cannot read.

For all those lines and circles, to me, a mystery.
Eve pull down the apple and give taste to me.
If she could it would be wonderful.
Then I wouldn't need someone else's eyes to see what's in front of me.
No one guiding me.

It makes me humble to be so green
at what every kid can do when he learns A to Z,

but all those lines and circles just frighten me
and I fear that I'll be trampled if you don't reach for me.
Before I run I'll have to take a fall.
And then pick myself up, so slowly I'll devour every one of those books
in the Tower of Knowledge.

—10,000 Maniacs, "Cherry Tree"

Consider what happens in *Stanley and Iris* (1990), made in the years following "A Nation at Risk," President Ronald Reagan's National Commission on Education's report proclaiming the disastrous state of educational achievement in the United States and warning of the "rising tide of mediocrity that threatens our very future as a people." In the film, Robert DeNiro plays a cafeteria worker who by chance meets Iris (Jane Fonda) when her purse is snatched. Their friendship develops, and Iris discovers that Stanley sustains an eccentric lifestyle: he lives with his father and rides a bicycle to work. Stanley works to hide his "condition," but is finally found out when Iris learns that he can't read well enough to produce the correct bottle when asked for aspirin. It turns out that Stanley has been living a life of enforced dependence, shame, and deception. Stanley confesses to Iris: "Sometimes I don't even feel human."

Set in 1945 at the end of World War II and the start of the Cold War, Stanley Cukor's *Born Yesterday* is a striking expression of the political sentiment of its era—in this case, of the ideals of liberal democracy in contrast to the oppression of German facism, on the one hand, and Soviet communism, on the other. In contrast to functionally illiterate Stanley in *Stanley and Iris*, Emma "Billie" Dawn (Judy Holliday) in *Born*

Yesterday (1950) is capable of performing the fundamentals of reading and writing. However, as a trophy girlfriend who is supported by Harry Brock (Broderick Crawford), a rich junk dealer involved in shady deals, she sees little purpose in reading for education and self-improvement. Early in the film, ex-chorus-girl Billie expresses her philosophy of education: "As long as I know how to get what I want, that's all I want to know." But when Brock seeks to influence congressmen in Washington D.C., he hires journalist Paul Verrall (William Holden) to "smarten Billie up a little" and make her over so that she will behave appropriately with the Washington set. Varall, a reporter with the *New Republic,* is initially motivated by the desire to learn more about Brock, but becomes more and more determined to educate Billie because he believes, as he says, that "a world full of ignorant people is dangerous." Billie's accumulation of literacy as knowledge drives the action of the story: The more fluently Billie learns to read, the greater her intellectual curiosity becomes and the more she wants to know.

Though both *Born Yesterday* and *Stanley and Iris* reflect the cultural and political climates of their eras, each features a main character who is fully transformed by literacy. Stanley sees literacy as the way to full, legitimate human status, but in very different terms from the ones Plato's Socrates set out. Stanley gives voice to a powerful tradition in Western thought connecting literacy not only with the ability to encode and decode written communications, but with being a socially and ethically viable human being. If you watch *Stanley and Iris,* you'll notice that as he moves further and further into the world of the Literate, the more he begins to take on the conventional markers of responsibility and good citizenship—he is neater, more confident in his demeanor, more elegant in his movements, even more nattily dressed. The more literacy Stanley acquires, the less he looks like a rumpled outcast and the more he looks like an

Stanley Before Literacy
STANLEY AND IRIS, 1989 Directed by Martin Ritt
THE KOBAL COLLECTION/MGM

especially well-heeled English professor.

Similarly, Billie Dawn in *Born Yesterday* begins wearing glasses and drawing on her expanding vocabulary (sometimes referring to a huge dictionary) to criticize her bullying sugar daddy Harry as "antisocial" and, later, a "big fascist." Whereas

Stanley After Literacy
MGM/The Everett Collection

Stanley and Iris implies that literacy makes you human, *Born Yesterday* directly links reading classic books to the preservation of civilization and government. At the same time that Billie begins to read classical philosophers that helped shape American government, Paul takes her to Washington, D.C., to visit the historic sites and texts of democratic government. Only when Billie becomes a real reader does she become a real citizen—a full participant in the democratic process.

Stanley's and Billie Dawn's transformations through literacy are good examples of contemporary thinking about the power and possibilities of reading and writing for literate individuals. For contemporary Americans who see literacy as a universal good, Socrates' distrust of literacy seems strange. Clearly, though, there are features of his thinking that *haven't* changed in conversations about literacy from 400 BCE to 2005 AD: First, there is the idea that literacy changes the way you think. And second, that this change has consequences: for morality, intellectual life, human relations, society in general. Indeed, as Billie continues reading and discussing questions of government with Paul, she also realizes how Harry and his lawyer have been using her signatures on company documents to cover up illegal business, which she now understands as a "cartel."

You could say that Stanley's lament is the flipside of Socrates' worry over the consequences of writing, and these oppositional sentiments are just complementary parts of our ongoing obsession with what literacy "means" and what the stakes are. Louise Phelps explains that since the time of Plato, we have continued to see speech and writing, orality and literacy, as fundamentally oppositional and "associated with different modes of thought" (1991, p. 61). So while Plato saw writing as a dehumanizing technology, the more common view these days is that it is the very thing that enables full human progress and achievement. When Stanley, after months of slow and painful instruction by Iris, *finally becomes literate*, we see him standing in the reading room of a library, glasses perched on nose, reading aloud haltingly at first but picking up speed and confidence as he masters more and more learned passages from more and more culturally important books—culminating, triumphantly, in a flawless rendering of the Creation in Genesis: "And the Lord said, *Let there be light!*"

Whereas Stanley's struggle for literacy culminates in the light of Creation, Billie's epiphany occurs when she revisits the Jefferson memorial after a major fight with Harry over his illicit deals and frustration with her awakening emancipation. As "America the Beautiful" quietly plays in the background, Billie reads the words, penned by Thomas Jefferson, that encircle the memorial: "I have sworn upon the eternal altar of God eternal hostility against every form of tyranny over the mind of man." She then phones Paul, her teacher of civilization, asking for him by the name

> **Focus Point**
>
> Claims for the effects of literacy:
>
> - abstraction
> - generalization
> - systematic thinking
> - metalinguistic awareness
>
>   leading to:
>
> - history
> - logic
> - science
> - democracy
>
> —*Cushman, Kintgen, Kroll, and Rose,*
> *Literacy: A Critical Sourcebook.*

Group Activity: With others in your group, locate three or four websites for organizations with missions to provide adult literacy education (maybe have each person in your group research one site). Look closely at the mission statements and the promotional material for the site(s) you find. What claims or attitudes about literacy do they implicitly (or explicitly) promote? What questions or complications seem to be less acknowledged, less visible? Compare your data and report your findings to the class.

Thomas Jefferson, to help her escape from Harry, whom she now, equipped with her new capacity to see things critically, recognizes as a source of exploitation.

Cunningham and Stanovich: Reading Makes You Smarter

Ideas about the direct humanizing and civilizing potential of literacy follow from the assumption that literacy helps you think better—that it helps you to be critical, reflective, to engage in rational thought. "The other side of the tradition," explains Phelps, "understands literacy as freeing humans from their bondages to the immediate and irrational," thus liberating them to participate fully in civic life. Consider educational researchers Anne Cunningham and Keith Stanovich, who believe, to quote the title of their recent essay, "Reading Can Make You Smarter." They write that "the amount of print children are exposed to has profound cognitive consequences," and that the intellectual improvements literacy brings should be the primary concern within an educational system that strives to produce good citizens (2003, pp. 34–39).

Cunningham and Stanovich cite empirical evidence (that is, real data from research) for their assertions, but such claims for the transformative potential of the written word have deep roots in modern Western thought. Historians, philosophers, and anthropologists have claimed that profound consequences accompany the spread of literacy in a society. The argument goes something like this: writing, with its visual dimension, demands abstraction, distance, and rationality. In their introduction to *Literacy: A Critical Sourcebook*, editors Cushman, Kintgen, Kroll, and Rose summarize well the general argument: "As opposed to their non-literate counterparts, literates engage in abstraction, generalization, systematic thinking, defining, *logos* (an emphasis on rational and logical thought)

> **Focus Point**
>
> *Great divide* theories of literacy refer to those that assume fundamental differences in ways of thinking in societies rooted in print culture versus those that are not saturated by the production and consumption of writing. Great divide theories assume that the cognitive changes that literacy brings give rise, in turn, to more advanced forms of social organization.

rather than *mythos* (an emphasis on narrative and myth), puzzlement over words as words, and speculation on the features of language," cognitive consequences that "lead to history, logic, astronomy, taxonomic science in the modern sense, and even to democracy" (1991, p. xii). In *The Psychology of Literacy*, Scribner and Cole identify (and ultimately challenge) theories that posit alphabetic literacy as "the key ingredient in the packet of social change that separated primitive from civilized, concrete from abstract, traditional from modern thought" (1981, p. 235). The "Great Divide" theorists of literacy claim deep and radical differences between the cognitive styles or capabilities of "oral" and "literate" societies, and they assume fundamentally different qualities of oral and literate communication. Chandler, for example, offers a list to indicate how these essential differences typically get represented in Great Divide theories of literacy:

Spoken word	Written word
Aural impermanence	Visual permanence
Fluid	Fixed
Rhythmic	Ordered
Subjective	Objective
Inaccurate	Quantifying
Resonant	Abstract
Time	Space
Present	Timeless
Participatory	Detached
Communal	Individual

(From Chandler, "Biases of the Ear and Eye,"
http://www.aber.ac.uk/media/Documents/litoral/litoral1.html)

Literacy and the "Great Divide"

The Great Divide theorists of literacy, then, hold in common the idea that cognitive changes brought about by the qualities of the written word themselves bring about grand and sweeping changes in the organization and development of societies. Literacy, from this perspective, has revolutionary potential. With new technologies of human communication come profound and irreversible changes in civilization. Implicit in such a view is the idea that the new modes of thought are not only new but improved, and that social progress follows—that is, people become more rational, more humane, more civilized. Literacy thus becomes a moral issue: if literacy causes human thought and civilization to "advance," then it becomes an ethical imperative to spread literacy and foster these changes. Names most commonly associated with Great Divide thinking are Walter Ong, Jack Goody and Ian Watt, Eric Havelock, and David Olson. Goody especially championed these theories because he also sought to challenge earlier historical and anthropological assumptions of the inherent racial superiority of people from European descent. Through their Great Divide theories of literacy, these scholars contended that the development of cultures had more to do with the cognitive shifts brought about by literacy than inherent European superiority.

> **Definition**
>
> **Walter J. Ong** was a Catholic priest, philosopher, cultural historian, and prolific literacy scholar. He published many works on religious and secular cultural history, but his book *Orality and Literacy: The Technologizing of the Word* (1982) has been most influential to literacy theorists and researchers. In it, Ong posited changes in human consciousness and social organization from the spread of print literacy— though Ong himself warned against reductive readings of his work as indicating deterministic views of literacy.

To get a better idea of how literacy works its magic from this theoretical perspective, let's look at what the famous theologian-philosopher Walter Ong had to say. Ong is perhaps one of the most well-known and widely read scholars of literacy, and his writings have had a huge impact on theoretical debates of the meaning and effects of the written word on social organization. Ong wrote of the revolutionary potential of writing and "literate cultures" to influence human organization and, ultimately, to rewrite human history. At the very foundation of these claims is the idea that, in Ong's words, "writing restructures thought": "A deeper understanding of pristine or primary orality enables us better to understand the new world of writing, what it truly is, and what functionally literate human beings really are: beings whose thought processes do not grow out of simply natural powers but out of these powers as structured, directly or indirectly, by the technology of writing. Without writing, the literate mind would not and could not think as it does, not only when engaged in writing but normally even when it is composing its thoughts in oral form. More than any other single invention, writing has transformed human consciousness" (Ong, 1982, p. 78). That's an ambitious claim, all right—that writing changes the mechanisms of human thought. But how, exactly does this work? What are the assumptions that lie behind this claim? One way writing changes thought is that it liberates the mind from memory, largely by freeing it from the mundane job of storing details of events so that it can devote itself to more complex intellectual operations. Complex lines of reasoning can't be easily stored in memory, said Ong, so that in societies with no writing, intellectual activity has inevitable limits. Ong asks us to imagine a scenario:

> Suppose a person in an oral culture would undertake to think through a particular complex problem and would finally manage to articulate a solution which is itself relatively complex, consisting, let us say, of a few hundred words. How does he or she retain for later recall the verbalization so painstakingly elaborated . . . How, in fact, could a lengthy analytic solution ever be assembled in the first place? An interlocutor is virtually essential: it is hard to talk to yourself for hours on end. Sustained thought in an oral culture is tied to communication. (1982, p. 30)

In other words, you can't think complex, memorable thoughts all by yourself without writing them down unless you have somebody else to help you test and elaborate them (and here Ong puts his finger on Socrates' preference for speech over writing—speech forces your ideas directly into contact with others). But Ong saw other ways in which writing changed thought as well. He argued that orality is

- **additive rather than subordinative** (speech doesn't specify relationships between narrative events—it operates in the mode of "and . . . and . . . and" rather than indicating cause-and-effect relationships between events);

- **aggregative rather than analytic** (works through conventions and clichés instead of through analysis);

- **redundant or "copious"** (oral communication has to build in lots of redundancy or overlap to keep both speaker or hearer "on track");

- **conservative or traditionalist** (since it takes so much energy to engage in intellectual inquiry through speech, oral communication tends to favor the old and established rather than the new and experimental);

- **close to the human lifeworld** (Socrates' idea that speech establishes close relationships because knowledge has to be personally passed on);

- **agonistically toned** (since oral communication *is* so highly interpersonal, it responds to the intensely conflictual nature of close and dependent human relationships);

- **empathetic and participatory rather than objectively distanced** (in an oral culture, you have to be closely connected with other people and to think together with them since meaning is controlled by the community—if you want to know what something "means," for example, you have to ask somebody else);

- **homeostatic** (more or less stuck in the present, since histories are hard to maintain and thinking about the future requires too much abstract speculation); and

- **situational rather than abstract** (closely tied to the immediate and concrete).

Above and beyond these qualities of oral language, wrote Ong, there is the matter of how the *medium* of oral communication—sound—is different from the visual medium of print communication. That is to say, we experience the world differently through hearing and sight, and this matters for how we think about things in relation to other people. For Ong, sound is a sensory mechanism that brings us closer to things, while sight has a distancing property: "sight isolates, sound incorporates."

> Whereas sight situates the observer outside what he views, at a distance, sound pours into the hearer . . . Vision comes to a human being from one direction at a time: to look at a room or landscape, I must move my eyes around from one part to another. When I hear, however, I gather sound simultaneously from every direction at once: I am at the center of my auditory world, which envelops me, establishing me at a kind of core sensation and existence . . . By contrast with vision, the dissecting sense, sound is thus a unifying sense. (1982, p. 42)

Ong contended that these qualities of the aural medium of oral communication have profound implications for how people in oral cultures locate

Activity: Experimenting with Oral Versus Written Argument
Plato's Socrates believed that writing interfered with inquiry, pro-
hibiting dialogue and interfering with critical evaluation of ideas. On
the other hand, theorists such as David Olsen and Walter Ong argue
that writing frees the memory from mundane tasks and documents
extended processes of inquiry, allowing for richer intellectual activity.
Working with a partner, test Socrates' claims against Ong's.
Choose a controversial issue and have a face-to-face conversation in
which you attempt to understand all possible "sides" of the issue.
Then, spend some time on your own exploring multiple perspectives on the same issue in writing. Afterward, report your experiences to the rest of the class: which mode, oral conversation or
written exploration, allowed you to get "deeper" into the issue?
What was gained and what lost, in each approach? How did literacy
enter into each version?

themselves in the tangle of experience, thought, language, and sociability.
People whose communicative medium is sound experience acts of language
as whole, organic events—as, in Ong's words, "always momentous in psy-
chic life" so that "the cosmos is an ongoing event with man at the center"
(1982, pp. 42–43). With literacy, however, people come to see themselves as
situated in time and space, rather than as at the center of all events and
meaning. It follows, then, that as literacy spreads throughout populations
and becomes more prevalent as a means of human interaction, the very
structure of culture and society undergoes big changes—specifically, developing complex administrative systems—so that "civilization" becomes possible (as Billie's transformation in *Born Yesterday* seeks to demonstrate).

    This idea of literacy as a history-making civilizing force is central to
Jack Goody and Ian Watt's famous "Consequences of Literacy" (1968).
For anthropologist Goody and historian Watt, language is the essential
feature of humanness; print, the enabler of the highest human achievement, rational thought. In their essay, they make exactly this claim: that
print communication, once it reaches a critical mass in a society, brings
inevitable changes in terms of social organization. Goody and Watt list
the same qualities of writing to argue for its capacity to enable knowledge
production as Plato lists as evidence of its ability to undermine it: written language stabilizes ideas into text so that they can be extended in time

> **Group Activity: Testing Ong's Categories**
> Look again at Ong's categorical characteristics of orality and literacy.
> Have everyone in your group think of one or two counterexamples
> for these categories: of instances of writing that are "agglutinative,"
> for example, or instances of orality that are "empathetic and
> participatory."
>   Examine the examples you've collected, and discuss what you
> found. Can you draw any useful conclusions about the viability—
> and usefulness—of Ong's categories?

and space. For Goody and Watt, the emergence of literate culture in the classical world made intellectual intercourse rooted in logic and rationality possible on a wider scale, such that more complex social organizations and institutions founded on rationality could now emerge.

Ironically, Goody and Watt believe that the appearance of Plato on the scene marked the beginnings of literate culture. Although historians claim Socrates never wrote anything down, Plato immortalized Socrates by writing him into his dialogues. Rhetoric scholar Jasper Neel (1988) points out that, even as Plato derides writing as immoral, frozen, and too mediated to be ethical, what we know of him is given through writing. Plato's dialogues are, after all, written—written and crafted as *writing*. Each of Plato's dialogues has a claim, a beginning, middle, and end; a distinctive voice and style. What Plato represents, argues Neel, is the voice of an emerging literate culture. What makes the argument for oral discourse and dialectic possible is, paradoxically, writing itself.

Literacy, Literacies, and Schooling: The Case of the Vai

But not all scholars of literacy buy into the stronger claims of the Great Divide theorists. For many, the idea that literacy arrives on the scene, revolutionizes thought, and advances civilization is not only wrongheaded but downright ethnocentric and elitist. Once you believe that literacy inevitably makes people and cultures better, then you also believe that nonliteracy marks nonliterates as intellectually inferior, less humane, and uncivilized. Indeed, long before the Great Divide theorists of the 1960s and 1970s, this view pervaded popular thought in 19th-century England and America, where people who couldn't read were often associated with problems of sanitation, immorality, and disease. Chandler lists research and scholarship on literacy that she sees as "correctives" to the generalized views of literacy offered by Great Divide theorists: Ruth Finnegan's *Literacy and Orality*, Brian Street's *Literacy in Theory and Practice*, Michael Cole and Sylvia Scribner's *The Psychology of Literacy*, and Harvey Graff's *The Labyrinths of Literacy*, among many others.

Perhaps the most widely cited challenge to Great Divide thinking appears in *The Psychology of Literacy* (1981), in which cognitive psychologists Sylvia Scribner and Michael Cole contest the idea, based on their research with the Vai people in Liberia, that literacy has generalizable cognitive "consequences." Scribner and Cole weren't entirely convinced that alphabetic literacy *per se* could be held responsible for bringing the revolutionary changes in thought and culture Great Divide scholars had claimed for it. Part of the problem with that work, they pointed out, is that if you're doing historical research, you can't see what goes on inside people's heads to *see* how they're thinking differently. Another difficulty is that it's difficult to assume that causes and effects at work in a particular time in history operate exactly the same way at other times (so, for example, there's no telling that a nonliterate child in a literate society will need to acquire literacy him- or herself in order to attain ways of thinking [abstraction, etc.] associated with literacy). Finally, the Great Divide theorists operate at the level of speculation, with no real grounded evidence for their claims. Of the kinds of generalizations about literacy made by such scholars as Ong and Goody and Watt, Scribner and Cole wrote that "these are perfectly satisfactory *starting* points [emphasis theirs] for a theory of the intellectual consequences of reading and writing but they do not warrant the status of conclusions" ("Scribner & Cole, 2001, p. 60).

With the assumptions of Great Divide causes and effects in mind, Scribner and Cole traveled to Africa to study uses of written language among the Liberian Vai. What made the Vai especially interesting to Scribner and Cole as research subjects was the unusual fact that they had reading and writing practices that were *not* learned in school—a situation that meant that the researchers wouldn't be inclined to confuse the effects of written language acquisition with the effects of *schooling*. Another thing that made the Vai an interesting "test case" to Scribner and Cole was that they practiced three distinct forms of literacy depending on their status and life situations:

- reading and writing in the language Mande using an indigenous Vai syllabary
- Qu'ranic literacy using Arabic script
- Western school literacy in English using the Roman alphabet

Scribner and Cole further noted that these forms of literacy were *not* randomly used or distributed—instead, each form had its own distinct set of uses. Native Vai literacy, for example, is deeply rooted in local cultural history and is used primarily to preserve traditional social roles and relationships. People pass Vai literacy down through generations and through their own social networks outside of schools or formal education. In contrast, the Vai use Arabic literacy learned in Qu'ranic schools and study groups for religious education, and they learn to read and write Arabic mostly through direct instruction and rote learning: "teachers emphasize recitation; they provide little explanation of the meaning of the texts being read, and the children have virtually no knowledge of the meaning of individual words or phrases" (Scribner & Cole, 1989, p. 69). English literacy, the official government literacy, had a religious impetus as well—that is, it was originally introduced into Vai culture by Christian missionaries—but for present-day Muslim Vai, reading and writing in English has mainly secular uses. Those Vai who aquire English literacy learn it exclusively in Western-style schools, and this literacy is used primarily for business transactions and nonlocal communications.

About a third of the Vai are literate in one of these ways—the Vai syllabary, the Arabic script, or the English alphabet. Some have two literacies; a smaller number have three. Each writing system corresponds to a different language, and the settings in which they are learned and used are very different. Scribner and Cole wondered: since the Vai had three very different kinds of literacies—and the three literacies used different writing systems that corresponded to different languages and were learned and used in different settings—did these have the same demonstrable "effects"?

Different Literacies, Different Cognitive "Consequences"

You can see how the Vai, with their three distinctly different forms of schooling, languages, and scripts, afforded the ideal context within which Scribner and Cole could put the idea that literacy has predictable cognitive consequences to the test. In their psychological research, they found that indeed they did not: different "literacies" could be related to different habits and capabilities. Qu'ranic literacy, for example—because it relied heavily upon ritual memorization and recitation—could be correlated in some cases to increased ability to do rote memory tasks. When Scribner and Cole looked across "effects of literacy" categories such as "communication skills," "memory," and "language analysis"—all categories named as universally subject to the consequences of literacy by Great Divide theorists—they found very different outcomes depending on the nature of the task and the kind of literacy in question. "The consequences of literacy that we identified," explain Scribner and Cole, "are all highly specific and closely tied to actual practices and scripts" (1981, p. 90). In fact, conclude the researchers, the capacities associated with literacy are more easily tied to forms of schooling—the pedagogies used to teach literacy—than to literacy practices themselves.

In learning about Vai ways of using print, Scribner and Cole concluded that the Great Divide theory in its strongest form was incorrect, or at least too ambitious in its claims. On the idea that literacy inevitably produces more logical or "higher-order" thought, they write,

> On no task—logic, abstraction, memory, communication—did we find all non-literates performing at lower levels than all literates.... We can and so claim that literacy promotes skills among the Vai, but we *cannot and do not claim that literacy is a necessary and sufficient condition for any of the skills we assessed.* (Cole & Scribner, 1981, p. 251; emphasis added)

Scribner and Cole argue for a more modest conception of what literacy "does," in keeping with their conclusion that "particular practices promote particular skills." They concluded that it was the process of education—or schooling—rather than literacy in isolation, that fostered new ways of thinking. It was, they concluded, *not* print literacy per se that led to "logical" thought, but rather schooling in the Western tradition that produced this result. Just being able to read and write, in other words, doesn't equip you for "logic"—instead, learning "logic" as a schooled practice is what equips you for these ways of making knowledge.

Scribner and Cole's findings led them to insist that an understanding of how literacy is *used* in particular social situations is essential to an understanding of literacy more generally, and that we should be careful of imagining that literacy operates in widely transformational or revolutionary terms. In other words: literacy might in fact change things, but it doesn't change things for everyone in the same way, and it's not always obvious what these changes are and how they work. As we'll see, the range of cultural variety in uses of literacy make it difficult to predict, with any real accuracy, what the precise social effects of literacy will be in a given situation—and also to make authoritative claims about how literacy changes thinking.

Interestingly enough, claims for the universal effects of reading and writing are best supported by claiming the same "consequences" in very different times and places. Such claims are provocative in thinking about how literacy operates as a technology—and now, in the age of digital communications, they are in wide circulation again (as we'll explore later, in Chapter Five). But where do they leave us in terms of understanding how literacy works in diverse locations and in real time? This is the question we'll take up in Chapter Three.

ACTIVITIES AND PROJECTS

1. **What's in a List?** Anthropologist Jack Goody has contended that the creation of written lists for various historical, social, and economic purposes "represented a significant change not only in the nature of transactions, but also in the 'modes of thought' that accompanied them" (1977, p. 33). One way to test claims that literacy produces major cognitive shifts is to experiment with creating lists—both oral and written.

   With others in your class, try making lists first orally and then with the aid of writing. Work in a group of four: three to act as "list makers" and one to be an "analytical observer."

   ### Part 1: Create lists orally
   1. After receiving a list of words (orally) from the instructor, the three list makers will create lists of like items (again, orally). List makers should discuss the words to determine organizing categories for the lists.
   2. Meanwhile, the person acting as observer records the process (i.e., decisions made, strategies used by the list makers), saving these notes for later group and class discussion.
   3. Then, everyone in the group orally describes the created lists and explains to the class their logic.

   ### Part 2: Create lists with the aid of pen and paper
   1. This time your group will receive written words that you can organize to make multiple lists however the group chooses. As before, work on creating several kinds of lists using various logical connections or categories.
   2. As your group discusses and formulates your various lists, also discuss and write down the logic of your categories and strategies.
   3. Report to the class the lists you made and the logic behind them.

   ### Part 3: Further reflection and analysis
   1. Still with others in your group, discuss in a general way the problems you encountered and the solutions you employed for the oral and written lists you made. How would you compare and contrast these two approaches?

2. Finally, identify two or three claims from Ong and the Great Divide theorists, and prepare to discuss with your classmates how your group's experiences with this activity affirm and/or complicate these claims about orality and literacy.

2. **Dialogue in Writing?** A question that continues to surface for those of us who study how writing works has to do with whether writing constrains or enables philosophical inquiry—and whether all forms of writing work the same way in this regard. As we saw in the *Phaedrus,* Socrates believed that writing would close down possibilities for conversation, that it would get in the way of real inquiry. Contemporary rhetoric scholar Jasper Neel has argued, however, that the Socratic dialogues needed to be written to realize their full potential *as* inquiry. To explore for yourself whether the dialogue (a) operates as an oral or written genre (or in some ways both); and (b) which mode or genre works best to fully *inquire* into the questions and assumptions that lie under the surface of a given issue, try the following exercise:

1. Choose a controversial topic of your choice—an *issue,* something you know people argue about a lot. Pick something about which you know you disagree with others around you.
2. Find a person with whom you know you *disagree* to discuss the issue with. Have a 30-minute conversation with your partner about the issue (during which each of you should explain, justify, and defend your positions).
3. Then write a traditional five-paragraph essay in which you explain a possible perspective on the issue. Within the constraints of this essay form, explain, justify, and defend this position.
4. Now create a written dialogue about the same topic. The rules for the dialogue: there must be three voices representing three different positions on the issue; each "voice" must be presented as equally intelligent, thoughtful, and well-informed.
5. Finally, consider: What does each form (oral discussion, traditional essay, and the written dialogue) allow you to do—to discover, to understand, to defend? Which leads you to a better understanding of the issue you chose? What does this activity lead you to think about Socrates' claims about the dangers of writing, or Neel's claims about the benefits?

3. **Email: An Oral, Literate—or Hybrid—Genre?** In the chapter you've just completed, you've explored ideas about how speech and writing differ, how "orality" and "literacy" have different forms, effects, and patterns of cultural distribution. Much of what you've read so far, however, addresses how oral and literate forms have developed in other times and places. It's important to think as well about how categories of orality and literacy might apply now, in the 21st century, when digital technologies mediate so much of what we communicate. Here's one way to begin thinking about how orality and literacy—as modes of discourse—look nowadays:

   1. Select three or four longer email messages from different social and institutional sources (personal communications with friends, exchanges related to schoolwork, work correspondences, solicitations from advertisers, etc.).

   2. Look closely at how the senders use language in each of the messages. Using the contrasting lists from Chandler and Ong in this chapter as your guide, ask yourself: what evidence of oral and literate processes do I see in these emails' language, tone, and organization?

   3. Based on these contrasting lists of "features" of orality and literacy, and the uses of language you see in these emails, give your analysis of email as a "hybrid genre." Use the following questions to guide your analysis:

      - Which of the email sources you selected would you say tend more toward oral or literate forms and structures? What reasons might you offer for your assumptions?

      - What specific oral and literate features seem to be combined in the discourse of various kinds of emails?

      - In looking at these patterns of orality and literacy in email, what does your investigation of email texts lead you to believe about what kind of communicative society 20th-century Americans have? What does it lead you to believe about the nature of "orality" and "literacy"?

4. **Research on Attitudes About Literacy and Intelligence.** As we saw, the belief that there is a strong causal connection between literacy and "intelligence" is pervasive in modern life. To find out more about what people believe about the correlation of literacy and intelligence, conduct brief

informal interviews with five or six people you know—parents, friends, siblings, co-workers, teachers—and ask them what they think about the relationship between literacy and smarts. Here are some questions to ask:

1. How would you describe the relationships between a person's literacy "ability" (fluency in reading and writing texts) and his or her intelligence?
2. How would you describe the relationship between a person's literacy *habits* (uses of reading and writing in his or her everyday life) and his or her intelligence?
3. If you think literacy enables or creates intelligence, what *kind* of intelligence do you think this is?
4. What have you seen and experienced that has led you to your conclusions about literacy and intelligence?
5. What is your own educational level? What is your occupation?

After you've collected your data, look for patterns in your informants' responses (setting aside the data from question 4 for the moment—you can come back to that later, for other purposes). Do you find general agreement about the correlation between literacy and intelligence? What are the areas of agreement and divergence? Now, triangulate your data (compare your results) with others in your class or work group. What is the "bigger picture" that emerges?

5. **Is There Speech in Writing?** Have you ever been advised by a writing teacher to "write as you speak"? Or have you, on the other hand, been told to practice a less "colloquial" style of writing? For this activity, explore these assumptions that often show up in teachers' expectations about writing by interviewing writing teachers about the connections they see between oral and written language.

1. First, choose three teachers you believe would be available and willing to talk with you (they don't have to be teachers you currently have for classes).
2. To prepare for interviews, develop at least ten questions about forms and uses of oral and written language that address these connections in regard to (a) your interviewees' *own* writing, (b) their ways of teaching writing, and (c) their experiences with students and their writing. (Possible questions could be, for example, Does the way you speak "affect" how you write? Do you advise your students to "write like you speak"? Do you believe that articulate speakers always make good writers?)

3. Ask questions to follow up on your interviewees' initial responses. You want to get your interviewees to give you examples, stories, and situations that you can then analyze more fully.

4. After you finish your interviews and record the results, work with one or two classmates to see what patterns or assumptions about literacy and writing and teaching practices you can collectively discover when you compare the statements, stories, and examples from each interview.

5. Still working with your group, create a written report interpreting your findings from your "data" from both interviews with teachers and discussions with others. In doing so, consider: How would you compare these teachers' assumptions and practices to the claims of the Great Divide theorists and the research of Scribner and Cole? How would you account for the differences between these teachers' responses? How much would you attribute the differences to their experiences and social and cultural backgrounds?

6. **Film Analysis: What Does Literacy Look Like?** If, as has been claimed by Great Divide theorists, literacy has the power to confer the capacity for higher-order reasoning and to make people "civilized," then is it possible to know a literate person when you see him or her? If literacy changes people, then how would we imagine a literate person to "wear" his or literacy in contrast to a nonliterate? For this activity, explore the assumptions of what literacy, or the presumed lack of it, "looks like" in the popular imagination, and whether or how the "look of literacy" might be changing. Just as we did with *Stanley and Iris* and *Born Yesterday*, explore how literacy/illiteracy is represented in popular media.

1. First, choose a film, a television show, or several magazine advertisements that depict any aspect of literacy in American or world contexts.

2. With the help of the following questions, discuss in groups and/or write individually about the assumptions about literacy that you think underlie these images and visual narratives.

   ▪ What do the image(s) suggest about how literacy is understood as a matter of class, race, gender, region, religion, body type, or other means of identity formation? How do things such as class operate as a "code" to communicate assumptions about how literacy works and where it's located?

- What is the scene and context for the actions of the people in the image? What do any objects in the foreground or background or scenes tell you about what kinds of assumptions about literacy are at work? What objects seem to represent the enabling or hindering of literacy?
- Based on the visual arrangement of people and objects in this image or scene, what can you interpret about the power dynamics regarding literacy concerns and the people represented in the image?
- What might the image(s) suggest about historical changes in literacy (in terms of who in society has authority through literacy, or in terms of technological changes in literacy)?
- How do the implied meanings of these visual markers and symbols of literacy or illiteracy compare to the Great Divide theories?

7. **Parody Advertisement.** Using military recruiting posters as a model, create a parody advertisement for "joining the literacy club." In your ad, create persuasive text and visuals to "sell" literacy: Here's what literacy can do for you and for civilization!

8. **Photo Collage.** Create a photo collage that advances a visual argument in favor of claims for the civilizing potential of literacy. To accompany your collage, compose a short (one to three pages) critical reflection in which you explain (1) how your collage works as an "argument" about literacy, and (2) your ideas on the effects of representing claims about literacy *visually*.

9. **Silent Speech?** As you've learned in this chapter, literacy theorist Walter Ong described "orality" as a communicative mode for which the particular "psychodynamics" depend on the properties of sound. Ong makes a careful case in "The Psychodynamics of Orality" that the physical production of orality defines its psychosocial features, but he gives less attention to the ways in which the acquisition of print literacy might also "rely" on sound. In "Learning How to Read and Bypassing Sound," scholars of Deaf education Supalla and Blackburn (2003) describe the special predicament deaf students face in learning how to process written information. They write,

> For signing deaf students, we encounter a unique linguistic situation. American Sign Language and English are not simply two languages. They

are languages that rely on separate modalities, one in hearing, the other in sight (Singleton, Supalla, Litchfield, & Schley, 1998). In this sense, hearing students enjoy at least two advantages compared to deaf students in learning how to read. For hearing students, the text is consistent with the way they speak. Further, they can use a system of phonetic skills to decode individual words and discover their meanings. Deaf students, on the other hand, are confronted with sentences that are constructed differently from what they sign. There is a gap between the deaf student's knowledge—his or her competency in American Sign Language—and how print represents English, a language that he or she cannot hear. (*http://clerccenter2. gallaudet.edu/KidsWorldDeafNet/e-docs/Keys/learning.html*)

Recall that Ong characterizes orality as "additive, aggregative, redundant, close to the human lifeworld, agonistically toned, empathic and participatory, situational," and so on (1982, pp. 36–57); from this he concludes that speech permits different kinds of social relationships from those possible through writing. Yet one communication medium that uses neither sound nor text is signing. Even though they don't use sound in their talk, deaf people using ASL (American Sign Language) are engaging in a highly interpersonal, nonmediated form of communication. What can this mean for Ong's early claims about the dependence of orality on sound? Read Supalla and Blackburn's article describing how deaf children learn print literacy, and then speculate on the implications of what you've learned for Ong's claims for orality and literacy.

FOR FURTHER READING

Cunningham, Anne, & Stanovich, Keith. (2003). "Reading Can Make You Smarter" Principal: What Principals Need to Know About Reading. 83(2): 34–39.

Cushman, Ellen, Kintgen, Eugene, Kroll, Barry, & Rose, Mike. (2001). Introduction: Surveying the field. *Literacy: A Critical Sourcebook* (pp. 1–17). Bedford/St. Martin's.

Goody, Jack. (1977). What's in a list? *The Domestication of the Savage Mind* (pp. 74–111). Cambridge: Cambridge University Press.

Goody, Jack, & Watt, Ian. (1962). The consequences of literacy. *Comparative Studies in Society and History*, 5(3): 304–345.

Goody, Jack, & Watt, Ian. (1968). The consequences of literacy. In *Literacy in traditional societies* (pp. 27–68). Cambridge: Cambridge University Press.

Havelock, Eric. (1982). *The Literate revolution in Greece and its cultural consequences*. Princeton, NJ: Princeton University Press.

_____. (1986). Writing is a technology that restructures thought. In Gerd Baumann (Ed.), *The written word: Literacy in transition*. Oxford: Clarendon Press.

Neel, Jasper. (1988). *Plato, Demdu, and Writing*. Carbondale: SIU Press.

Ong, Walter. (2002). *Orality and literacy: The technologizing of the word*. London: Routledge.

Olsen, David R. (2001). Writing and the mind. In Cushman, Kintgen, Kroll, & Rose (Eds.), *Literacy: A critical sourcebook* (pp. 107–123.) Bedford/St. Martin's.

Plato. (2005). *Phaedrus*. New York: Penguin.

Scribner, Sylvia, & Cole, Michael. (1981). *The psychology of literacy*. Cambridge, MA: Harvard University Press.

_____. (2001). Unpackaging literacy. In Cushman, Kintgen, Kroll, & Rose (Eds.), *Literacy: A critical sourcebook* (pp. 138–156). Bedford/St. Martin's.

Supalla, Sam, & Blackburn, Laura. (2003). Learning How to Read and Bypassing Sound. *Odyssey* (5)1.

3

Literacy and Culture

Before You Read. Consider your response to the question about literacy and cognition in Chapter One. Now that you've been invited to think of literacy as a cultural phenomenon, ask yourself how your response to that question might change. Does literacy now seem more like a practice, or a possession? Which of your "literacy habits"—your attitudes about, uses of, and practices of literacy—now seem to be explainable in terms of your cultural environment? What does inviting ideas of "culture" into the conversation change about how you understand the kind of literacy you "have" or "do"?

Into the Field: Ethnographic Research on Literacy

Community Reading in Trackton, South Carolina

One way to think about literacy is to imagine the scenes in which it happens. We tend to think about the "scene" of literacy as a schoolroom, an office, a library. But imagine instead the following scene, which takes place in South Carolina in the1970s. Lillie Mae, a resident of Trackton, a small African American working-class community in the Carolina Piedmonts, has just received a letter from the state daycare program she wants for her 2-year-old son Lem. Lillie Mae steps out onto her front porch to consult with her neighbors, who work nearby sweeping their porches or doing other chores in the large open space between their homes. She reads from the letter as she talks to her neighbors:

> **Lillie Mae:** You hear this, it says Lem might can get into Ridgeway, but I hafta have the papers ready and apply by next Friday.

Visiting Friend: You ever been to Kent to get his certificate? [the friend is a mother of three children in school]

Mattie Crawford: But what hours that program gonna be? You may not can get him there.

Lillie Mae: They want the birth certificate? I got his vaccination papers.

Annie Mae: Sometimes they take that, 'cause they can bout tell the age from those early shots.

Visiting Friend: But you better get it, cause you gotta have it when he go to school anyway.

Lillie Mae: But it says here they don't know what hours yet. How am I gonna get over to Kent? How much does it cost? Lemme see if the program costs anything (she reads aloud part of the letter). (quoted in Heath, 1983, p. 197)

The discussion continues for almost an hour as Lillie Mae's neighbors contribute their interpretations of the various sections of the day-care letter based on their personal and communal experiences. How would she get a ride to Kent to get Lem's birth certificate, which was required for the local daycare program, when she and many of her neighbors didn't have a car? What were the pros and cons of these daycare programs as other neighbors had experienced them with their children?

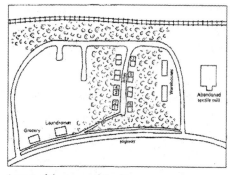

A map of the town of Trackton

Shirley Brice Heath. Ways with Words: Language, Life and Work in Communities and Classrooms. Cambridge UP, 1983. Reprinted with the permission of Shirley Brice Heath

Here in Trackton, people tend to talk together to make sense of texts that will likely influence their lives. Notice in this scene how literacy is not—in this case—something people do alone in their living rooms or dorm rooms or offices. For the people of Trackton, reading a letter is done in a public space with a group of people—people who are looking on, listening, helping to interpret the text. In this scene, even reading, something we often think of as a private act, happens as much "out there" in the community as it does "inside the head" of a single person.

To say that literacy happens "in culture" as well as in the mind is to acknowledge scenes such as this one in Trackton as being important to an understanding of how literacy works. To say that literacy is a cultural thing is also to acknowledge that what exactly literacy *is* and *means* and *does* depends on where the cultural scene is, and who is involved.

In this chapter, you will learn more about the research methods and analytical tools to help you study how and why people use literacy within specific cultures. Through discussion of ethnographic studies of literacy and examples of literacies in various cultures (ranging from ethnic communities to youth basketball players to Star Trek fans), you will learn to:

- Identify and research a *literacy event* in a culture, subculture, or group.
- Analyze five key *elements of literacy* for a culture, subculture, or group, and how to discern the significance of these elements for this culture.
- Examine how people seek and use power through these five elements of a literacy event: *text, context, function, participants,* and *motivation.*
- Recognize the traits of *essayist literacy* and analyze its possible impact upon a given culture, subculture, or group.
- Understand how ethnographic research of literacy can help communities and institutions.

What Is Ethnographic Research of Literacy?

The scene in Trackton comes from an anthropological study of reading and writing within communities by Shirley Brice Heath, *Ways with Words: Life, Language, and Learning in Communities and Classrooms,* published in 1983. According to Heath, who spent over 10 years in the Piedmonts researching how people in three local communities speak, read, and write, almost all acts of reading, and many of writing, in Trackton become a social activity. Trackton residents only tend to read as a solitary activity when the information has to do with economic competition for jobs. Heath says of reading in Trackton: "Authority in the written word does not rest in the words themselves, but in the meanings which are negotiated through the experiences of the group" (1993, p. 196). In this case, Lillie Mae repeatedly returns to the words of the daycare letter, testing its possible meanings against the interpretations of her neighbors to weigh her choices.

Heath's anthropological approach to literacy research is *ethnographic* (*ethnography* means "writing culture": *ethno* refers to culture, and *graphic* refers to writing). The method of ethnography comes from cultural anthropology. An ethnographer is a researcher who seeks to understand the beliefs, values, and unspoken social rules of a culture or group as people who have membership or who participate in the culture understand it. To accomplish this goal, ethnographers rely on research

methods of *participant-observation* and *ethnographic interviewing*. When ethnographers simultaneously participate in and observe the activities of a culture (sometimes called *cultural practices*) as they happen, they stand a better chance of understanding the motives, values, and social roles of the activities in ways a group's members understand them. Ethnographers also continually test out their hunches about these insider perspectives of the culture by informally interviewing members of the culture to get a fuller picture of these cultural practices.

Heath's book paved the way for other ethnographic studies of community literacies, and it remains a central work in the field today. What ethnographic research on literacy like Heath's study can help us see is how differences in people's literacy and the ways they use reading and writing are cultural—not cognitive—differences. Unlike researchers like Ong, ethnographers of literacy show how literacy looks in local scenes—they tell the "little narratives" of literacy rather than creating "big narratives" of literacy that assume dramatic, large-scale changes in human cultural organization.

So ethnographies of literacy offer readers particulars of people's lives, not information applicable to a variety of contexts. We get details and unfolding narratives, as with our opening scene of Lillie Mae's letter. Ethnographers represent evidence for their arguments more as lived experiences, as stories to help readers see from the ethnographers' and participants' eyes as much as possible. In this way, ethnographies best help us understand complexities of cultures and test theories about cultures against people's lived realities in ways that scientific data cannot. Because ethnography focuses on particulars of local contexts, however, the knowledge from its research is often not portable, like scientific studies, to other situations. This is a major reason why the world of standardized testing and its climate of literacy as science, as discussed in Chapter One, tends to ignore ethnographic knowledge of community literacies.

Studying Literacy Practices in Cultures

To understand how ethnographers think of culture, recall the scene in teen movies (like *Mean Girls*) where the main character is shown in the high school cafeteria, which is divided into different groups of students—jocks here, burnouts here, band kids here, geeks into Dungeons and Dragons over there, and so on. An ethnographer would recognize each of these groups as a different subculture with its own unspoken social rules for behaving, talking, and interacting with others (what might be cool for a D & D gamer, for example, would be a sign of hopeless geekdom for a jock). An ethnographer would also be interested in the individual differences *between* people in these groups that defy the usual teen-movie stereotypes. After all, you may very well have been into Rage Against the Machine *and* took a role on the prom committee or debate team.

Ethnographers of *literacy,* then, explore how and why each of these subcultures uses (or doesn't use) various kinds of reading and writing and, more important, what meanings they associate with these uses. Ethnographer Amy Shuman was also interested in teen culture. In the 1980s, she compared the kinds of writing middle school girls in Philadelphia *chose* to do on their own—diaries, notes passed in class, manifestos related to school issues—to the writing they *had* to do for their classes. Ethnographers refer to a culture's or group's various ways of using literacy as *literacy practices.* Through her careful observation and participation in the culture of these girls as they wrote, Shuman was able to analyze when and why the girls would use various genres of writing to resist authority in the school.

> **Definition**
>
> **Literacy Practices**
> A culture's or group's various ways of reading, writing, and talking about texts

For instance, the girls collaborated on forging excuse notes that the school administration most often did not question. The school principal, however, did not accept the authority of the girls' collaborative efforts when they wrote a petition to allow a talent show act based on Pink Floyd's anti-school rock anthem, "The Wall." From this and other data, Shuman infers that school authorities overlooked the excuse notes because they didn't disrupt any power relationships, while the collaborative petition was an effort to legitimately challenge the principal's authority. If Shuman were to do this research today, she would very likely want to include as part of her data the messages and photos girls would be sending by cell phones across the cafeteria and in the hallways.

Activity: Comparing Literacies in Different Parts of Our Lives
One of the ways that ethnographers research the many kinds of literacies people use in specific communities is through *domain analysis*. To better understand this kind of research, try mapping out a domain analysis of your own.

1. Divide a piece of paper into four boxes with these headings:
   - Institutional (schools, religious contexts, public institutions)
   - Home
   - Neighborhood/Friends/Community
   - Workplaces

2. For each box heading, list memories of the kinds of literacy practices and the ways you use them in this domain. Try to get at least three for each. These literacy practices do not need to be special memories.

3. Now, share and discuss your literacy map of domains in small groups.
   - How did the situations you encountered in these domains influence the purpose or structure of these literacy practices in each particular domain? What has been the influence of larger social contexts?
   - How much do the literacy practices overlap in, or conflict with, these domains?
   - What do the literacy practices in these domains suggest about culture and identity?

Literacy in Action: Understanding a Literacy Event in Trackton

Heath's Idea of a Literacy Event—Where Talk, Reading, and Writing Come Together

Because Heath recognized that different uses of literacy had more to do with cultural differences than innate mental abilities, she believed ethnographic research would help her understand better why the children of Trackton, a working-class African American community, and Roadville, a working-class White community, rarely succeeded in the nearby middle-class schools of Gateway despite each community's concern for its children's success in school. She observed and tried to infer patterns in local uses of (and occasions for) talk, reading, and writing in Trackton and Roadville. Heath then compared these patterns of literacy practices to the assumptions about literacy implicitly held by the middle-class "townspeople" in Gateway. Heath's book helped open the door for ethnographic studies of literacy practices in other communities outside schools and middle-class institutions. Her book remains central to the field of literacy studies today.

Unlike the cognitive theorists who saw a great divide between orality and literacy, Heath and other ethnographers of literacy believe that the social meanings of a culture's literacy can only be found in the *relationships between* acts of reading, writing, and talking in the community. Literacy ethnographers believe that because it's important to understand whole systems of meaning and use within cultures, you can't separate people's talk from their ways of using literacy.

When literacy researchers want to discern meaningful intersections of talk, reading, and writing in a culture or community, they use the idea of a *literacy event* to help them interpret what they see and hear. In her work with these Carolina communities, Heath defined a literacy event as "any occasion in which a piece of writing is integral to the nature of participants' interactions and their interpretive processes" (1983, p. 350). This means that a literacy event refers to any moment when we interact with reading or writing or talk about those materials we read and/or write. As this definition suggests, then, a literacy event can refer to everyday moments, such as Lillie Mae consulting her neighbors about her daycare letter, as much as any special event.

Defining a Literacy Event

As a concept that comes from research methods in anthropology, this cultural approach to researching language gives us methodological tools that help us better analyze the *social meanings* of talk and literacy practices in a culture. Heath drew the concept from the term *speech event* (created by Dell Hymes from the language philosophy of J. L. Austin) used in sociolinguistics and the ethnography of communication. Speech events follow unspoken social rules for how to talk with others in a given community. When sociolinguists identify which people in the Boston area pronounce their city "Bahstan," they are researching people's unspoken, and sometimes subconscious, identification with the values of a particular social class, race, or region.

In the case of literacy events, unspoken (tacit) social rules tend to govern what a particular culture or group reads and/or writes, how to read and write it, and how to talk about it with others in particular contexts. Just think of the difference between how you talk about an entertainment or sports magazine among friends and how the same material would be "analyzed" in a college classroom. Because what people read and write in various groups and cultures can vary so much, ethnographers refer to any written products as *literacy materials*, be they racing forms or weblogs.

So when a literacy ethnographer studies a *literacy event*, she is looking for the implicit rules within a specific community, culture, social group, or institution for *how* participants

a) read or write particular literacy materials,

b) talk about the reading and writing of the materials, and

c) understand the social, cultural, economic, and historical relationship between the participants' talk and reading and writing.

From both his or her participation in and observation of these literacy events as they occur and the interviewing of community members about how they view these events, the ethnographic researcher of literacy hopes to better understand the cultural assumptions and values of the participants that become apparent in the intersection of all three elements.

What Cultural Values Underlie Trackton's Social Approach to Reading?

So now let's return to Lillie Mae and her neighbors' social reading of the daycare letter in Trackton. When Heath observed and participated in this literacy event, she was also asking: what cultural assumptions and values underlie this highly social approach to reading? She also wanted to know how these practices related to larger social contexts that affect the community, contexts such as social class, race, and the schools' (and other dominant middle-class institutions') approaches to literacy. Over time, Heath could see connections between these social acts of reading and writing and the ways Trackton parents habitually taught their children to interact with most people and objects in their daily lives.

Heath saw that, unlike the more middle-class parents in Gateway who tended to label objects in their children's everyday experiences and in books ("this is a cat"), to ask rhetorical questions about objects ("what does the cat say?"), and explain items for their toddlers ("this cat is like our kitten Boots"), Trackton adults didn't ordinarily talk this way to their children. Instead, they expected their children to be observant and to figure things out for themselves without such explicit prompting. Heath quotes Annie Mae, another Trackton resident, who explains this view. (Note that Heath uses unconventional spelling to approximate the sounds of Annie Mae's rural southern African American dialect.)

> He gotta learn to know bout dis world, can't nobody tell 'im. Now just how crazy is dat? White folks uh hear dey kids say sump'n, day say it back to 'em, dey aks 'em 'gain 'n 'gain bout things, like they 'posed to be knowin'. You think I kin tell Teege [her grandson] all he gotta know to get along? . . . he see one thing one place one time, he know how it go, see sump'n like it again, maybe it be de same, maybe it won't. He hafta try it out. If he don't, he be in trouble. (quoted in Heath, 1983, p. 84)

When Lillie Mae seeks out her neighbors to help her interpret the meanings of the daycare letter, she enacts the cultural assumptions of the community expressed here by Annie Mae. The Trackton residents do not immediately trust the text itself of the letter. First, it must be tested by their experiences and their own understandings in the particular contexts of their lives. They recognize that meanings in texts can change depending upon the situation and the people involved in the transaction of the written communication. Moreover, most Trackton residents are rightly wary of texts from outside the community that often hold institutional power over them.

Informal Teaching of Literacy Use in Trackton

Heath shows how the community members implicitly teach these "meanings" of literacy to their children when she describes how parents let other adults in the community tease their children by, for example, temporarily withholding treats from the children until they learn how to spar verbally with the adults. She points out that the adults often change the rules in their games of playful teasing, so that children have to learn how to read each situation and context as it emerges. "Preschoolers, especially boys, are always presented with situations and being asked, '*Now,* what you gonna do?'" (1983, p. 84). Cultural practices like these foster great verbal and interpretive flexibility and creativity as well as a highly social approach to interpreting others' language, such as in Lillie Mae's approach to interpreting the situation and context of the daycare letter.

These attitudes and behaviors toward improvisation and social interpretation suggest that Trackton parents recognize that their children need to learn to improvise to prepare for future struggles with institutionalized racism that they themselves have experienced. As Annie Mae put it, "Maybe it be de same, maybe it won't. He hafta try it out. If he don't, he be in trouble."

By comparing these cultural practices to the literacy expectations of middle-class schools in Gateway, we can see the social implications of these practices for the children of Trackton (and possibly, children of other working-class African American communities). As Heath mentions, the middle-class schools in Gateway do—to a degree—value this kind of use of imagination. But they also expect students to be able to practice "book talk" (to be able to use language that comes from books that are outside the students' immediate situations) and to develop accuracy in reconstructing the details and implied meanings of written texts. These are cultural expectations of literacy that put the African American working-class children at a disadvantage in school despite their keen improvisatory abilities. Only by spending considerable time with the people of Trackton was Heath able to discover these meanings of language use, meanings that influenced community members' practices of reading and writing. You can't find out these local understandings of literacy only through historical research, or only by theoretical speculation.

Talkin' Story: Texts in Literacy Events

What Counts as a Story in Roadville?

But the concept of *literacy event* can also help researchers see how written texts influence ways of talking. For instance, Heath saw that the ways people read the Bible in Roadville, the White working-class community she studied in the Piedmonts, influenced what they believed counted as a "story" and what counted (by contrast) as "truth." These literacy expectations differed greatly from those of the families in middle-class

Gateway. In *Ways with Words*, Heath provides an example of a typical moment of storytelling among women in Roadville when Sue tells a story of a baking recipe gone awry:

> **Mrs. Macken:** Sue, you oughta tell about those rolls you made the other day, make folks glad you didn't try to serve fancy rolls today.
>
> **Mrs. Dee:** Sue, what'd you do, do you have a new recipe?
>
> **Mrs. Macken:** (speaking at same time as Sue) You might call it that
>
> **Sue:** I, wanna. . .
>
> **Martha:** Now Millie [Mrs. Macken], you hush and let Sue give us *her* story.
>
> **Sue:** Well, as a matter of fact, I did have this new recipe, one I got out of Better Homes and Gardens, and I thought I'd try it, uh, you see, it called for scalded milk, and I had just started the milk when the telephone rang, and I went to get it. It was Leona. I thought I turned the stove off, and when I came back, the burner was off, uh, so I didn't think anything about it, poured the milk in on the yeast, and went to kneading. Felt a little hot. Well, anyway, put the stuff out to rise, and came back, and it looked almost like Stone Mountain, thought that's a strange recipe, so I kneaded it again, and set it out in rolls. This time I had rocks, uh, sorta like 'em, the kind that roll up smooth at the beach. Well I wasn't gonna throw all that stuff out, so I cooked it. Turned out even harder than those rocks, if that's possible, and nobody would eat 'em, couldn't even soften 'em in buttermilk. I was trying to explain how the recipe was so funny, you know, see, how I didn't know what I did wrong, and Sally [Sue's daughter] piped up and said 'like yeah, when you was on the phone, I came in, saw this white stuff a-boiling, and I turned it off.' (pause) Then I knew, you know, that milk was too hot, killed the yeast. (looking around at the women) Guess I'll learn to keep my mind on my own business and off other folks. (quoted in Heath, 1983, pp. 151–152)

Heath points out that unlike the Trackton residents who value improvisation to cope with social injustice in their everyday lives, people of Roadville—who follow a strict southern Christian morality in their lives—expect a story to be, in their words, "a piece of truth." To conform to community norms, stories must be factual accounts that make fun of the storyteller, showing what she or he has learned from the transgression of these norms, just as Sue does here.

How Storytelling Can Enforce Community Values

Heath first emphasizes Roadville residents' concern for the enforcement of community norms when she points out that Mrs. Macken is more of a newcomer to the community and doesn't have as much authority to nominate Sue, a longtime resident, to tell her story. This is why Martha implicitly puts Mrs. Macken in her place in the social hierarchy of the town: "you hush, and let Sue give us *her* story." One of the strongest moral norms in Roadville is telling the truth, even in one's own stories. That's why Heath notes that Sue is careful to qualify each of the metaphors she uses: the bread dough is "almost like Stone Mountain" (a state park in Georgia) and "sorta like" the rocks on the beach that the women often bring back from their vacations to put in their flowerpots.

The transgression that Sue's story narrates is gossip: all of the Roadville women identify Leona, the woman with whom Sue converses too long on the phone, as a notorious gossip. So Sue's story, through the example of the storyteller, is meant to remind all the women present of their failings—and the importance of trying to do the right thing next time: "Guess I'll learn to keep my mind on my own business and off other folks." By emphasizing Sue's need to summarize her story with a moral, Heath likens these oral stories to two favorite genres used by Roadville residents—prayer testimonials and Biblical parables.

Heath argues that it is exactly this need for stories to contain clear morals that stick to the meaning of the biblical Word that creates difficulties for the working-class Roadville children when middle-class teachers want them to use their imagination and consider alternatives to a situation in their reading and writing. Roadville kids have trouble with this expectation because from their perspective these forms of intellectual creativity are lies. And because this kind of storytelling and these uses of stories are not encouraged by their parents, the Roadville children have a difficult time adapting to these different literacy practices. In contrast, the Trackton children run into trouble in the middle-class schools for the opposite reason—because Trackton residents value creative storytelling more than analyzing the truth of situations. From the study of these two communities, we can see how complicated things get once you start to hang around and pay attention to literacy in action and when you analyze the social implications of those complications.

Activity: Finding the Literate in Oral Storytelling

Heath's research suggests that we can almost always find traces of written genres and styles within our talk, and particularly in our storytelling, as we see with the Roadville women and their use of the Bible. Here's a way to explore this weaving of the written and the oral for yourselves.

1. Individually, ask someone in your family to orally retell a familiar family story to you. As they tell you the story, you can either record their story on tape or a digital recorder or you can write down as much as of the original language as possible as it's told to you.

2. Now, in a group, share your recordings and notes of the stories. As a group, assume you will find traces of the written until proven otherwise.

3. Discussing and writing together, ask:
   - How much of written genres or styles can you find in the style and content of these family stories?
   - In what ways might they resemble other well-known written stories?
   - If any trace of the written seems absent, how would you explain that absence?
   - What cultural values seem to underlie the message of this story, and what properties of telling the story orally may help foster those values?

Wired Reading, Writing, and Talking: Redefining the Literacy Event

But being "literate" these days is more complicated still. You know how to interpret, and probably produce, not only print texts, but also texts together with images. If you've ever played a Game Boy, built a website, or knew what would happen next in a movie or TV show based on the camera angle, then you've exercised a kind of literacy that was much less important in the 1970s, when Heath hung around the Piedmont Carolinas. When Heath developed her approach to researching literacy events, literacy researchers focused entirely on print literacy and orality, having been deeply influenced by the cognitive researchers like Ong and Goody. Yet today literacy researchers recognize the increasingly important role *visual literacy* plays in our lives. Rapid changes in technology, such as the Internet and visual media such as television, have increased our need to interpret and analyze the unspoken narratives and arguments embedded in multiple kinds of images every day.

At the same time, cultural studies approaches in academic disciplines have argued that we are always reading some form of text, whether it be print, visual media, or oral genres in our conversations (such as storytelling in Roadville or the way someone might argue using logic learned in a philosophy course or a bar room).

Definition
Redefining Literacy Event
When people interpret and talk about *texts*
-print
-visual
-other mediums
according to cultural expectations of group, community, or institution

For these reasons, literacy researchers have tended to redefine *literacy event* as any occasion in which people interpret and talk about texts (whether these are print, visual, or some other form of texts) according to cultural expectations for meanings and behaviors. This is important to keep in mind as we consider the "cultural" meanings of literacy nowadays—and we'll return to this discussion in Chapter Six when we consider how new technologies are quickly changing what it means to read and write.

Analyzing the Narco Corrido on Popular Television

The idea of *literacy event*, then, is useful not only for anthropologists, but for anyone who wants to think about how literacy works in everyday life, including in representational media. We can also apply the concept of a literacy event to analyze representations of literacy in popular culture. For instance, in one episode of the Los Angeles police drama "The Shield," Vic Mackey (Michael Chiklis) and his strike team of detectives had to learn how to interpret the cultural assumptions underlying the popular Mexican cultural genre of *narco corridos* in the context of a suspected murder. At the beginning of this episode, a distraught mother, whose daughter has been missing for 6 months, comes to the police station with a CD given to her by a friend. She fears that the song on the CD provides proof that her daughter has been murdered by someone she knows in their Latino neighborhood: "It says he killed her. He killed

Reina!" In anthropological terms, the CD is a *literacy artifact*, a product made by the culture using writing that can provide clues to the culture's values and beliefs. To solve the crime, the police need to become ethnographers and gain an insider's perspective of the *narco corridos* culture. In the next scene, several of the officers listen to the CD. First, the White officers can't make sense out of the recording, which sounds to them like Mexican polka: "This is supposed to be hip?," one of the officers comments, "Sounds like a Chihuahua threw up on an accordion." Although several of the officers speak some Spanish, David Ascevido (Benito Martinez), the captain of the Farmington, Los Angeles, precinct, knows the language better and, more important, the CD's genre of songwriting: "It's a *narco corrido*, a song about crimes, very popular in Mexico." To which Vic replies, "must be making its way up north." Actually, as music critic Sam Quinones points out, the genre of *narco corridos*, songs about Mexican drug lords and smugglers, has enjoyed popularity with portions of the Mexican immigrant population living in America for 30 years. Vic's assumption that *narco corridos* is a relatively new form of music suggests how much of an outsider he is to a culture that may be invisible to many White Americans.

Claudette (CCH Pounder), an African American officer ranked above Vic, translates the first lyric on the CD as a love song, but Ascevido corrects her, explaining that the rest of the song depicts the grisly details of the murder of the girl as well as the burial location of the body. When he orders Vic to check out the location, Vic mocks the claims of the song, "We're going to bring in Eminem every time he raps about killing his ex?" Ascevido then proclaims with certainty, "Rap songs are not fantasies. *Narco corridos* are recorded history." When Vic finds eight bodies rather than the one they assumed to find, he then refers to the *corrido* as a "map." Soon after, we see officers cracking two other cases using songs from the CDs they confiscate from the *corridor*, the songwriter and singer.

Thinking Ethnographically to Solve a Crime

Later when Vic and his crew interrogate the *corridor* who wrote the song, they gain a more complex insider understanding of what Ascevido claimed earlier about the genre. The *corridor* declares, "I don't commit crimes. I'm a journalist . . . I just write the truth. Arrest me, arrest the *LA Times* too." When asked who commissioned him to write the *corrido*, he replies, "a reporter protects his sources." The songwriter claims journalistic integrity of objectivity and accuracy rather than artistic integrity of creative license. As a literacy artifact whose social meanings and functions can be read in several ways depending on the cultural background of the listener, the song is then a map, newspaper, and folk history. With this knowledge, Vic and his team come to understand that the *corridor's* reputation, and his music's cash value in the open market, rests on his street credibility for getting the facts straight in his songs.

In fact, the criminals involved have used this knowledge of the genre to mislead the police, slipping the *corridor* false information about this murder and who was buried. When Vic figures this out, he begins to turn his newfound knowledge of the literacy practices in the culture of the *narco corrido* to his advantage. He taunts the songwriter with the knowledge that he was duped: "How's that going to play down in the barrio? Wouldn't want your fans paying good money for a *corrido* con job, huh?" With this strategy, the strike team eventually finds the real crime—the forcing of illegal immigrant Mexican women to manufacture methamphetamine.

But here's where the analysis of a literacy event drawn from a popular culture representation, such as "The Shield" television show, can only go so far. Ethnographers also need to understand the historical and socioeconomic contexts that influence insider perspectives. In that regard, it's worth asking: Why have the *narco corridos* been so popular? Where have they come from, and why have they become such an important form of entertainment in Mexican and Mexican American life? When we researched critical writings about the genre, we found out that it evolved from the earlier form of *corridos*, which dates back almost a hundred years to the revolutionary days of Pancho Villa and Emilio Zapata. In general, the *corridos* are songs of underdog rebels and gangsters who challenge, or are depicted as challenging, the government system that oppresses the poor of Mexico. The portrayal of these men is similar to American folk songs' sympathetic portrayal of outlaws like Jesse James as western Robin Hoods.

In the 1970s, when Mexican government corruption was on the rise, the increase of drug smuggling across the American border helped many Mexican farmers who would grow opium make a living. In this manner, the drug lords were seen, and may still be seen in some areas, as the benefactors and traditional underdogs of the *corridos*. The drug smugglers in the *corridos* become a symbol for some in the working class to identify with against (the popular view of) the government as economic oppressors. And so the heroes of the *corridos* changed, influenced also by the trappings

Activity: Analyzing an Object Related to a Culture's Literacy

Ethnographers of literacy analyze the web of human relations attached to material objects, like the *narco corridos* CD. They ask: what groups are involved in the production, distribution, and various uses of this artifact?

1. Choose an object or short text that suggests some of the literacy practices of a culture, subculture, group, or institution. This object may be as simple as a business card or as complicated as a short multimedia text created on computer by a local group. Here are some other ideas to suggest the range of literacy domains and types of objects and texts:
   - section of a newspaper or a particular magazine often read by a group
   - song shared among a group of friends
   - a scrapbook of photos
   - a particular textbook
   - pamphlet, program, or flyer from a church or community group

2. Now consider and write about:
   - When, where, and how is it used, and by whom?
   - What cultural values are often associated with its use? (To help you identify some of those values, you might also consider what values users do not often associate with its use as well).
   - What kind of physical or mental labor goes into the creation of this object and its possible circulation among a group?
   - What kinds of social roles and functions does this literacy artifact promote and why?

3. If you can, also briefly interview someone who would have an insider's perspective toward this literacy artifact. Write about how his or her view compared to your own.

of American gangsta rap culture in the 1980s and 1990s. Although most bands that write and play *narco corridos* do not directly associate with drug smugglers, a few bands do seek patronage and commissions from drug lords.

Yet even all of this social and cultural knowledge only goes so far— it doesn't, for example, help us understand how people create culture from these songs and other experiences in the farms, fields, and cities of

Mexico and immigrant America. Nor can we attain a more complex picture of how the social meanings underlying these literacy practices evolve from the local perspectives of these bands, songwriters, and fans. For these perspectives, literacy researchers would need—in the manner of Shirley Heath—to participate in and observe the lives of these Mexican farmers and immigrants to better understand how they integrate the meanings of these songs into the experiences of their daily lives.

Who's Got the Power?: Analyzing Power Dynamics in Literacy Events

As the example of the clash between the Los Angeles cops on "The Shield" and the culture of the *narco corridos* suggests, researchers of literacy can also use ethnographic methods to gain a deeper understanding of the power dynamics involved for participants in literacy events. At the local level of this literacy event, it initially appears that Vic's strike team calls the shots, but it is actually the criminals who are in control because of their knowledge of the genre. At the level of the larger social context, we find that the culture of the *narco corridos* is partially a folk response to the economic and cultural power of the Mexican and American authorities.

Similarly, we can see that the Trackton residents' highly social practices of reading collaboratively with neighbors are in part based on a history of distrust of the local bureaucracies and institutionalized racism. Ethnographic researchers of literacy want to understand who gets to

> **Definition**
>
> *Power Dynamics in Literacy*
> The social forces between participants in a literacy event that are determined by social, economic, or cultural power

say what counts as authoritative literacy when people talk, read, and write in a particular situation. Often the dynamics between participants and larger socioeconomic forces involved in these literacy events determine who maintains and who is denied social, economic, or cultural power.

Power Dynamics for Trackton Residents at the Loan Office

To better understand how the relations between people's reading, talk, and writing can influence and be influenced by power structures, let's look at how Heath analyzes the uneven power dynamics involved when Trackton residents meet with loan officers at the local banks and credit unions. Heath observed that, in an interaction between a Trackton resident and a loan officer, the loan officer never physically shared the Trackton client's loan file although the financial and personal information recorded in the files should belong to both parties. The loan officer typically requested that the Trackton client orally tell him the needed information. But in making this request, he held the file away from the view of the client and never showed the print material he read from during the meeting. Here, only the bureaucracy has the authority to read the Trackton client's information.

Moreover, only the loan officer's talk about what is in the print material counts as authoritative, and that talk can make a difference between an acceptance and a rejection of the client's request. The Trackton client has no idea what the loan officer is withholding in the reading from the file or what is being written down in the file during the meeting, even though "the client is repeatedly asked to supply information as though she knows the contents of the written document" (Heath, 1983, p. 364). So the client must habitually guess at the loan officer's assumptions even though the officer often speaks in incomplete sentences that don't clearly state what information he is referring to. Heath's recorded transcripts refer to statements from the loan officers such as "let's see, we're gonna combine this" (p. 361)—statements that don't provide clear "visual and verbal cues" about its meaning for the client.

Local government assistance agencies near Trackton often assumed that Trackton residents badly needed adult literacy programs that offered education in higher-level reading skills. But when Heath participated in and observed the lives of the Trackton residents, she frequently heard Trackton residents claim they did not, in fact, need programs in higher-level reading. Instead these Trackton residents wanted *training in the oral practices* (in this case, the ways of talking using written materials) of the institutions—such as the bank, credit union, and the personnel office in the textile mill where they worked—that controlled their economic opportunities. That is, they wanted to learn more effective "ways of getting through such interviews or other situations (such as visits to dentists or doctors) when someone else held the information they needed to know in order to ask questions about the contents of the written material in ways that would be acceptable to institution officials" (p. 364). In other words, they wanted to be more proficient in the ways of talking to officials about the information written about them that these officials held (and often withheld).

Ideological Versus Autonomous Models of Literacy Research

In the early 1990s, literacy scholar Brian Street claimed that ethnographic research (rather than exclusively "theoretical" work) offered one of the best ways to investigate these kinds of power dynamics in literacy events and their implications for those involved. Advocating for "new literacy studies," Street noted how ethnographic researchers "paid greater attention to the role of literacy practices in reproducing or challenging structures of power and domination" (1993, p. 7). For instance, we see the significance of power dynamics in the literacy practices of Roadville and Trackton compared to the expectations of the mainstream schools. Although Heath did not necessarily intend to portray issues of social power in her study of these communities, her use of ethnographic methods led her more in the direction of what Street then identified as an ideological model of research. Similarly, when Amy Shuman closely participated with and observed the literacy practices of adolescent girls in a Philadelphia school, her approach to the research inevitably led to concerns of social power between the girls and adult authorities in their lives.

Street was one of the first to draw strong distinctions between the earlier claims of the Great Divide theorists and the emerging work of ethnographers of literacy like Heath. Street identifies Great Divide theories as advancing an *autonomous model* of literacy as opposed to an *ideological model* of literacy.

In the *autonomous model*, theorists claim that

- the technology of writing *by itself* promotes the universal development of societies independent of specific social contexts.

- writing as a technology fosters civilizations independent of the array of social and cultural factors that influence, and are influenced by, people's approaches to literacy in various local scenes.

In contrast, the *ideological model* of ethnographic (and some historic) research

- emphasizes the investigation of the power structures within the literacy practices of cultures and institutions.

- asks questions such as: Whose literacy (ways of reading, writing, talking) is authoritative in each cultural or institutional situation, and What's at stake when people practice habits of literacy that dominant cultures do not see as authoritative?

Seeing Literacy in Five Dimensions

So what general terms most help ethnographers of literacy conduct this kind of research on literacy events and literacy practices in a culture, and what is that research good for in practical terms? Around the same time that Heath was publishing her study of Trackton and Roadville, Anthropologist John Szwed proposed that if we want to understand how literacy is meaningful to members of a particular group and how they *use* literacy, we need to pay attention to the intersections of five main elements:

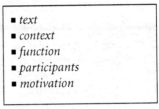

- *text*
- *context*
- *function*
- *participants*
- *motivation*

Like other early ethnographic work in literacy studies, Szwed's proposal defined literacy as reading and writing any kind of print literacy, but we can easily see how these five elements apply to our broader understanding of literacy that includes visual and oral forms as well.

But why do we need these terms when researching how literacy works culturally for a group or individual? For one thing, they provide a methodology— a way of seeing things systematically in cultural scenes—that can help us suspend our judgment of others' literacy practices. They can also help prevent us from applying our *own* cultural assumptions about literacy when we conduct participant-observation in, or interview members of, a community or cultural group. This is *not* to say that the ethnographer is an objective scientist, viewing his subjects under a microscope. Participant-observation in real people's lives gets way too messy for that. Moreover, the ethnographer's body and emotions are her research instruments, and her individual responses to people's behaviors help her

> **Key Idea**
> *Discerning Cultural Patterns of Literacy Practices*
>
> - use the five elements of literacy
> - test hunches of cultural analysis through ethnographic interviewing

make sense of their perspectives. Looking for the interplay among the various elements of literacy can act as a kind of check-and-balance between subjective and objective ways of seeing culture. When we look for these elements in people's uses of literacy, it can help us see patterns that may reveal to us people's deep cultural assumptions and values. We can then check our hunches about these patterns and assumptions through informal interviewing and our own experiences of participation in the culture.

Observing the Five Elements of Star Trek in a Basement

To better illustrate Szwed's five elements and how much they can overlap each other, we'll put them in the context of a local literacy subculture from David's early teens (coincidentally also in the early 1970s). This part of David's own cultural history clearly reveals the geekish side of his background. In David's small town in New Jersey, Erik, an older friend of David's who also happened to be an electronic genius, built in his basement a replica of the bridge of the *Starship Enterprise* from the original Star Trek show. The set included working lights on consoles modeled after the show and buttons that would play tape loops of the various original console sounds. Erik also had a video camera, long before they were sold in most stores. A few of Erik's friends, including David, wrote a couple of scripts using characters they created based on the show's premise, which they, and others in the neighborhood, then performed and videotaped.

> *Text*
>
> When we observe and ask questions about texts, we ask: What is it that people read, write, and then talk about?
>   As we suggested earlier, *texts* could refer to many things. When we read, write, see, and hear texts, we make decisions about what we want to do with them and how we feel about them. We might understand the text differently for ourselves; we might resist it or we might embrace it. Literacy ethnographers try to understand how people are relating to texts in certain situations.

In the context of David's local Star Trek subculture, he and his friends drew on the general plots and themes from reruns of the show to create and produce, on a nothing budget, their own show. In this regard, they were practicing fairly sophisticated acts of reading (of television texts) and writing outside of school, drawing from popular culture but then making it their own with the help of then-emerging technologies.

As cultural studies scholar Jonathan Fiske has suggested, we can define *mass culture* as whatever entertainment products the industries churn out in an effort to gain consumers' interest and money. Every fall, for instance, TV producers try to gain audiences' loyalty to new shows. In contrast, we can define *popular culture* as those shows people select regularly from what the entertainment industry puts out there. Popular culture is the entertainments that groups of people develop loyalty to because these entertainments help them, in one way or another, make meaning in their lives.

Ethnographers of popular culture study how people produce, rather than exclusively consume, cultural meanings from the entertainment they watch and listen to. Henry Jenkins, another popular culture studies scholar, did an ethnographic study of *Star Trek* fans who produce their stories, scripts, pictures, and graphic novels based on ideas and themes from the various *Star Trek* series and other science-fiction entertainments. He called people in this subculture textual poachers because fans who create their own texts based on these shows "poach" from the larger entertainment industry's cultural products to revise and produce their own social meanings from these shows. At the time, David and his friends would not have explicitly described their motives for their makeshift *Star Trek* productions in this way, but clearly their actions indicate what television texts they did value. Rather than just consuming other, less thought-provoking TV products, they chose to use their literacy abilities to expand the worlds from TV that did spark their imaginations and intellects.

Context

When ethnographic literacy researchers ask questions about the *contexts* of a group's literacy practices, they ask: When, where, and under what circumstances is this reading, writing, and or talking about particular kinds of texts being done?

Context, such as time of day or locations that require particular identity roles, will deeply influence what we read and write at any given moment, as well as our motivation toward that activity. In addition to local contexts, we should also think about the influence of larger historical and social contexts on the literacy practices and their meanings for members of a group.

In David's example, all of this production work took place outside of the school, although David does recall some covert script writing during some classes or in study periods. If we consider that this production could have made a substantial integrated curriculum project for a group of students in a classroom, it suggests how rarely most schools allow for, or have the capacity and money to foster, this level of creative collaboration using different media. In that regard, David remembers now that his friends valued the control and authority they had over their own production compared to the more conventional writing projects assigned by their school. Even so, the school David attended in the early 1970s was a progressive middle-class elementary school, and it's likely that some teachers' encouragement of creative freedom fostered his and his friends' interests in producing something like these video episodes outside of classes.

Function

When ethnographers of literacy look at patterns related to function, they ask: What values and assumptions are associated with these uses of literacy? What might these literacy practices have to do with the social structures and dynamics of the group? What might these literacy practices suggest about the individual's identity within the group and the group's role within the larger society and its structures?

In terms of the homemade *Star Trek* shows, the production work created opportunities for David and his friends to show off their creativity in several areas: technology, design, writing, and acting. David would also now claim that, within his own social context, this production work functioned as a form of status and distinction. Although David and his friends would not have recognized this identity role at the time, their interests in all things *Star Trek* was one way to be different from the prevailing mass culture. Clearly other neighborhood kids couldn't have cared less whether they were part of this activity. But for the core participants in this group, it did provide a pride of distinctive insider status. From this perspective, we can also see how these efforts at distinction connect literacy not only to "culture," but to social class. In particular, this group implicitly looked to cultural texts, such as *Star Trek*, to develop a sense of distinction from the "masses." In Chapter Four, we will return to these issues of social class and literacy in greater detail.

Participants

When we consider the importance of the participants in a literacy event, we ask, Who is involved in these intersections of reading, writing, and talking about particular texts? What are the relationships between these participants, and what power dynamics do those relationships suggest? What roles do they assume or perform through these literacy events? Of what are they trying to persuade others—or themselves—through these literacy practices?

What David recognizes now about the participants in the basement *Star Trek* productions is the significance of gender differences. As with many literacy subcultures, there was a core group of insiders—in this case, insiders who wrote the few scripts and worked out the details of the productions. Not too surprisingly, these four or five insiders were all boys. Girls involved with the productions, either sisters or friends from a local youth theater workshop, helped with the construction of the sets and often also acted along with some of the core boys and one or two other boys. So because of the gender imbalance, the themes for the amateur scripts tended to mirror those of the actual TV show. Like the original show, the scripts emphasized more masculine values of confrontation, albeit ones fostered by 10- to 12-year-old science-fiction geek boys, even while they promoted somewhat less violent means of conflict resolution than were common on most television shows and in schoolyard playgrounds.

Motivation

Szwed views *motivation* as the nexus of the other four elements. So based on the factors of contexts, texts, and various kinds of functions (such as social, economic, psychological), literacy researchers should ask: What motivates these people to participate in these literacy practices or to resist them in various ways? And what social meanings do individuals and others in this group attribute to these ways of reading, writing, and talking?

As our discussion of David's group demonstrates, his friends' motivations to participate in the productions varied depending on the individuals

---

Activity: Looking Closer at Your Domain Analysis

Earlier in the chapter, we suggested you try a domain analysis of your literacy practices in different locations and situations. Look back at the domain map you created, or go back to the earlier activity and create one now.

Using Szwed's discussion of the five elements of literacy, choose some of the literacy practices in each domain to analyze more fully in some written notes. Consider David's examples as a model.

Now, share and discuss your analysis in small groups. You might want to consider:

- How did, or does, local and larger social contexts influence these literacy events in each particular domain?

- What functions did these literacy events serve for the people involved? Consider identity roles, social functions for the group, and functions for maintaining (or resisting) larger social structures.

- What other elements of literacy that Szwed discusses play a part in your group's analyses?

---

and their part in the process. So for the writers, it provided an opportunity to be creative within a genre they appreciated. For the technicians and set builders, it offered a chance to show off their skills and creative approaches to problem solving. For the actors, they enjoyed the chance to perform different characters. While the motives for all these activities varied, all participants in the productions shared the motivation of creating an identity in the group process, separate from their school and family. Literacy researchers may not always consciously categorize their observations using Szwed's five elements; nevertheless, any strong ethnographic analysis will include some form of them.

What Literacy Ethnography Is Good for: Uses and Applications

Once an ethnographer has systematically observed, analyzed, and interpreted these elements of literacy from the perspectives of those inside a particular culture, how can his or her research help others in that culture?

Ethnographies of literacy tend to serve three overlapping goals:

1. to develop more culturally appropriate and effective approaches to literacy education

2. to build cross-cultural understanding of communication and knowledge-making between groups and institutions

3. to better understand the socioeconomic issues and power structures related to the resources of literacy and their distribution.

As we'll discuss in the rest of this chapter, literacy educator Jabari Mahiri's research with African American boys in the Chicago Youth Basketball Association provides a good example of this first goal. Our discussion of Marcia Farr's analysis of "essayist literacy" and a Chicago Mexicano community will demonstrate the importance of this second goal. And in the next chapter, we will show how the third goal relates to studies of literacy and social class.

Shooting Hoops: Ethnography, Coaching, and Literacy Education

Jabari Mahiri's research shows how the study of community literacies can help revitalize teaching and education in public schools. Mahiri identified the positive learning within the communication patterns and sports knowledge of African American boys in the Chicago Youth Basketball Association. He then examined and tested out how school curriculums could build on the strengths he identified.

As a high school teacher in the Chicago public schools, Mahiri saw a deep disparity between schools' unimaginative teaching of functional literacy skills to many African American boys and the complex literacy behaviors these boys demonstrated when motivated by their participation in their neighborhoods' Chicago Youth Basketball Association (YBA) program. To better understand the motivations of these boys' literacy behaviors, Mahiri conducted ethnographic research through participant-observation in his role as assistant coach on one of the city's YBA teams.

Mahiri draws on Heath's research to define the term *literacy skills* in contrast to *literacy behaviors*. Literacy skills are "mechanistic linguistic abilities which focus on separating out and manipulating discrete elements of text, such as spelling, vocabulary, grammar, topic sentence, outlines, etc." (1998, p. iv). In most schools, the teaching of literacy skills is all too often divorced from any meaningful context and motivation for the learner. Consider, for example, an exercise on correcting subject–verb agreement that doesn't require students do any actual writing of their own. In contrast, literate behaviors are higher-order cognitive abilities to "analyze, discuss, interpret, and create extended chunks of language types of discourse that lie at the heart of academic study." Mahiri found that the YBA boys' deep interest in sports culture motivated more meaningful literacy behaviors than those they were required to exhibit in their working-class schools. Outside of school, the boys would carefully read and interpret sports articles from newspapers, statistics from basketball cards, complex instructional materials for computer sports games, and examine diagrams related to games. In the process, they would perform complex analysis and synthesis of teams and individual players in the NBA, NCAA, and fictional teams they would create on computer games. As Mahiri points out, "Just to stay abreast of the active players in the NBA in any given year entailed knowledge of twelve players on twenty-eight teams or 336 individual players in the league" (p. 47).

> **Definition**
>
> *Literacy Skills.*
> • Writing skills such as spelling and grammar
> • Separate from meaningful acts of writing
>
> *Literacy Behaviors.*
> • Higher cognitive abilities such as analysis and interpretation
> • Essential to complex acts of thinking and writing

Through his research, Mahiri found that the boys' development of these literacy behaviors built on their verbal and social interactions with their YBA coaches. Mahiri only researched those coaches the boys respected and admired, not ones who acted like abusive marine drill sergeants. So he focused on the best practices of those coaches who viewed their job as mentoring the boys' social development and communicative skills. Mahiri asserts that these coaches' style of communicating helped build an educational environment that fostered the boys' social and intellectual development—which then led to the boys' more complex literacy behaviors over time. Consequently, Mahiri proposes reforms in literacy education based on the metaphors of teachers as coaches, students as players, and education as learning games.

Coaching as Adaptation, Improvisation, and Fostering Communicative Styles

Over the course of his participant-observation and ethnographic analysis, Mahiri identifies three main elements of this model of coaching that he believes are necessary for persuasively teaching students so deeply influenced by African American and youth popular culture in the 21st century. Mahiri claims the best teachers, like the coaches, (a) adapt to the situation, (b) allow for improvisation, and (c) nurture communicative styles of their students/players. First, like the YBA coaches, teachers need to be flexible to the changing motivations of their players/students, and adapt to different game plans as situations evolve. As an example, Mahiri describes how he prepared before teaching each of his own college writing classes so he would have more flexibility as a teacher to work with groups' and individual students' writing concerns as they arose in each class.

Second, Mahiri's research suggests that teachers, like coaches, should embrace the practice of improvisation within an established set of game rules as a means to develop motivated learning. In his ethnographic research of a few high school English teachers admired by their urban multicultural students, Mahiri identified two approaches to improvisation in the classroom these teachers used The first approach was to help students become co-creators of the classroom culture and curriculum. These successful teachers worked to provide a curricular and social framework in which students feel motivated to discover and develop their particular interests through their work with various kinds of texts. In one class, students researched and created personally motivated projects centered on issues and themes of hip-hop culture.

The second approach to improvisation these teachers used involved the use of team-oriented competition to motivate improvisational learning in these classrooms. The students in these classes did not appreciate the pressures of individual competition. They did, however, claim they gained new perspectives and problem-solving approaches through team debates and other games based on a curriculum focused on a theme, such as identity and youth culture, that required complex literacy behaviors of analysis, synthesis, and various rhetorical strategies.

Finally, Mahiri concludes that in order to achieve the kinds of curricular flexibility and improvisation that can lead to students' greater motivation, the teacher/coach must first establish an open yet structured approach to students'/players' communicative styles and expressions. In his research with the YBA teams, Mahiri found that the coaches would first ground the team members' communications in ritual forms of call and response in order to build team relationships. For example, Coach Carl emphasizes the first main themes for the team members' social development—respect, listening, and brotherhood—through call and response. Carl calls out, "The key to success and winning is what?" and the players respond in unison, "Respect for each other." [...] Carl shouts, "What's the word?" and the players answer "Brotherhood!" (1998, p. 33). Mahiri recognizes how these ritual unified responses serve to bond the group and discipline the team. More important, Mahiri asserts these rituals of communication helped structure a model for talk that players later took up and elaborated upon among themselves.

Through this model of talk that Mahiri analyzes in greater detail, the coaches helped the boys develop more mature communicative and reasoning abilities in which they could also incorporate the language styles of their communities. By respecting these language styles, the coaches helped the players to maintain their cultural identities, and so earned the players' greater motivation to develop these more mature forms of communication and analysis. Mahiri's research demonstrates how the boys draw on these forms of reasoning and talk (as well as using the texts of sport culture) to also develop their literacy behaviors. Mahiri found that when high school English teachers practice these coaching-style approaches, their students are more likely to draw on these approaches to develop the complexity of their own literacy behaviors.

Literacies in Conflict: Essayist Literacy and Other Cultural Literacies

Mahiri's research helps us see how literacy teachers can build from students' cultural styles of communication through a coaching model for learning. Marcia Farr's research examines the hidden rules of the dominant cultural style of literacy used in schools in comparison to students' other cultural styles. Unlike Mahiri, Farr does not intend for her ethnographic work to have direct applications to teaching. Instead, she means to broaden educators' understanding of the cultural conflicts that arise when students from various cultural backgrounds encounter these unspoken rules for literacy in public schools and colleges. Drawing on the work of earlier anthropologists and language scholars, Farr labels this dominant form of school-writing and school-speaking *essayist literacy.* Essayist literacy is the conventional style for writing and speaking in school and college—think of your average textbook, lecture, or argumentative essay. Farr (1993) identifies these main traits of essayist literacy as the culturally dominant style of language used in institutions such as schools, corporations, and government offices.

Essayist literacy:

■ Assumes lack of shared context(s)

The writer/speaker generally assumes readers/listeners do not share the same context of experiences and knowledge. Just remember when a writing teacher advised you to, "put in everything in your essay that you just told me. Don't assume that the reader will know what you mean here." Consider also the strange writing situation of an essay exam in a college course: you know that the professor knows all about the subject, but you must *write as if* your audience required the detail and explanation to understand your essay.

> **Key Idea**
> *Essayist Literacy*
> • assumes lack of shared context
> • states logic of argument
> • maintains plain style and voice
> • claims objectivity and neutrality

■ Explicitly states logic of argument and organization of text

When teachers require you to state your thesis, points, and claims, and show readers what to expect in each part of your argument and analysis, they are practicing essayist literacy. For example, just think of the forms of the five-paragraph essay that you learned in high school where the writer is expected to set up navigational signposts along the way. In contrast, many Asian styles of writing influenced by cultural values of deference and politeness allow the reader to infer the writers' arguments from the text without these openly stated guideposts.

- Maintains an impersonal voice and plain style of writing/speaking

Anthropologist Clifford Geertz once referred to writing that Farr calls essayist literacy as "author-evacuated prose"—all the personal or cultural style has been sucked out of the choice of words. When we write or speak in the style of essayist literacy, we assume that the facts and ideas are more important than the words chosen or the personality of the writer/speaker. Indeed, we assume that facts are not part of, or derived from, personality and culture.

- Claims objectivity, neutrality, or balanced positions

Practitioners of essayist literacy tend to count "the giving of reasons and evidence" as legitimate means of argument and analysis and generally dismiss "opinions, feelings, and experiences" (Elbow, p. 140, quoted in Farr, 1993, p. 9) as irrelevant to persuasive argumentation. When we write and speak in (and read and listen for) the style of essayist literacy, we look for balanced viewpoints and the deliberate consideration of counterarguments more than emotional appeals and metaphorical language.

The style of essayist literacy emerged from the Enlightenment period of the 1700s, primarily in England and France. With the rise of empirical methods of research in the growing sciences of the Enlightenment period, European scholars sought changes in writing and speaking that favored plain style and openly stated logic. Writing and speaking was to serve science and a new efficiency of management for a growing middle class.

Today this style, and its claims of logical and/or scientific objectivity, dominates writing and speaking in our schools, government, corporations, and many other institutions. When most of the Great Divide theorists we discussed in Chapter Two spoke of the civilizing forces of literacy, they were often implicitly thinking of the logic and organization of essayist literacy style and ignoring the multiplicity of styles we find in different cultures. Ethnographers of communication, however, assume that people can carry out and demonstrate reasoning and rational thought in a variety of writing and speaking styles.

What Is Communicative Competence, and Why Does It Matter?

In contrast to the ethnographers' interest in multiple literacy styles, mainstream institutions assume that essayist literacy is *the* language of the

Activity: Playing with Essayist Literacy

One way to examine the social functions and effects of the style of essayist literacy is to see it through the lens of other writing styles. These two activities do just that.

Cultural Rewrite

1. Find a text that you think could be categorized as essayist literacy based on the traits we have discussed. Be prepared to point to examples of organization, language choices, tone of voice, and so forth.

2. Describe why this text fits these traits and qualifies as the style of essayist literacy.

3. Now rewrite this text using a different cultural style (such as the example of Mexicano speech style Farr studied, discussed next). To help choose a cultural style of speech, consider the language of other contexts, such as a sports locker room or a country-and-western bar, or an IM session online. You could also consider styles of different speakers, such as a particular talk show host or a wrestling star.

4. Discuss in groups:
   - what happens to the content of the original text when you rewrite it in this other style?

Parodying Essayist Literacy

1. In pairs, choose a familiar fairy tale or well-known popular story and write a brief parody version of the story as an essayist literacy text, exaggerating the essayist literacy traits identified by Farr.

2. Consider also how the language of your parody can include the cultural assumptions (such as objectivity) that Farr suggests underlie their use in mainstream literacy practices.

3. Once you have shared your parodies, consider:
   - What aspects are lost in this rewritten version?
   - What can be the gains and losses of emphasizing essayist literacy in first-year college composition classes? In schools with more "non-mainstream" students?

educated. Consequently, they often use the style and forms of essayist literacy to judge and sort others. Just think of what kinds of literacy skills are required for SATs/ACTs, GEDs, college entrance essays, and many job interviews. As Farr points out, the concept of *communicative competence* from the field of sociolinguistics shows what is at stake when those in power assume that only one particular style of literacy demonstrates a logical and rational mind. The term *communicative competence* refers to how people's use of language tends to overlap in all their speech, writing, and even nonverbal gestures. Most often it's the ways of using language that we learn in the family and home communities that most stay with us. So for families that have gained economic and cultural power from the essayist literacy of mainstream schooled education—perhaps over several generations—their communicative competence in "essayist" forms of speaking and writing will pervade communication in their homes and possibly neighborhoods. Consequently, kids who grow up in these homes are already familiar with the forms and expectations of essayist literacy by the time they get to school. Heath's research in the Carolinas showed how the middle-class townspeople of Gateway implicitly taught this communicative competence of essayist literacy style, as in their practices of labeling and discussing book characters, to their children. This familiarity with essayist literacy style gains them a substantial advantage over those kids who come from cultures, like Trackton and Roadville, where essayist literacy is not a major communicative competence practiced in their homes and neighborhoods.

> **Definition**
>
> *Communicative Competence*
> * How people speak and write to function effectively within a culture
> * How people's use of language tends to overlap in speech, writing, and gestures

So, you may ask, if people from various cultures want to succeed in these institutions, why don't they just take on the traits of essayist literacy as part of their repertoire of communicative competence? Clearly many people do, but as the research of Heath and other ethnographers shows, it's also not that simple when you consider the complexities of culture and identity in matters of communicative competence. First, in terms of culture and identity, people may consciously or often subconsciously resist assimilation to the communicative competence of essayist literacy forms because they do not value the cultural assumptions that underlie these forms of language use. They might associate these literacy practices with the attitudes of the dominant class, gender, race, region, or other form of power. We can see this cultural response in the people of Trackton and Roadville. Some of the core values of both of these rural working-class communities conflicted with the assumptions underlying the language use and literacy practices of the middle-class schools. Second, and equally important, the process of gaining and practicing communicative competence in speech styles, and to a degree in writing styles, most often occurs at the subconscious level. It's not a matter of consciously turning off and on a switch.

"Hablar Sabroso": A Mexicano Literacy Event in Chicago

With these conflicts between essayist literacy and other cultural styles of communication in mind, Farr's ethnographic research in a Chicago neighborhood contrasts the public speech styles of Mexicano immigrants (and also Mexicanos who move between Mexico and the United States) to the essayist literacy styles of U.S.-educated Mexican Americans. Farr's field research helps "show that what is considered persuasive—and how and in what contexts the persuasion is displayed—can vary dramatically from one culture to another" (1993, p. 32).

To conduct her ethnographic research, Farr interviewed Mexicano community members and families in a Chicago Latino neighborhood to find out which qualities make for a good and persuasive speaker from the perspective of community members. In her essay, "Essayist Literacy and Other Verbal Performances," Farr lists four related qualities of speech that community members frequently identified:

gracia/wit: refers to wittiness in talk and those speakers who can include clever and appropriate jokes in their comments.

sabor/flavor: refers to the pleasures of a conversational style. *Hablar sabroso* means "to talk deliciously," such as through direct contact with the listeners and through mimicking of voices.

sinceridad/sincerity: refers to the "genuineness and honesty evidenced by a speaker . . . tell[ing] a story with earnest desire" (1993, p. 19). Community members spoke about being able to "read other's faces for *sinceridad* to determine whether or not their words can be trusted: 'When someone truly respects you, look the person in the face and in the person's eyes, and you will see the expression.'"

emocion/emotion: refers to the quality shown by people who "speak from the heart," who put emotion into their talk and/or who gain emotional pleasure from talking with others.

In sharp contrast to the traits of essayist literacy, the qualities most valued by the community emphasize the *person* of the speaker, or writer, in relation to the group, rather than the facts or ideas in the content of the text itself.

Researching a Verbal Performance as an Act of Literacy

At the same time she conducted these interviews, Farr observed and taped public meetings of local politicians and community organizations in the neighborhood. She then listened to the tapes for *verbal performances* that embodied the community traits of a good persuasive speaker. The term *verbal performance* refers to the ways we speak to others using different oral genres, such as telling a story or joke, arguing a position, giving a lecture, and so on. Finally, Farr looked for how different audience members at those community meetings "evaluated" these performances. The term *evaluation* in the ethnography of verbal performance refers to audience members' responses to someone's speech or talk—whether they laughed, nodded, looked puzzled, interrupted the speaker, and so forth. One can then roughly gauge how persuasive a speaker is for particular audience members by observing their various evaluations of the speaker's verbal performance. Farr found that the Mexicano community members evaluated the verbal performances of the Mexicano speakers at many of these meetings very differently than did the American-educated Mexican Americans, despite their often shared political concerns.

> **Definition**
>
> ***Verbal Performance*** How well we speak in different oral genres, such as stories, jokes, arguments, lectures
>
> ***Evaluation*** How an audience verbally or nonverbally responds to a speaker's verbal performance

For example, Farr analyzes the verbal style of, and contrasting audience evaluations for, Sr. Martinez, a politically active church member in the Mexicano community. Martinez spoke during a ward meeting to discuss which candidate the community should support for mayor in an upcoming election. In this election—a contentious mayoral race rife with racial politics—Juan Soliz, a local Latino alderman, was running for the office. Called upon by one of the Mexican American leaders of the meeting, Martinez encourages the audience to ignore Soliz's racial identity and, instead, to look critically at Soliz's poor record within the Latino community. Here Farr describes how Martinez uses the four traits of persuasive speech valued by the Mexicano community.

> Sr. Martinez argues that it is the person who is important ("who that person is"), not whether he is Black, White, or Hispanic. He shows sincerity by including personal testimony: "I was . . . one of the first who went with Juan Soliz. When I did not know him, you see." He adds flavor and wit to his argument by claiming that during the last election this particular incumbent received only two percent of the vote of "his own people," and insists that this time it would be even less! Pointing out that this man was barely elected by his own people is somewhat embarrassing in this public setting; it makes fun of the candidate and draws laughter from the audience. Finally he relies on shared values to persuade by urging his audience to take actions ("tell the people about Juan Soliz' history) for the larger good: "for our community, for our children, for our families." In using the pronouns we and us (rather than you) and by using both Spanish and English, he identifies himself closely with the audience, positioning himself and his audience within the same communities. (1993, pp. 25–26)

As Farr suggests, Sr. Martinez does offer a critical perspective in the logic of his impromptu speech. And the Mexicano audience's evaluation of laughter, clapping, and nods of heads clearly indicates the persuasive quality of Martinez's words and verbal performance. But we see the conflict of literacies when the college-educated Mexican Americans conducting the meeting interrupt the speaker twice, believing that Martinez's speech does not stick to his points or make a clear argument free of poetic qualities of speech. One of the leaders commented after the meeting, "sometimes that guy just goes on and on."

Expanding Understanding of Literacy Styles in Education

Through her ethnographic study, Farr hopes to broaden literacy teachers' and educational administrators' understanding of cultural styles of argumentation, analysis, and persuasion. Farr suggests that teachers frequently take the underlying cultural assumptions of essayist literacy for granted. So if teachers better understand these assumptions, they will be better prepared to teach these traits of essayist literacy to students whose cultural backgrounds do not include these forms of speaking and writing.

Farr contends that we should not, in fact, dismiss essayist literacy's (a) potential for critical thought and democratic process, as in its emphasis on counterarguments; and (b) power to influence students' economic futures. Yet Farr also believes that teachers should learn how to help students integrate the strengths from their cultural speaking styles and literacy practices into their uses of essayist literacy. In this manner, teachers can help their students rejuvenate the often alienating "author-evacuated prose" and pseudo-scientific claims of objectivity in the writing demanded by many schools and institutions. Moreover, Farr points to the changing racial demographics in the United States, what some have referred to as the "browning of America," to indicate that these cultural changes in essayist literacy are inevitable.

ACTIVITIES AND PROJECTS

1. **Doing Participant-Observation Research of a Culture's Literacy Practices.** Ethnographers believe that the only way to get insider perspectives on literacy in a culture is to conduct field research through firsthand participant-observation.

   In the Project Appendix, you will find detailed guidelines for conducting participant-observation research that you should follow for this project.

   When choosing a field site to study literacy and culture, you will likely want to consider groups that are:
   - part of a much larger cultural identity (such as gender, ethnicity, religion, etc.),
   - a subculture (like a fan club, sports team, community group), and/or
   - an academic disciplinary culture (classes and/or clubs related to a specific major or professional field in school).

2. **Interviewing Someone About Their Literacy Practices in a Culture.** To explore connections between identity, culture, and literacy, you can conduct ethnographic interviews of another person. Ethnographic interviewing can help you better understand and analyze this person's literacy history, behaviors, attitudes, and values from the context of his or her experiences with a specific culture or subculture.

   We have provided detailed guidelines for conducting ethnographic interviews in the Project Appendix. Here, we focus on supplemental advice for writing an interview paper about someone's literacy behaviors and cultural practices.

   1. For your interviews, choose someone you know who belongs to a particular culture or subculture. Remember that an ethnographic definition of culture can be very wide: you could choose to study a church group, a rock band, a sports team, a community organization, or even a particular business or profession. Consider people you know who might
      - represent and/or challenge literacy researchers' claims about literacy and culture,
      - challenge public stereotypes about literacy, and/or
      - suggest interesting connections or conflicts between literacy behaviors in different parts of their lives.

2. Once you have decided whom you will interview, choose literacy interview questions from the Project Appendix to adapt and to develop your own questions. You will need to customize the appendix interview questions to your knowledge of your interviewee's background and experiences with his or her culture or subculture.

   Here also are some general categories often used to develop questions for interviewing someone about their various literacies:

   - family and neighborhood
   - education
   - oral practices (types of talk, ways of talking, in what contexts of the person's life)
   - writing and reading in various contexts
   - stories associated with the person's culture and experiences

     Looking at the style and phrasing of interview questions in the Project Appendix will help you create questions in these and other categories as appropriate for this person and your goals of the project.

3. For the rest of the process of ethnographic interviewing and writing your paper, see the Project Appendix.

3. **Doing an Autobiographic Ethnography of Your Literacy in a Culture (or Subculture).** Although ethnographers of literacy concentrate on firsthand participant-observation of literacy within particular groups, we can also learn from critical reflection on our past experiences within specific subcultures, as we saw in David's example of his makeshift Star Trek production crew.

1. Your analysis can take the form of a narrative story or a more explicitly analytical style or something in between these two forms, just as long as you analyze the literacy practices in this subculture through the lens of Szwed's five elements of literacy.

   First, use our discussion of the five elements of literacy to take some notes about your experiences with this subculture.

   - What elements seem most important to helping others understand these literacy practices from an insider's perspective?
   - How do these elements relate to the dynamics, identity roles, social functions, and cultural values of the group, and in contexts of the larger society?

2. If you choose to write your analysis as a critically reflective narrative, select a specific incident, or a short series of incidents, from your

experience with this subculture that you believe can show others the elements of your analysis. The guidelines for memoir writing in the Project Appendix can also help you. Concentrate on showing your readers your analysis of these elements through descriptive scenes containing dialogue, setting, character, and your reflections as an observer today on these scenes. You can choose to present the whole scene to readers and then step back to offer your analysis drawn from the questions in step 1, or you can step back at moments in your narrative scene to offer that analysis along the way.

3. If you choose to focus on an analytical style, consider the overall argument or claim about the literacy behaviors in this subculture that your analysis notes about the five elements suggested to you. Then work to organize your paper by this main thesis argument with supporting claims that develop this main claim. To better demonstrate your supporting claims, use specific descriptions, or smaller scenes, of literacy practices you remember from experiences with this group to illustrate your analysis of these supporting claims.

4. **Analyzing the Culture of a Literacy Event in a Movie or TV Show.** Occasionally, movies give viewers a more authentic glimpse of a particular culture's (or subculture's) literacy behaviors and values. For this activity, choose a scene from a movie or show that relates to a particular culture's ways of reading and writing verbal and/or visual texts. Here are some suggestions. Look them up on the Internet to see what interests you and possibly to help you make a better choice of your own outside this list.

Once Upon a Time When We Were Colored

Inherit the Wind

Tortilla Soup

The Dangerous Life of Altar Boys

NightJohn

Il Postino

Songcatcher

Central Station

Spellbound (documentary)

Hoop Dreams (documentary)

1. Once you have chosen and viewed your movie or show, choose a scene to analyze through an ethnographic lens. Consider if you were Heath, Mahiri, or Farr: what would you notice about the ways people use language and texts within this scene?

2. Use the various analytic tools we have discussed in this chapter to develop your analysis of these people's literacy behaviors and possible cultural assumptions that underlie them.

   - How do you identify and define the literacy event(s) here? What unspoken social rules of this culture do they suggest?
   - How do you identify the five elements of literacy here? What does the interaction of these elements (text, context[s], functions, participants, motivations) suggest?
   - What can you discern about the power dynamics within this group and/or within the larger social contexts that influence this culture?
   - What can all these aspects of your research suggest about the roles of literacy, culture, and power for the people involved in this scene?

FOR FURTHER READING

Bauman, Richard. (1977). *Verbal art as performance.* Prospect Heights, IL: Waveland Press.

Briggs, Charles, L. (1986). *Learning how to ask: A sociolinguistic appraisal of the role of the interview in social science research.* Cambridge, UK: Cambridge University Press.

Farr, Marcia. (1993). Essayist literacy and other verbal performances. *Written Communication, 1*(10), 4–38.

Heath, Shirley Brice. (1983). *Ways with words: Life, language, and learning in communities and classrooms.* Cambridge, UK: Cambridge University Press.

Mahiri, Jabari. (1998). *Shooting for excellence: African American and youth culture in new century schools.* Urbana IL: National Council of Teachers of English Press.

Moss, Beverly. (Ed.). (1994). *Literacy across communities.* Cresskill, NJ: Hampton Press.

Street, Brian. (Ed.). (1993). *Cross-cultural approaches to literacy.* Cambridge, UK: Cambridge University Press.

4

Literacy and Class

Before You Read. Look back at your response to the prompt at the beginning of the previous chapter. Before reading any further, think about your developing literacy in relation to various institutional and cultural sites: your family, your community, your educational experience. Next, consider whether/how these literacy experiences can be understood as experiences shaped by *social class*—for example, think about Heath's research in Roadville, Trackton, and Gateway, and ask yourself: which of these communities practiced literacy in ways most like the community I grew up in? Finally, think about how literacy experiences up to now relate to your plans for the future. How do you think your literacy history has shaped your expectations about what your future relationship with literacy should be? What do you expect your habits of literacy to cost you or to buy you as you think ahead to your future? In what "markets" will they be most valuable?

In the United States, we live the mythology of a classless society. We believe our society provides equal opportunities for all and promises success to those who work hard to achieve it. We believe the key to achievement is education, and we believe the heart of education is literacy. In a society bound by such a mythology, our views about literacy are our views about political economy and social opportunity . . .

—J. Elspeth Stuckey, The Violence of Literacy

In a famous episode of *The Sopranos*, HBO's popular drama about a suburban mob family, Tony Soprano, well-to-do mob boss and father of college-bound Meadow, drives Meadow to Maine to interview for admission to Ivy League colleges. As father and daughter stroll companionably on the lush campus of Bates College, the moment is right for exchanging father–daughter confidences. Meadow asks her father about his own experience with higher education:

Meadow: Dad . . . how come you didn't finish college?

Tony: I had that semester and a half at Seton Hall.

Meadow: Yeah? And?

Tony: [chooses words] Grandma and Grandpa didn't stress college. They were working-class people.

Meadow: Even Grandma? With her whole 'tude?

Tony: What 'tude?

Meadow: "The D'Agostinos are from Providence and we're a couple notches above the Sopranos. The Sopranos are . . ." what is it?—"car phones."

Tony: [laughs] *Cafone.*

Meadow: What does that even mean?

Tony: Peasants. Low-class mutants.

Meadow: How come your parents were anti-education?

Tony: [uncomfortable] Not anti. Look, I can't lay it all on them. I got in trouble as a kid.

Later, dining with her proud father at a restaurant near campus, Meadow looks radiant at the prospect of the educational adventure before her. Tony gazes at her affectionately and tells her: "I can't tell you how proud I am—a real student at Casa Soprano."

In the previous chapter, we saw how literacy operates within, and takes its meaning from, cultural contexts. We learned that understandings of literacy as a cognitive process that brings predictable social changes can be productively complicated by ethnographic research, which uses methods of participant-observation within cultural scenes to learn how people *use* reading and writing in their everyday lives. The more localized understandings of the everyday, highly contextualized nature of literacy such research enables can further help us to see what happens when we look at literacy as a social practice. We can easily read the previous scene with Tony and Meadow as a story of literacy: It dramatizes, and evokes for our purposes, many of the points where culture meets class. *To understand what happens when we locate literacy in relation to social class, we need to recognize that literacy is tightly linked not only to particular cultural histories and scenes but to social power—to economic and social mobility.* How this works, exactly, is a difficult question: literacy's relationship to class is hard to assess directly and sometimes contradictory in its social and economic effects. What makes the educational predicaments narrated in *The Sopranos*—a cultural text critic Fred Gardaphe calls "a commentary on not only the genre [of the gangster film] but on contemporary life in the United States" (2002, p. 90)—particularly interesting is that the characters' relationships to higher education reveal complexities and contradictions that define the relationship of literacy to culture and social class. Tony Soprano—arguably a postmodern gangster version of *Born Yesterday's* shyster Harry Brock—is himself a contradiction: he is, by virtue of his criminal activities, economically upper-middle class. Wealthy enough to send his daughter to an expensive Ivy League college, Tony still demonstrates the beliefs, values, and social behaviors of his immigrant working-class parents, who "didn't stress education." The Soprano family's financial access to, and conflicted relationship with, higher education and its prestigious ways with words are but one illustration of the difficulties in accounting for all the ways in which literacy is a function of class. If it's true, as Elspeth Stuckey (1991) argues, that "the heart of education is literacy," and "our views about literacy are our views about political economy and social opportunity," then the saga of family Soprano and its story of the nightmarish side of the American Dream is also a story of literacy, as we will see.

To say that literacy is in some way connected to socioeconomics is a proposition that most people would probably accept. They would agree, for example, that, as Bush education secretary Rod Paige remarked in an October 2004 press release, "The need for literacy in reading and mathematics is a prerequisite for almost every job" (2004). They would also probably agree that, apart from the economic potential of literacy, the things you read and the written language you use give you more or less status and make it more or less possible to hold social power. But given what we know so far about literacy and culture, we can predict that the relationship between literacy, power, and socioeconomic status is going to be complicated. One way to sort out the questions and issues is to consider not only what literacy *means*, culturally, but also what literacy *does*.

We might say that there are three things literacy does if you look at how it operates in relation to social class: (1) it lets you in; (2) it keeps you out; (3) nothing. The question we begin the chapter with, then, is this: How does it do these things?

The Work of Literacy

In the first chapter, we explored some common ideas of what literacy is supposed to do for you: in the Western humanistic tradition, the idea is that literacy is supposed to make you smarter, more humane, more receptive to change. And as J. Elspeth Stuckey (quoted earlier) suggests, in America we believe that the benefits of literacy entitle you to enjoy the benefits of class mobility: with the right education in reading, writing, and communicating, you can acquire wealth and prestige and enjoy a better quality of life. But what does this look like in practice? How does this happen?

Stuckey is among many commentators and critics who have observed that here in the United States, land of opportunity, we don't much like to talk about class—or even recognize its existence. Thinking too much about how American society is divided into economic strata gets in the way, it seems, of our will to believe in the American ethos of individuality and equality, and in the American Dream of social mobility. But historians, sociologists, and anthropologists have long understood American society to be *stratified,* that is, to contain more or less stable socioeconomic "layers." There is considerable disagreement about just how much mobility there is between layers, but in May of 2005, the *New York Times* ran a special series on social class in America, "Class Matters." The authors introduced the series, which ran for several weeks, with a reminder that class does, in fact

> **Definition**
>
> **Stratification** is a term sociologists use to describe the organization of a society into a hierarchy of status groups (for example, socioeconomic classes) or "strata."

"matter," and that it matters more and more in a time of a rapidly closing window of economic opportunity:

> Over the past three decades, [class] has come to play a greater, not lesser, role in important ways. At a time when education matters more than ever, success in school remains linked tightly to class. . . . At a time of extraordinary advances in medicine, class differences in health and lifespan are wide and appear to be widening.

And new research on mobility, the movement of families up and down the economic ladder, shows there is far less of it than economists once thought and less than most people believe. . . . In fact, mobility, which once buoyed the working lives of Americans as it rose in the decades after World War II, has lately flattened out or possibly even declined, many researchers say. (Scott & Leonhardt, 2005)

If Scott and Leonhardt are right, and if it's also true that literacy is connected to economic opportunity, then the stakes of literacy are high indeed. In such a scenario, how literacy "works" can be a matter of survival. J. Elspeth Stuckey, author of *The Violence of Literacy* (1991), makes the argument that it's hard to understand the nature or effects of literacy in the United States without taking a broad economic view. For Stuckey, questions of literacy are directly connected to matters of access: What forms of access to economic benefits does literacy allow, and in what ways is literacy used *against* people to limit access to such benefits?

To help us think through this question with a living example, let's take a look at another ethnographic study of literacy in a community setting: Ellen Cushman's *The Struggle and the Tools: Oral and Literate Strategies in an Inner-City Community* (1998), published 15 years after Shirley Heath's study of literacy practices in the

Definition
Gatekeeping is a term literacy researchers use to refer to an institutional process in which literacy functions as a criterion for blocking access to avenues of social mobility and economic opportunity.

Carolinas. In its aims and methodology, Cushman's study is very much like Heath's: Cushman was interested in the complexities surrounding literacy practices in nonmainstream (for Cushman, an urban African American neighborhood in the Northeast) communities. Like *Ways with Words*, Cushman's study seeks to find the meaning in everyday practices; like Heath, Cushman wants to create a picture of what literacy *means* in the lives of a particular group of people in a particular time and place. Cushman herself is a participant-observer, so she spends time with the members of the community, living with and learning from them. Cushman's research participants have adapted literacy to their culture, just like the people of Roadville and Trackton. And for Cushman's research community as well, what is cultural is also socioconemic. Like Tracktonites, Cushman's Quayville residents have their own ways of using literacy to survive in the world. But whereas the *economic* forces to which "culture" is adaptive are implicit for Heath, Cushman foregrounds the economic forces and predicaments relevant to meanings and uses of literacy.

The setting of Cushman's study is a town she calls "Quayville," a poor African American community in the urban northeastern United States. Cushman found that residents of Quayville, who had limited economic opportunity and who were forced to rely on government subsidies to survive, had to struggle daily within and against the institutions that controlled their access to the resources they needed for survival—food, money, housing, and so on. "More often than not," writes Cushman, "individuals in Quayville's inner city encountered gatekeepers who obstructed their efforts to gain resources and debased residents as they did so" (1998, p. 16). Quayville residents had to persuade the gatekeepers in their communities—courts, landlords, welfare agents—to provide them with these resources. The oral and written strategies they used to do this rhetorical work constitute a form of cultural literacy—one that includes tactics for protecting cultural values while it works to procure resources. Like the residents of Trackton, Quayville residents read and interpret texts collaboratively, locating acts of reading in episodes of talk. Cushman observed that "over and over again, community members collectively practice strategic readings of letters, applications, notices, ad information packets" in which they "collectively construct the power relations between themselves and wider society's organizations," and "through these constructions they develop plays and skills to move through institutional influences in their daily lives" (p. 110). In her book, Cushman gives examples of these collaborative literacy events. In the following scene, a woman reads a letter from the Department of Social Services to others in her home:

> "They say I didn't recert [recertify], so they gonna sanction my ass for three goddamn months."
> "Did you recert?"
> "You know it. That day Shantel with me and we saw you coming out of Cost Hacker?"
> "Well haul her ass down there and tell them there a mistake. You got a witness to prove it."

. . . and troubleshooting what do about an overdue bill:

> "Now where I gonna get the money for this?"
> "Just pay what you can. They won't cut you off if you given' 'em a little somen.' They just like men!"

"You know it, girl. I'd just call they and say you're in a tight situation and can you please set up a payment plan with them?' Number's right there [pointing to the upper left-hand corner of the bill]."

The literacy that children acquire in Quayville, then, includes "ways to read in to an organization, to find an access route to opportunity, to find a way out or around or through" (Cushman, 1998, p. 111). The people of Quayville "need" literacy, all right, and they need it for economic survival—but it's a kind of literacy practice that's under the radar of many conversations about how literacy is tied to economics, which more commonly focus on how technical literacy skills can be directly cashed in for upward mobility.

It's easy to see how the literacy practiced by Quayville residents—like the residents of Trackton or Roadville or the members of an English department—works to sustain cultural values. How the women value literacy, and what they do with it, is clearly a cultural issue—like Heath's portrait, Cushman's intimate view shows how written and oral uses of language work together in relation to a community's everyday practices, beliefs, and commitments. What Cushman's study *explicitly* does that Heath's does not is to show how cultural values are adaptive to economic conditions: cultural literacy practices in Quayville are shaped by the forms of powerlessness Quayvillers have relative to those people and institutions who *do* have the power to control their lives. Significantly, how and why the poor need literacy—that is, what they have to *use it for*—is different from how and why middle-class people need it. Quayvillers routinely experience literacy as a thing used against them, and they in turn use literacy to resist and struggle against its explicit control over them. Their particular literacy practices, then, include pragmatic strategies for interpretation of institutional documents, ways of taking action in *gatekeeping* situations in agencies that stand between them and economic survival, and cultural tactics for resisting the effects of literacy used to demean and disempower them.

Ellen Cushman's study is important in that it shows not only how cultural literacies have socioeconomic dimensions for their practitioners, but also how forms of reading and writing are used to guard the gates of social institutions. Quayvillers feel the power of literacy as a gatekeeping tool very acutely in their everyday lives, but even people who are not directly disenfranchised by institutional literacy experience the exclusive power of literacy practices. Anyone who has, for example, had his confidence shaken by a teacher's response to his culturally different ways with words in a written composition, or who has been relegated to "remedial" classes on the basis of her writing, has experienced the effects of literacy-as-gatekeeping.

Consider the predicament of Rita, heroine of the British film *Educating Rita*. Rita is a working-class woman in England who goes to university to become educated. She arrives at the university with none of the cultural experiences that might have prepared her for the work of higher education. She ends up studying with Frank, a jaded professor of poetry who first sees Rita as something of a joke in her naïveté about literary study, but who eventually comes to see in Rita everything that he feels is missing in his life as a middle-class intellectual: embodied energy, forthrightness, childlike wonder, the will to action. On one level, *Educating Rita* is about the relationship between a cynical mentor and his eager student, but on another, it's about the relationship between literacy and class.

Rita's earnest determination to get the kind of knowledge she believes the university can provide drives the action of the film. When Frank first meets Rita and asks her why she wants to come to Open University, she says, "Because I want to know. Everything." Rita's unaffected, energetic mind and sharp wit impresses Frank very much, even as he recognizes that she doesn't "do" reading and writing in ways that show her to have a legitimate claim to a place in the university, a situation that creates much of the dramatic tension in the film. Rita demands that Frank teach her, but he is ambivalent, recognizing how little Rita's very-real-but-working-class intellectual capabilities will be valued within the institution in which he, as professor, serves as gatekeeper. In one scene, Rita, after having been lectured by Frank about how literary criticism should be "purely subjective," delivers to him the product of his assignment to write an essay about E. M. Forster's *Howard's End*. The scene opens as Frank, having evaluated the paper, confronts Rita with her failed attempt to produce acceptable criticism:

> **Frank:** [thrusting a sheet of paper at Rita]. What's this?
> **Rita:** It's a bleedin' piece of paper, isn't it?
> **Frank:** It's your essay. Is it a joke? Is it?
> **Rita:** No, it's not a joke.

Frank: Rita, how the hell can you write an essay on E. M. Forster with almost total reference to Harold Robbins?

Rita: Well? You said bring in other authors.

Frank: [clucks his tongue and shakes his head]

Rita: Don't go on at me. You said—you said: "Reference to other authors will impress the examiners."

Frank: I said refer to other works, but I don't think the examiner, God Bless him, will have read, ah, . . . [looking at the paper] *A Stone for Danny Fisher.*

Rita: Well, that's his hard luck, isn't it?

Frank: It'll be your hard luck when he fails your paper.

Rita: Oh, *that's* prime, isn't it?? That's justice for yer. I get failed just 'cause I'm more well read than the friggin' examiner!

Frank: [with thin patience] Devouring pulp fiction is not "being well read."

Rita: [searching for a cigarette] I thought reading was supposed to be good for one.

Rita knows that knowledge of books—reading many books and being able to name them—is important when it comes to displaying the kind of literacy the university expects and values. What she does not yet know, however, is that in this context, some books count more than others, and that some (those considered to be "common" or "popular") actually *subtract* from the value of her demonstrated literacy. Harold Robbins, a bestselling novelist whose work most often features the sexual adventures of rich people, is not an author who produces what specialists in literary criticism regard as "literature." Even though Robbins has sold 50 million books and has fans all over the world—and arguably *because* he has sold tens of millions of books and has fans all over the world—he is not seen as "good" or "important" enough to find a place in academic literary studies. In showing her lack of knowledge of the difference between "pulp fiction" and "real literature," Rita makes her first cultural mistake; in showing her specific knowledge of Harold Robbins's work, she makes her second; in claiming to *like* Robbins's writing, she commits a third. As a person hungry for knowledge who has had no prior access or exposure to middle-class literacy as it is enacted in a university setting, Rita has, up to this point, had no experiences that lead her to the understanding that, if you want to show that you have the literacy of an educated person, certain kinds of knowledge can actually count *against* you.

> **Focus Point**
>
> Can you think of a time when your knowledge was held—or used—against you? What was the knowledge? What was the situation? What were the consequences?

Cushman's study and Rita's predicament remind us that *the socioeconomic gates literacy keeps are often locked with cultural keys.* Apart from the economic consequences of literacy, it's not just that literacy "opens doors" economically by providing skills you need to navigate social institutions, or to do a particular job. It also has symbolic value—that is, it indicates to people in positions of power that you're one of *them*, that you have a rightful claim to the benefits of the institutions they control. Sociologist Pierre Bourdieu would call this function of literacy *cultural capital.* While having prestigious forms of literacy doesn't seem to guarantee economic success (just ask any English Ph.D. who, unable to get a full-time university job after years of professional training, has to teach several classes at different institutions merely to make ends meet), it does seem to be the case that *not* having socially valued forms of literacy can constrain your chances.

> **Definition**
>
> *Cultural capital* refers to inherited cultural habits and competencies that can be transformed first into *social capital* (membership in social groups and networks with power and access) and then into economic capital—real money.

But wait, you say. Isn't there a way around this? If you've got real money, is middle-class literacy really useful or necessary? Or, in Bourdieu's language, if you have real, material capital, then why bother with the symbolic kind?

We began this chapter with a scene from *The Sopranos* in which Meadow, in a conversation with her father on the campus of Bates University, asks Tony about his own educational history. In that conversation, Meadow wants to know about her father's *own* parents' expectations for higher education. Even though her father is the son of working-class immigrants, Meadow herself has access to the kind of prestigious literacy associated with an Ivy League education because her parents have money acquired through Tony's "career" as mob boss. Culturally, Tony has more in common with his own working-class parents than with the other Bates parents—and much of the dramatic tension in *The Sopranos* comes from the family's split-class status as people whose income puts them in an upper-middle-class tax bracket while their old-country traditions, patterns of kinship, social networks, and ways with words tend to be marked as working-class. The dramas of Soprano family life are often driven by this tension. Tony asserts his authority as traditional family patriarch while Meadow seeks middle-class cultural legitimacy through education and Carmela rejects the role of passive housewife to present herself as fashionable, upwardly mobile soccer mom pursuing her own version of the American Dream. While Tony has his main office at the Bada Bing, a South Jersey bar featuring nude dancers, Carmela presides over a suburban home in the most upscale neighborhood of New Jersey, in an upper-middle-class subdivision where her neighbors are highly educated professionals. While Tony is embroiled in old-world gangsterish scenarios of corruption, intimidation, and violence, Carmela bakes ziti in her gourmet kitchen and manages the construction of a new home theater for the Soprano's expansive living room.

One episode of *The Sopranos* ("Rat Pack") illustrates these tensions around class and culture with respect to literacy particularly well. Carmela organizes a ladies' film club, the purpose of which is to introduce several of her friends to the American Film Institute's Top 100 Best American films. Carmela selects *Citizen Kane* to be viewed at the club's first meeting, introducing it to others by saying that "it's supposed to be a classic." But we watch the women in the film club as they view the movie, first looking eager, then bored, then half asleep. Carmela weakly attempts to encourage some dialogue about the film, but the collective analysis never makes it beyond Adriana La Cerva's observation about the final plot revelation: "So it was the sled, huh? He should have told somebody." Thus endeth the "reading" of the film, and the conversation moves on to more everyday concerns.

In many ways, the *Citizen Kane* scene is a demonstration of schooled, middle-class uses of literacy: A group of people are spending leisure time consuming a "classic" work of art, and have convened for the purposes of interpreting the work. Carmela, as an upwardly mobile consumer of culture, knows full well that knowledge and consumption of "great films" function as cultural capital—the kind of capital that the Sopranos, as much cash as they have stashed in their pool shed outside, don't have. Yet Carmela and her friends lack deep knowledge of the literacy practices that count as capital—they may organize a club and watch the right movies, but they don't know how to talk about them. Nothing in their class experience or cultural background has equipped them with the knowledge of how to perform the highly specialized discourse that marks middle-class literacy. Carmela fears that the gate separating her from true middle-class legitimacy will likely remain closed in spite of her material wealth.

What Carmela is struggling to acquire, and what Meadow is mortified that Tony doesn't have, is what Pierre Bourdieu calls *cultural capital*—that is, a form of knowledge that earns her social rewards and has the potential to become real, material capital. For the highly educated middle class, *Citizen Kane* and specialized interpretations of it are symbolic claims to class privileges. When Pierre Bourdieu conducted a series of surveys intended to discover the range and variety of social meanings in people's patterns of consumption and display (their choice of clothes, furnishings, food, recreation, etc.), his data led him to conclude that instances of consumption and social production, far from being random or "innocent," are means of securing "distinction," or social prestige. One practice that is conventionally employed to secure social distinction, in Bourdieu's analysis, is performed knowledge of which cultural texts and artifacts are "good" or "tasteful" and which are not. To "know" *Citizen Kane*—to know that one *should* like the film, as well as to know *how* to consume it (as a text to be analyzed) are both ways of accumulating cultural capital and, ultimately, social power. In her efforts to acquire the prestige literacy to match her other patterns of middle-class consumption, Carmela knows that *Kane* should be regarded as a good film, and that it should be treated as an occasion for displays of textual critique. She and her friends can't quite muster this literacy, however, as they ultimately lack the cultural knowledge—just as Rita does—of *how* to conduct "critique."

And yet as we know, currencies have different values in different marketplaces. Bourdieu would say that when it comes to the "value" of literacy, there is a dominant "marketplace" defined by middle-class financial and educational institutions that determines what literacy will be worth as cultural capital. Within this larger market system, however, people still value things differently according to their own local needs. Consider, for example, the reading habits of people who frequent the Smokehouse Inn, a working-class bar south of Chicago where Julie did research on working-class uses of discourse. At the Smokehouse, where it's rare to find a person with a college diploma and common to encounter people who didn't finish high school, many people read voraciously for their own purposes (for information or for pleasure). They trade books, recommend reading material to others, are often highly skilled in ways of using print to enable their working lives, and use specialized print and visual texts related to hobbies or personal interests (woodworking, music, etc.). Many take pride in their expertise at trivia games or word puzzles. What Smokehousers do *not* do, however, is to assert their reading habits—or knowledge of the "right" books or films (such as *Citizen Kane*)—as cultural capital. Certainly Smokehousers are literate by most definitions, but their uses of literacy differ from middle-class practices in the sense that cultural prestige does not rest on these uses or practices. In fact, group solidarity is implicitly threatened by displays of "high" literacy, which is often perceived as an obvious sign of disloyalty to collective interests in favor of individual class prestige. Smokehousers would feel no pressure to watch *Citizen Kane* because middle-class film experts believe it's important, or to "analyze" the movie like a text. In fact, someone who did so might well be seen as a "phony," as somebody making an obvious play for the kind of social prestige Smokehousers reject—although they would *not* reject the kind of display of material assets in which Carmela routinely engages (the home theatre, for example). This is not to say that Smokehousers don't think deeply about things or even that they don't display knowledge publicly—they very clearly do—it only means that that they don't have the same uses and expectations of literacy as cultural capital. A sociolinguist observing Smokehousers rejecting the practice of using reading as cultural capital would say that they are participating in forms of *covert prestige*. A Smokehouse regular would likely say that somebody who *does* expect to acquire status by reading E. M. Forster is a phony and a snob.

Consuming Literacy, Cashing in (on) Culture

Why is it so important for Carmela to know about *Citizen Kane?* And what does Carmela and friends, watching a movie at home, have to do with what happens in schools?

Schools are important institutions in setting the terms of literacy as capital. In fact, schools help to control the marketplace—they are instrumental in deciding what the costs and rewards of literacy will be— what "cultural capital" is worth, and what it can eventually buy you. Americans believe schools to be sites for the upward mobility and class security. In an online question-and-answer forum on the Department of Education's website, Bush administration Education Secretary Rod Paige denies the significance of racial and socioeconomic differences in educational opportunity, saying that disparities in the quality of schooling can be addressed through schooling: "A quality education and high expectations are what will lift kids out poverty and break the cycle which leads to this segregation" (Ask the White House, 2004).

"Reading is definitely much better for you. I don't even own a TV anymore."

© *Mike Baldwin, Cartoonstock.com*

If upward mobility is related to the conversion of cultural capital to economic capital, then shouldn't schools simply *give* students the forms of cultural capital they need to succeed? Since it's hard to change stable social organizations like educational institutions, shouldn't literacy instruction for kids consist of the very cultural forms that are considered by mainstream institutions to be important? The idea that schools should do exactly these things is the rationale for E. D. Hirsch's *Dictionary of Cultural Literacy* (1998; written with James Trefil and Joseph Kett), a bestselling reference volume (now in its third edition) based on Hirsch's earlier *Cultural Literacy: What Every American Needs to Know*, a philosophical manifesto in which Hirsch introduces and elaborates his theory of literacy as specific cultural knowledge. Hirsch is well aware that having the "right" kind of literacy is cultural power. For this reason, he advocates that schools directly teach cultural information that marks people as "literate." In his introduction to the first edition of *The Dictionary of Cultural Literacy* ("The Theory Behind the Dictionary"), Hirsch explains his rationale for advocating literacy education as content knowledge. Hirsch explains his approach, grounded in the idea that "true literacy depends on a knoweldge of the *specific* information that is taken for granted in our public discourse" (p. xi), as follows:

> . . . learning depends on communication, and effective communication depends on shared background knowledge. The optimal way to fulfill

this requirement is simply to insure that readers and writers, students and teachers do in fact share a broad range of specific knoweldge. This makes good communication possible, which in turn makes effective learning possible, which also enables a society to work. . . . An important key to solving the twin problems of learning and literacy is to attain the broadly shared background knowledge I have called "cultural literacy." (p. xiii)

Hirsch goes on to explain that cultural literacy "can be taught systematically to all our students," thereby leveling the socioeconomic playing field and ensuring equal middle-class access for all. Hirsch admits that the "background knowledge" that the entries in the *Dictionary of Cultural Literacy* supply is fairly superficial, that it provides just enough information for readers to acquire frames of reference that allow them to participate in "literate" conversation. The entry for **Orson Welles**, for example, reads as follows:

> Welles, Orson. An American actor and filmmaker of the twentienth Century. His masterpiece is *Citizen Kane*, the story of a newspaper TYCOON, which he directed, and in which he played the title role.
>
> ■ For Halloween of 1938, Welles wrote a famous radio Dramatization of *The War of the Worlds*, by H. G. WELLS, the story of an invasion of the EARTH by warriors from MARS. Welles's play included several fictional radio news reports about the invasion. Many listeners who missed the beginning of the play thought that they were hearing about an actual Martian attack, and panicked. (p. 188)

A person armed with this bit of essential information about Welles will, the theory behind *The Dictionary of Cultural Literacy* has it, possess enough "cultural knowledge" to participate in public discourse (i.e., the kind of mainstream institutional discourse controlled by the educated elite).

Let's assume for the moment that Hirsch is right, and that "success" according to Hirsch's definition of access and mobility comes with knowledge of the right cultural "stuff." It would seem, then, that schools could educate children in the kind of "cultural literacy" Hirsch, Trefil, and Kett catalogue in their *Dictionary*. Yet as we have seen, students, far from arriving at school as human receptacles to be filled with literacy learning, already arrive at school socialized into particular uses of literacy, with plenty of cultural literacies of their own. How students fare in acquiring schooled literacy has much to do with the *kind* of cultural literacy they arrive with, and with what their investments are in retaining it.

Activity for Discussion

1. Spend some time looking very closely at the latest edition of Hirsch, Trefil, and Kett's *Dictionary of Cultural Literacy*. Then ask yourself the following questions:
   - What entries seem to be missing from the *Dictionary*?
   - To whom might the missing entries be important?
   - What did you find included in the *Dictionary* that surprised you?

2. Compare your findings with others in your work group or class (Did you notice the same things? Very different things?). What do you make of the differences in your observations? Can you, based on your observations of what is and is not in the *Dictionary*, begin to formulate a theory of how the authors made decisions about what counts as "cultural literacy"?

A quick tour of Paul Fussel's scathing and cantankerous *Class: A Guide Through the American Status System* (1992) suggests why Hirsch's "cultural literacy" might come up short in ensuring access to upward mobility. Fussell is no sociologist, but he offers extravagant descriptions of the social and material worlds of Americans—worlds that include geography, architecture, education, tastes, clothing styles, language, and, most important for our purposes, habits, artifacts, and symbols of literacy behaviors. According to Fussell (as for Bourdieu), Americans communicate (sometimes deliberately, more often unwittingly) their class affiliations symbolically in everything they own, everything they say, and everything they do. Matters related to the production and consumption of literacy are no exception—so those aspiring to class status display symbols of the "right" reading and writing habits (which means that, conversely, they distance themselves from knowledge-making and communicative textual practices associated with lower-class status, such as television viewing). For this reason, even the television itself—*as an object*—is a cultural artifact with rich potential to signal literacy habits and class affiliation, as Fussell notes:

> An observer with little time to spend in a house can make a fair estimate of the class of the occupants by noting the position of the TV set. The principle is that the higher in class you are, the less likely it is that your TV will be exhibited in your living room. Openly and proudly that

is: if you want it there for convenience or because there's no other place to put it, you'll drain away some of its nastiness by an act of parody display—indicating that you're not taking the TV at all seriously but using the top as a shelf for ridiculous objects like hideous statuettes, absurd souvenirs, hilariously awful wedding presents, and the like. (p. 90)

So confident is Fussell that artifacts are symbolically loaded when it comes to class membership that he provides a "scoring" rubric by means of which the reader can assess his or her own class location by comparing his or her own environment against a checklist of things that communicate class affiliation. Not surprisingly, Fussell's inventory includes literacy artifacts:

Bookcase(s) full of books	add 7
Overflow books stacked on floor, chairs, etc.	add 6
Hutch bookcase "wall system" displaying plates, pots, Porcelain figurines, etc., but no books	subtract 4
Wall unit with built in TV, stereo, etc.	subtract 4

The following satire from *The Onion*—which Paul Fussell would no doubt appreciate as correctly describing the relationship between displays of literacy behaviors and artifacts and class identifications—plays on the idea that you communicate your class status and class identification (not only what class you are, but also what class you would like to be) in *how present yourself as a consumer of literacy.*

Volume 39 Issue 24
25 June 2003

Area Man Constantly Mentioning He Doesn't Own a Television

CHAPEL HILL, NC Area resident Jonathan Green does not own a television, a fact he repeatedly points out to friends, family, and coworkers as well as to his mailman, neighborhood convenience-store clerks, and the man who cleans the hallways in his apartment building.

"I, personally, would rather spend my time doing something useful than watch television," Green told a random woman Monday at the Suds 'N' Duds Laundromat, noticing the establishment's wall-mounted TV. "I don't even own one."

According to Melinda Elkins, a coworker of Green's at The Frame Job, a Chapel Hill picture-frame shop, Green steers the conversation toward television whenever possible, just so he can mention not owning one.

"A few days ago, [store manager] Annette [Haig] was saying her new contacts were bothering her," Elkins said. "The second she said that, I knew Jonathan would pounce. He was like, 'I didn't know you had contacts, Annette. Are your eyes bad? That's a shame. I'm really lucky to have almost perfect vision. I need reading glasses, but that's it. I'm guessing it's because I don't watch TV. In fact, I don't even own one.'"

According to Elkins, "idiot box" is Green's favorite derogatory term for television.

"He uses that one a lot," she said. "But he's got other ones, too, like 'boob tube' and 'electronic babysitter.'"

Elkins said Green always makes sure to read the copies of *Entertainment Weekly* and *People* lying around the shop's breakroom, "just so he can point out all the stars and shows he's never heard of."

"Last week, in one of the magazines, there was a picture of Calista Flockhart," Elkins said, "and Jonathan announced, 'I have absolutely no idea who this woman is. Calista who? Am I supposed to have heard of her? I'm sorry, but I haven't.'"

Tony Gerela, who lives in the apartment directly below Green's and occasionally chats with the 37-year-old by the mailboxes, is well aware of his neighbor's disdain for television.

"About a week after I met him, we were talking, and I made some kind of *Simpsons* reference," Gerela said. "He asked me what I was talking about, and when I told him it was from a TV show, he just went off, saying how the last show he watched was some episode of *Cheers*, and even then, he could only watch for about two minutes before having to shut it off because it insulted his intelligence so terribly."

Added Gerela: "Once, I made the mistake of saying I saw something on the news, and he started in with, 'Saw the news? I don't know about you, but I read the news.'"

Green has lived without television since 1989, when his then-girlfriend moved out and took her set with her.

"When Claudia went, the TV went with her," Green said. "But instead of just going out and buying another one, which I certainly could have afforded, that wasn't the issue. I decided to stand up to the glass teat."

"I'm not an elitist," Green said. "It's just that I'd much rather sculpt or write in my journal or read Proust than sit there passively staring at some phosphorescent screen."

"If I need a fix of passive audio-visual stimulation, I'll go to catch a Bergman or Truffaut film down at the university," Green said. "I certainly wouldn't waste my time watching the so-called Learning Channel or, God forbid, any of the mind sewage the major networks pump out."

Continued Green: "People don't realize just how much time their TV-watching habit or, shall I say, addiction, eats up. Four hours of television a day, over the course of a month, adds up to 120 hours. That's five entire days! Why not spend that time living your own life, instead of watching fictional people live theirs? I can't begin to tell you how happy I am not to own a television."

"Area Man Constantly Mentioning He Doesn't Own a Television," *The Onion*, Volume 36, Issue 04. Copyright © 2008, by ONION, INC. Reprinted with permission of THE ONION, *www.theonion.com*.

The joke, of course, is that Green will give himself away every time as a wannabe—he's trying too hard to display a superior literacy (one that he believes doesn't include television watching)—a literacy that marks him as "classy." It's difficult to simply pick up a book like Fussell's, note his observations about how the various classes behave, and (if you happened to be so inclined) "pass" as a member of a particular class by observing and mimicking the habits of that class. This is in large part because cultural dispositions, including those related to literacy practices, are deep, lived, and embodied. Sociologist Pierre Bourdieu would call these deep cultural dispositions *habitus*, a way of *being in one's body* that tacitly expresses one's position in the social order. From Bourdieu's perspective, your ways of using language are ultimately controlled by *habitus*—which doesn't mean that you don't have any control over them and can't change them, but it does mean that they're "in" your bones and muscles as much as in your brain, and that, for this reason, they have staying power.

Bourdieu's concept of *habitus* helps to further explain what's missing in Hirsch's definition of "cultural literacy"—specifically, that literacies

---

Activity for Discussion: In *Class*, Paul Fussell catalogs behaviors associated with class membership. Fussell's book is by no means a sociological study based on careful collection of data, but it's often cited in support of the idea that class is cultural as well as economic. Think of examples of how people might use literacy to convey class membership or mobility. What literacies do you associate with "classy" or "classless" behavior? With others in your group, develop a taxonomy of working-, middle-, and upper-middle class literacy behaviors. On what do you easily agree? Disagree? What might be the uses, and dangers, of such taxonomy?

are carried in people's bodies, in their ways of moving and relating and being in the world. Carmela "knows"—just as Hirsch's *Dictionary* insists—that *Citizen Kane* is an important thing to know, but this knowledge isn't organically integrated into her identity and everyday life (watching the scene, you'll note how stilted and artificial Carmela is with respect to the "classic" reputation of the film, and how little she knows about how to respond to that knowledge about it). Carmela knows she's *supposed* to like the film, but she has no idea *how* to like it. Anyone who has been assigned a piece of "great literature" to read in an English class, who approaches it in good faith under the assumption that the intellectuals who decide this stuff *must* know more about it than she does, and who is mystified as to how such a thing got to be considered to *great*, will know exactly what we mean here.

Like the work of Shirley Heath and Ellen Cushman, Annette Lareau's recent ethnographic study of child-rearing practices in Black and White working- and middle-class families (*Unequal Childhoods: Class, Race, and Family Life*, 2003) describes how children develop class *habitus* with respect to literacy. Lareau's findings confirm what Heath observed in the working-class communities of Roadville and Trackton in contrast to the middle-class community of Gateway, where middle-class children are actively and persistently *created* by their parents as users of language and literacy whose "ways with words" will earn them rewards within schools. Lareau names this middle-class tendency to control and orchestrate children's' experiences *concerted cultivation*, a process through which "a robust sense of entitlement takes root in the children." This "sense of entitlement," writes Lareau, "plays an especially important role in institutional settings, where middle-class children learn to question adults and address them as relative equals" (p. 2). The poor and working-class households Lareau observed, by contrast, enacted a very different approach to child-rearing, one she calls *the accomplishment of natural growth*. For these parents, the crucial responsibilities of parenthood do not include self-conscious and deliberate cultivation of decision-making skills—rather, they include keeping children safe, preparing them for the "real world" of uncertainty and lack of control, and allowing them the space to problem-solve with peers to learn independence from constant adult intervention.

Lareau's study offers us yet more evidence—to further supplement the findings of literacy researchers like Shirley Heath and Ellen

Cushman—that the relationship between literacy and schooling begins long before classes begin. While Lareau is careful to point out that both "methods" of bringing up children are morally equivalent and carry benefits and liabilities in terms of what children can do in the world, she shows how these class-based patterns of interaction with children around language have consequences for children's experiences of schooling. Once children arrive in schools, other forms of sorting with respect to class-based literacy practices kick in. Yet schools don't just teach forms of literacy that will allow the educated to sort themselves upward—they sort at the front end, as people try to gain access in the first place (as Rita learned). To get to a place where you can begin to cash in on culture, you need access to the institutions where literacy has exchange value. In other words, the kind of schooling you get follows from, as well as affects, your class position.

Take the example of Mike Rose, a professor of education at UCLA who began his academic career as a remedial student. The story of Rose's educational history is remarkable for two reasons: one, because it's exceptional; and two, because it's ordinary. As the story of a working-class student who is tracked into remedial classes and alienated from education who grows up to be one of the most successful voices in the field of education, Rose's history is exceptional. But as a narrative of the educational predicament of working-class students everywhere, Rose's story speaks for many. It's a vivid example of how school sorts and differentiates the experiences of working- and middle-class students, and how the literacies of these students are shaped by the identities school creates for them.

In "I Just Wanna Be Average," a chapter in his educational autobiography *Lives on the Boundary: A Moving Account of the Struggles and Achievements of America's Educationally Underprepared* (1989), Rose situates his introduction to schooling within a larger story of his childhood as the son of poor Italian immigrants in a working-class east Los Angeles neighborhood. Though Rose's environment encouraged a view of life "that rendered it short and brutish or sad and aimless or long and quiet with rewards like afternoon naps, the evening newspaper, walks around the block" (p. 170), it's clear from Rose's story that, despite these prohibitive circumstances, he harbors a nascent intellectual curiosity (he writes of his passion for science fiction novels and of spending hours with his favorite toy, a chemistry set). Yet he is indifferent about school, and when, through an administrative error, he is relegated to the remedial-vocational track, his indifference deepens into real alienation: "During my time in Voc. Ed.," Rose remembers, "I developed further into a mediocre student and a somnambulant problem solver" (p. 177). Rose describes the experience of voc-ed this way:

> If you're a working class kid in the vocational track, the options you'll have to deal with [the challenges of school for adolescents] will be constrained in certain ways: You're defined by your school as "slow;" you're placed in a curriculum that isn't designed to liberate you but to occupy you, or, if you're lucky, train you, though the training is for work the society does not esteem; other students are picking up the cues from your school and your curriculum and interacting with you in particular ways. (p. 178)

Rose was powerless to forge for himself a different set of experiences within this track; his parents were ill-equipped to intervene in their son's predicament. Whereas middle-class parents with more resources—more inside knowledge of how schools work, more entitlement to challenge institutional decisions—might have been able to advocate on behalf of a child victimized by bureaucracy or bad administrative judgment, Rose's parents had no means to allow them to do so. Rose writes:

> The current spate of reports on schools criticizes parents for not involving themselves in the education of their children. But how would someone like Tommy Rose, with his two years of Italian schooling, know what to do? And what sort of pressure could an exhausted waitress apply? The error went undetected, and I remained in the vocational track for two years.

Annette Lareau would say that Rose's story is a typical story of how working-class children experience education. She found that working- and middle-class parents had much different expectations when dealing with educational institutions. Whereas middle-class parents were comfortable in their ability and entitlement to make demands of schools to secure individualized benefits for their children, working-class parents were not inclined to do so. Lareau writes that "working class and poor parents typically are deferential rather than demanding toward school personnel; they seek guidance rather than giving advice to them; and they try to maintain a separation between school and home rather than foster an interconnectedness" (2003, p. 198). She speculates that this is *not* because working-class parents are indifferent about their children's education, *nor* is it a result of general passivity when dealing with the "public." Rather, Lareau believes, these parents may "lack the requisite vocabulary to effectively challenge such individuals" (p. 199)—and because working-class parents may lack this vocabulary of expertise, they "view education as the job of educators and thus they expect teachers and school staff to be the ones primarily responsible for seeing that their children learn all that they should" (p. 199). Lareau observed that this pattern was in marked contrast to how middle-class parents contended with schools. At Swan School, the suburban middle-class school where Lareau and her research team spent time observing classes, Lareau learned that "parents frequently came barging into school to complain about minor matters," and that "parents of Swan students did not hesitate to criticize teachers' choice of projects, book report assignments, homework levels, or classroom arrangements" (p. 177). She cites as an example of this kind of intervention the case of Stacy Marshall, a middle-class student at Swan who missed the score cutoff for the school's gifted-and-talented program. Stacy's failure to meet this criterion for inclusion into the elite program prompted Ms. Marshall to take immediate action:

> Using informal advice from educators in the school, tips from friends in other districts, the family's substantial economic resources, and her own vast supply of determination, Ms. Marshall learned the guidelines for appealing a decision and followed them. She arranged to have her daughters tested privately (to the tune of $200 per child) and was able to get both girls admitted to the program. (p. 176)

Contrast Ms. Marshall's approach to her daughter Stacy's schooling with the approach of Ms. Driver, a working-class mother, to her daughter Wendy's educational needs. Though Wendy had learning disabilities and was struggling to read in the fourth grade, Ms. Driver did not directly intervene in her education (that is to say, she did not negotiate with the

"Where do you get off saying my kid is grade level?"

© *The New Yorker Collection 1999 Barbara Smaller from cartoonbank.com*

Lower Richmond school, where Wendy is a student, to create what she believed to be a positive educational experience for Wendy). Lareau describes the resources Ms. Driver would need to "make things happen" for Wendy in the same way Ms. Marshall made them happen for Stacy:

> To match Ms. Marshall's actions, for example, Wendy's mother would have had to engage in extensive discussions about the *substantive* nature of her daughter's educational problems. This in turn would have required a familiarity and facility with terminology such as "auditory reception," "language arts skills," and "decoding skills"... In a situation with many uncertainties, confronted by experts who did not agree about the best course of action, Ms. Driver would have needed a bedrock faith in herself as the person best able to determine the right course of action for Wendy... and have been willing to define her intervention as being as valuable, and possibly more valuable, than what would have happened had Wendy's education been left to school staff only. (p. 220)

Lareau's research led her to conclude that class may be more significant than race in predicting success in educational institutions: Stacy Marshall is Black; Wendy Driver is White.

With Lareau's observations in mind, let's return to the story of Mike Rose. Fortunately for Rose, the administrative mistake that tracked him into the voc-ed track was eventually discovered by a teacher, and Rose was reassigned to the college-prep track, where he found himself in classes driven by imagination and passion for inquiry. "The telling thing," reflects Rose, "is how chancy both my placement into and exit from Voc. Ed. was; neither I nor my parents had anything to do with it. I lived in one world during spring semester, and when I can back to school in the fall, I was living in another" (1989, p. 179). In the college-prep track, Rose was to encounter Jack McFarland, an inspirational teacher who would serve as an important figure in Rose's entrée into the "literacy club" (the kind of figure literacy researcher Deborah Brandt calls a *literacy sponsor*—more about this idea in the chapter to follow).

Rose's story ends well: he ultimately became a professor at UCLA, a widely read author, and an authority on literacy, class, and educational reform. But his story reminds us of how much one's experiences of schooling—and one's access to the kinds of literacy that correlate with class mobility—depend on the class position one has coming in to school.

Activity for Discussion: Read "I Just Wanna Be Average." Imagine how Rose's story of schooling might have been different if he had been the child of well-to-do, highly educated parents. Which elements of the story would be likely to change, and which ones do you think would remain constant?

Rose's narrative of his own schooling shows that schools sort students via tracking, that the categories into which students are sorted align predictably with socioeconomic classes, and that students' experiences of schooling (and access to uses of literacy that correspond with social power) are profoundly influenced by these classifications. Yet beyond these classed categories within schools there are differences in literacy instruction *between and among* schools that have class implications. Several education scholars interested in the relationship between educational institutions and social class formation and mobility have noted that educational curricula are conceived and delivered very differently for students at different places in the socioeconomic hierarchy. Jean Anyon, a scholar working in this tradition, did a large-scale sociological study to find out if this was true in American education. Anyon's work (1980) gives us "examples of differences in student *work* in classrooms in contrasting social class communities" from data gathered at five elementary schools in New Jersey (three in an urban district, the two at the highest socioeconomic level in proximate suburbs) defined by income, occupation, and features of social class memberships of the parents: "working class, middle class, affluent professional, and executive elite." Anyon concluded from her research that "there is a 'hidden curriculum' in schoolwork that has profound implications for the theory—and consequence—of everyday activity in education."

What Anyon found is that schools, far from giving pupils access to literacy practices that would ensure equal opportunities for social mobility, actually "trained" students to work within the literacy practices and environments functional in the work environments of the classes to which they already belonged. Students from the working classes, then, weren't learning the literacies they needed for life as bosses and managers; instead, they were learning ways of using literacy that would make them better workers. Meanwhile, children of the upper classes learned literate behaviors intended to prepare them to move into the professional leadership roles of their parents. Anyon found that curricula at the lower end were characterized by obedience and conformity to rules, codes, and systems (for example, as Anyon writes, "Work is often evaluated not according to whether it is right or wrong but according to whether the children followed the right steps"). Curricula for children of the wealthier and more powerful classes emphasized leadership, control, independent decision making, problem solving, and creative management of resources and environment. Consider, for example, Anyon's observations of the differences between language arts instruction in the working-class schools and in the "affluent professional" school. In the working-class schools,

> work in language arts is mechanics of punctuation (commas, periods, question marks, exclamation points), capitalization, and the four kinds of sentences. One teacher explained to me, "Simple punctuation is all they'll ever use." Regarding punctuation, either a teacher or a ditto stated the rules for where, for example, to put commas. The investigator heard no classroom discussion of the aural context of punctuation (which, of course, is what gives each mark its meaning). Nor did the investigator hear any statement or inference that placing a punctuation mark could be a decision-making process, depending, for example, on one's intended meaning. Rather, the children were told to follow the rules. Language arts did not involve creative writing. There were several writing assignments throughout the year but in each instance the children were given a ditto, and they wrote answers to questions on the sheet. For example, they wrote their "autobiography" by answering such questions as "Where were you born?" "What is your favorite animal?" on a sheet entitled "All About Me."

By contrast, in the more affluent, middle-class school,

> Each child wrote a rebus story for a first grader whom they had interviewed to see what kind of story the child liked best. They wrote editorials on pending decisions by the school board and radio plays, some of which were read over the school intercom from the office and one of which was performed in the auditorium. There is no language arts textbook because, the teacher said, "The principal wants us to be creative." There is not much grammar, but there is punctuation. One morning when the observer arrived, the class was doing a punctuation ditto. The teacher later apologized for using the ditto. "It's just for review," she said. "I don't teach punctuation that way. We use their language." The ditto had three unambiguous rules for where to put

commas in a sentence. As the teacher was going around to help the children with the ditto, she repeated several times, "where you put commas depends on how you say the sentence; it depends on the situation and what you want to say. Several weeks later the observer saw another punctuation activity. The teacher had printed a five-paragraph story on an oak tag and then cut it into phrases. She read the whole story to the class from the book, then passed out the phrases. The group had to decide how the phrases could best be put together again. (They arranged the phrases on the floor.) The point was not to replicate the story, although that was not irrelevant, but to "decide what you think the best way is." Punctuation marks on cardboard pieces were then handed out, and the children discussed and then decided what mark was best at each place they thought one was needed. At the end of each paragraph the teacher asked, "Are you satisfied with the way the paragraphs are now? Read it to yourself and see how it sounds." Then she read the original story again, and they compared the two.

Here working-class students are expected to enter into a powerless, passive relationship with literacy—learning how decode conventions, learning to stay within somebody else's rules. Upper-middle-class children, on the other hand, are actively shaping and forming literacy, using it to interpret their environment and to manage relationships with others. These are cultural uses of literacy with profound consequences for people's everyday lives and economic situations. Anyon concludes that schools, and the literacy instruction they provide, often work more to reproduce existing class relations than to make available real opportunities for students of the lower and working classes to move up.

Exploration for Discussion or Writing: Reflect on your experiences as a high school student. When you think about the kinds of institutional experiences you had there—the amount of control over or freedom with your time, the kinds of work you did in classes, your relationships with your teacher or school administrator "bosses"— what kind of working life would you say your high school *implicitly* prepared you for?

Costs of Literacy: Language and Class Identity

In "Stupid Rich Bastards" (1995) working-class-girl-turned-English-professor Laurel Johnson Black writes of the wrenching displacement from home she experienced in becoming educated, becoming academic, becoming middle class. As an example of the terms of this displacement, Black writes of a conversation she had as a graduate student with her younger sister, who telephoned her seeking advice after a fight with her boyfriend. Black remembers:

> I searched my brain for what little I remembered from my pre-law days at college, a decade earlier. Now in a Ph.D. program in composition and rhetoric, far away from the gritty New England town where my sister lived and near which we grew up, I felt useless. Again, I began to ask her about her lease, to tell her about the Legal Aid society. I even began to think out loud through cases from a textbook I remembered. Suddenly she interrupted me, screaming over the line, "Fuck you! Fuck you! Don't talk to me like college, talk to me like a sista!" (p. 23)

Black's story of alienation and loss renders a common theme in the stories working-class people who have acquired academic literacy tell about their experiences "moving up" from local to more prestigious ways of speaking and knowing. It's not the only theme in these stories—an equally common theme is that of gains in power, autonomy, and financial stability—but it does suggest that acquiring forms of cultural capital that "buy you more" in the dominant social economy can be experienced as a loss of value in local cultural marketplaces. In this case, what Black loses in calling upon the resources of her new literacies is the trust of her own sister, who perceives Johnson Black's invocation of legal cases—of schooled literacies—as a display of status and a distancing strategy.

As we have seen, the idea that acquiring middle-class academic forms of literacy brings losses as well as gains is a major thematic element in *Educating Rita* as well. While Rita is driven by her ambition to acquire the kind of literacy her more privileged classmates have, Frank, ironically, is less sanguine about the transformation Rita is hoping to effect. Frank is drawn to Rita precisely because she is not a cynical manipulator of literacy as cultural capital—really, because her energy and cleverness *don't* work well as commodities within higher education. Frank knows firsthand that academic literacy doesn't always lead to self-fulfillment, as Rita believes, and he has no desire to help her eradicate in Rita that which he most values in her. But Rita wants what Frank has (the ability to read the right books the right way and say the right things about them, and to smoothly negotiate the social contexts in which such knowledge is important) as much as Frank wants to divest from the pretensions he believes go along with these very skills. Frank worries that Rita is willing to pay for academic literacy with things that, to him, are more important: genuine feeling, optimistic energy, straightforwardness, and spontaneity. He knows that the kind of literacy Rita is after won't come without a price. Rita believes that literacy will liberate her, will make her more powerful and self-actualized. What Frank believes is that it in fact *will* change her—but not necessarily for the better. He understands that literacy comes with social power, but that it can be about social convention as much as about individual self-actualization.

As we saw, it's not necessarily the case that everyone who is working class can, by acquiring the right "literacy moves," become happily middle class—even if they have the money and/or connections to get them access. Cushman's Quayville residents are "double voiced" in their efforts to work within the system and hang on to their class dignity at the same time. What makes the acquisition of literacy for socioeconomic power difficult for people is that they *often stand to lose culturally what they gain socially.* Programs like the one Hirsch describes don't take this into account. In fact, one of the things that makes literacy education so difficult is, convincing people that they stand to gain more than they stand to lose. Julie learned (for example) from her research on rhetoric and identity at a working-class bar that people are sometimes reluctant to pay the costs to their identities that come with acquiring middle-class literacy practices associated with advanced schooling. She discovered that people at the Smokehouse, for example, want access to good jobs and resources to make their lives more comfortable, but also that they aren't necessarily willing to trade away their sense of *who they are* in order to do so. Smokehousers treated Julie, then in graduate school, as a symbol of the kind of upward mobility that trades on cultural capital rather than material capital (they were suspicious of the value of graduate study, tending to see it as a kind of betrayal of local origins that didn't yield corresponding economic benefits). In scripting her into their performances of arguments about politics, Smokehousers cast Julie in the role of "career student," one whose fancy literacies were inauthentic and of questionable worth when it came to the business of everyday life. In fact, having "street smarts" rather than knowledge associated primarily with the consumption and production of texts was a marker of

> **Definition**
> *Covert prestige* refers to the idea that nonstandard language practices can acquire status for their users by signaling group identification and solidarity.

cultural solidarity and, ultimately, of class identity. Were we to call once again on Bourdieu for help in understanding what's going on here, Bourdieu might explain this by saying that although the larger domain of social relations ultimately assigns market values to literacy practice so that some are "worth more" in the social and economic rewards they bring, these practices also take on their own value within local social settings. Sociolinguists call the social rewards (such as inclusion, status, and solidarity in a particular group of people) that come from *nonstandard* uses of language *covert prestige.*

For literacy scholar James Gee, acquiring and using literacy are processes and practices—like those associated with covert prestige in particular contexts—deeply rooted to identity. For Gee, any discourse practice calls upon an "identity kit," which, in Gee's words, "comes complete with the appropriate costume and instructions on how to act, talk, and often write, so as to take on a particular role that others will recognize" (2004, p. 526). Anytime someone uses reading or writing, they're inventing and performing a social identity. In this view, literacy is not a neutral technique or language ability—it is, as a larger pattern of discourse, an important piece in a person's repertoire of social resources. Writes Gee: "Discourses are ways of being in the world, or forms of life which

> **Definition**
> Gee's idea of *identity kit* refers, in his own words, to a "tool kit full of specific devices (ways with words, deeds, thoughts, values, actions, interactions, objects, tools, and technologies) in terms of which you can enact a specific identity and engage in specific activities associated with that identity" (2001, p. 6).

integrate words, acts, values, beliefs, attitudes and social identities, as well as gestures, glances, body positions and clothes" (p. 127). In a way, this is like Bourdieu's idea of *habitus.*

When someone who goes off to college from a home where people's identities aren't tied to—or are defined to some extent in opposition to—mainstream literacy practices has the experience, upon returning home,

---

Activity for Discussion: Unpacking Your Identity Kit
Unzip your own "identity kit." When you look inside, what do you
see there? What tools? What props? What costumes? What roles are
possible to "perform" with these tools/props/costumes? Discuss with
your group and with the class.

---

of suddenly feeling displaced or "different," you could say that they're
having trouble bringing new additions to the identity kit into the family
house. As we have seen, the costs of "retooling" one's identity kit is an ongoing theme in both *The Sopranos* and *Educating Rita*. After spending
time at Colombia and away from her home assumptions about how literacy fits into everyday life, Meadow has trouble reconciling her new
knowledge and perceptions with those of her old-world father—his ideas
about who is part of his community, about how men and women should
relate to each other—his ways of using language. As Meadow learns more
prestige forms, the working-class dispositions of her father become more
and more untenable. Similarly, Rita increasingly doesn't know how to
be—*who* to be—with her boyfriend or parents any more as she acquires
middle-class literacy.

Literacy, Class, and Power: Paulo Freire and Critical Pedagogy

Even though the identity kit reorganization that results from Rita's new
literacies has costs for her former relationships, in the end, Rita is grateful to Frank for being the kind of teacher who gives her the resources to
make the kinds of life choices she has always sought. From Rita's perspective, she has lost a part of her old self, her old life, but she has gained
much in the way of choice, control, and agency. In a sense, Rita is enjoy-
ing the benefits of what Brazilian educator Paulo Friere believed to be the
transformative power of literacy: For Freire, literacy must bring the
power to change—that is, it must give people control over their own
destinies—if it is to have any value at all.

If literacy is cultural capital, then it can be used to "cash in" for ownership in a share of middle-class culture and power. Some teachers and researchers of literacy, however, have wondered whether the purpose of
gaining power via literacy should be to *acquire* social power or to *critique*

it—and whether the responsibility of literacy teachers of working-class students should be to help students accumulate the things they need to gain entrance into cultures of power and access, or whether teachers should encourage these students to learn to exert some control over those cultures in the first place. The practice of teaching literacy as a way of *changing* rather than accommodating to the social systems already in place is associated with *critical pedagogy*, a practice named by Brazilian educator Paulo Friere. Freire is famous for the educational philosophy expressed in his hugely influential *Pedagogy of the Oppressed*, in which he elaborates a method of teaching literacy intended to develop "critical consciousness" in disempowered people. Freire believed that literacy is never a neutral tool, but rather a set of practices that enact *ideology*, or a deeply entrenched set of beliefs about the way the world works. In "The Banking Concept of Education," a chapter in *Pedagogy of the Oppressed*, Freire critiques the traditional model of teaching and learning, comparing it to the process of depositing money into a bank, so that students are "filled" with knowledge delivered to them from the teacher. "Education," writes Freire, "thus becomes an act of depositing, in which the students are the depositories and the teacher is the depositor . . . the teacher issues communiqués, and makes deposits which the students patiently receive, memorize, and repeat" (quoted in Adler-Kassner, p. 75). Freire sees this model of learning as one that preserves the existing arrangements of social class, because students don't learn to think for themselves, to ask questions and to see themselves as agents of change. He contrasts the banking model of education with liberatory pedagogy, which treats students as active rather than passive literacy learners, and which honors the knowledge students already have. Freire calls for a form of literacy teaching that enacts *problem-posing* pedagogy, which asks students to think critically about the political implications of literacy:

> Whereas the banking method directly or indirectly reinforces men's fatalistic perception of their situation, the problem-posing method

---

Definition

Critical pedagogy refers to the theory and practice of literacy education that seeks to make students more aware of—to help them develop "critical consciousness" about— oppressive social and political structures. Its ultimate goal is to transform the social order to bring about a more peaceful, just society.

A central feature of critical pedagogy is the *dialogic classroom*, which aims to redefine the traditional hierarchical student–teacher relationship and invite students to take active roles in their own learning.

presents this very situation to them as a problem. As the situation becomes the object of their cognition, the naïve or magical perception which produced their fatalism gives way to perception which is able to perceive itself even as it perceives reality, and can thus be critically objective about that reality. . . . A deepened consciousness of their situation leads men to apprehend that situation as a historical reality susceptible of transformation. (quoted in Adler-Kassner, p. 83)

It's questionable whether Rita, under the tutelage of Frank, has in fact achieved "critical consciousness" by these standards. Though she feels empowered in her life, she doesn't critique or take action against the educational system that supports the inequalities associated with her class predicament in the first place. For Freire and his followers, the idea is to develop in students literacy practices that can help them contribute to political change.

Freire's ideas about literacy and social change have been adopted and adapted in many U.S. college writing classes, even though Freire developed his educational philosophy and practice in his work with Brazilian peasants, not North American college students. Within the field of Composition and Rhetoric studies, Freire's ideas have been enthusiastically embraced as a method for teaching adult literacy. Yet literacy teachers and scholars have begun to point out the problems with "importing" Freire's ideas for American college students. The main problem they identify can be described as one of rhetoric and authority: If the goal of critical pedagogy is to get students to see forms of oppression, and students (for whatever reason) don't *want* to see these, what then? What if students *don't* want to engage in dialogue, and what if they seem perfectly happy to maintain the political status quo? When David did a study of working-class students in a first-year writing class with a critical agenda, he found that working-class students were often unwilling to buy in to critical pedagogy because thinking too much about social "limit factors" threatened to undercut the energy and optimism they needed to carry out their plans for upward mobility: As David writes in *Who Can Afford Critical Consciousnes?*, "critical pedagogy's aim is to dig up the social contradictions—to foster a skepticism of dominant ideologies"—even though "some students without economic and cultural privileges may be understandably reluctant to wholly embrace these critical assumptions" (Seitz, 2004, p. 165). In reflecting on his own upbringing in a family of middle-class social activists, David speculates that, in contrast to working-class kids who are never far from pressing economic needs, "a middle-class kid can afford to be pissed off at big issues" (p. 4). One difficulty in achieving the aims of critical pedagogy, it seems, is that working-class students can perceive the values of political skepticism and social critique as just another required performance of middle-class literacy imposed upon them in educational institutions—one they fear they may not be able to cash in as easily for material rewards.

Going Places: Mobility and the American Dream

Activity for Discussion: In the introduction to this book, we invited you to think about the (multiple) possible meanings of literacy by asking you to do the following analysis and reflection:

Focus Point

Consider the following posting from a political website following the election of President George W. Bush to a second term in office:

> Sure, you can get all upset about a nation of illiterate redneck cultists electing the anti-christ to a second term, or you can just warm up to the idea of an even better season of *The Daily Show*. We're tending towards the latter.
> *http://www.evil.com/archives/2004/200411/20041117.htm*

What, in your view, does the author of this posting mean by "illiterate"? What more general definition of literacy does this particular usage imply?

In light of the discussion and analysis in this chapter, consider what an understanding of literacy as a *class* issue adds to the understanding of this writer's use of the term *literacy*. Discuss with others in your group and prepare to report to the rest of the class.

We began this chapter with a question: What does literacy do for people? There seems to be no question that literacy plays some part in class membership, class identity, and class mobility—but we saw that just what kind of "factor" it is, and how it interacts with other social forces, is a much more complicated matter. Still, the power of literacy to afford upward mobility is a durable part of American lore, and a belief in literacy can be a powerful source of identity and inspiration. Perhaps the lesson here is this: we should believe in the power of literacy as long as we don't begin to see it as religion—as a form of salvation—such that we stop noticing the economic realities that often determine access to literacy and education in general, or such that we fail to recognize the political dynamics and institutional forces that affect access and mobility. In the next chapter, we explore the relationship between literacy and work. Everyone agrees that literacy is related to jobs and professional activity, but how? Questions of workplace literacy take up and further locate issues of mind, culture, and class that we've considered so far.

ACTIVITIES AND PROJECTS

1. **Visual/Audio Collage.** Choose a key concept pertaining to literacy and class: mobility, gatekeeping, cultural capital, identity kit, covert prestige, critical literacy. Create a visual (or sound) collage using popular print and/or media images or sounds/soundtracks illustrating the concept you've chosen.

2. **Memoir.** J. Elspeth Stuckey argues in *The Violence of Literacy* (1991) that literacy is just as often used to disempower people and to disable social mobility as it is to empower and create opportunities for mobility. Think about this argument in relation to your own experience with literacy: Have you ever felt that literacy was used against you? What "tests" of your literacy can you recall? What was the nature and form of these tests?

3. **Institutional Analysis.** Find out about curricula at two high schools—one in an upper-middle-class community, and one in an area that serves working-class and/or poor students. (You can do this by looking at websites and public literature/documents, by interviewing students or faculty, or some combination of these methods). What does each institution assume students need to know about literacy, and how does each curriculum express expectations about literacy, work, and social power? Do Anyon's observations about "hidden curricula of work" play out in the schools you have chosen to investigate? Write an essay in which you report and interpret the results of your research.

4. **Film Analysis.** The research of Jean Anyon and Annette Lareau—as well as the experiences of educator Mike Rose—suggest that educational inequalities are deep within social institutions. In movies like *Stand and Deliver* and *Dangerous Minds*, bad educational conditions are overcome by one charismatic teacher who pushes students to overcome these inequalities by force of will and imagination. Choose and watch a movie about education and write an essay in which you (1) discuss the vision of class and literacy you think the film promotes, and (2) tell whether you think such a vision is beneficial or harmful, how, and to whom.

5. **Critical Comparison Essay.** Compare the first and third editions of the *Dictionary of Cultural Literacy* by Trefil, Kett, and Hirsch. What

do you notice has been added? What has been omitted? How can you account for these changes? What additional entries would have to be included if your home literacy were to become the dominant one? Write a two- to three-page essay in which you reflect on the uses, functions, and limitations of the *Dictionary.*

6. **Position Paper.** In an opinion piece published in *The Wall Street Journal* online ("Class Struggle: American Workers Have a Chance to Be Heard," November 15, 2006), newly elected Senator Jim Webb of Virginia warned of a widening economic gap brought about by increasing globalization and job outsourcing. Find and read Webb's piece, and then create your own opinion piece in which you elaborate a position on the role of *literacy* in relation to Webb's claims about the growing class divide. Is literacy part of the problem Webb identifies, or is it part of the solution? Neither? Both?

FOR FURTHER READING

Anyon, Jean. (1980, Fall). Social class and the hidden curriculum of work. *Journal of Education,* 162(1).

Ask the White House. (2004). U.S. Department of Education. Available online at http://www.whitehouse.gov/ask/20040824.html.

Black, Laurel Johnson. (2005). Stupid Rich Bastards. In C. L. B. Dews and C. L. Law, *This fine place so far from home* (pp. 13–26). Philadelphia: Temple University Press.

Bourdieu, Pierre. (1987). *Distinction: A social critique of the judgment of taste.* Boston: Harvard University Press.

Bourdieu, Pierre, & Passeron, Jean-Claude. (1977). *Reproduction in education, society and culture.* London: Sage.

Cushman, Ellen. (1998). *The struggle and the tools: Oral and literate strategies in an inner-city community.* New York: SUNY Press.

Dews, C. L. Barney, & Leste Law, Carolyn. (1995). *This fine place so far from home: Voices of academics from the working class.* Philadelphia: Temple University Press.

Friere, Paulo. (2005). *Education for critical consciousness.* Continuum International.

Fussel, Paul. (1992). *Class: A guide through the American status system.* Touchstone.

Gardaphe, F. (2002). Fresh garbage: The gangster as suburban trickster. In *A sitdown with the Sopranos: Watching Italian American culture on T.V.'s most talked-about series.* New York: Palgrave McMillan.

Gee, James Paul. (2004). *Situated language and learning: A critique of traditional schooling.* New Jersey: Routledge.

Hirsch, E. D. (1988). *Cultural literacy: What every American needs to know.* Vintage.

hooks, bell. (1994). *Teaching to transgress: Education as the practice of freedom.* New Jersey: Routledge.

Lareau, Annette. (2003). *Unequal childhoods: Class, race, and family life.* Berkeley: University of California Press.

Lindquist, Julie. (2002). *A place to stand: Politics and persuasion in a working-class bar.* New York: Oxford University Press.

Rose, Mike. (1989). *Lives on the boundary: The struggles and achievements of America's underprepared.* New York: Free Press, 1989.

Scott, J. & Leonhardt, D. (2005, May 15). Class matters. *New York Times.*

Seitz, David. (2004). *Who can afford critical consciousness? Practicing a pedagogy of humility.* Utah: Utah State Press.

Stuckey, J. Elspeth. (1991). *The violence of literacy.* Portsmouth, NH: Heinemann/Boynton-Cook.

Zweig, Michael. (2004). *What's class got to do with it? American society in the twenty-first century.* ILR Press.

5

Literacy and Work

Before You Read. Comparing jobs you have had in your life or those of people you know, what were the literacy abilities required in each job? Was each kind of literacy necessary for all situations in each job, or was it limited to particular domains or duties? How might your analysis of literacy demands in jobs you have had and jobs you might assume in your future compare to literacy demands of a previous generation? How have the changing technologies and increasingly global economy affected specific practices of workplace literacy over these generations?

A Tale of Two Workplaces

Imagine the following scenes, the first one overheard in the office cubicles of the marketing department of a small corporation . . .

Laura: Don, you ready for the hatchet job today?

Don: I guess . . .

Laura: Yeah, I know what you mean. All those changes around here the past few months don't exactly inspire confidence. Upper management is looking for another way to "trim the herd." But what can we do? We've got to find a way to write this proposal with them, or it'll be *our* jobs on the line next time, right?

Don: True, but how can we get four other departments to agree to this plan and the language we know it needs to contain? It's hard enough to do it with our own team, much less 30 people. And when legal gets ahold of it, you know we're going to have to rewrite it again, for the fifth time, as I recall.

Laura: Yeah, well, see you in there. We'll find a way to make it work, we have before. I'm off for coffee, gotta pump myself up somehow.

And now on a manufacturing shop floor, we overhear two machine operators on their break. . .

> **Lev:** I hear they want to retrain us *again.*
>
> **Alex:** *And* redo the teams.
>
> **Lev:** Yeah, Carl just called another meeting for next week, on our time too. We still have to make the same quota, don't they ever think about that? Whaddya think they're bitchin' about this time?
>
> **Alex:** Bev in processing says they still don't like our team's paperwork, that it don't give enough detail about the "quality control."
>
> **Lev:** Well, hell, that's not what we were hired for, was it? And besides, we got a new kid on the shift. He's had some problems, but he's alright. If we wrote down all they wanted on those forms and that computer screen, it would make him and our team look bad. It's not our fault that the vendors can't get the plates to us in time to keep up with this new quota.
>
> **Alex:** I hear ya, man. I thought these teams were supposed to give us more control over our jobs. It worked for them over in assembly. Why don't Carl and those others just let us use our own notes rather than those stinkin' manuals?

What do these two scenes have in common? Both conversations reflect the workplace changes in literacy created by the knowledge economy and practices of total quality management, which we will examine in this chapter.

In this chapter, we will take a look at how workplace literacy has changed over the past 20 years in the corporation and on the manufacturers' shop floor. Using ethnographic studies of workplaces and examples from movies and television, we will examine how these changes may affect your future work and the work world around you. You will learn to:

- Identify the role *literacy sponsors* play in the changing literacies at work.
- Examine how the *knowledge economy,* globalization, and flexible capitalism shape the kinds of literacy practices often emerging in corporate and factory workplaces of the 21st century.
- Weigh the advantages and drawbacks of the teamwork increasingly expected in these workplace literacies.
- Recognize and analyze specific tensions between opportunity and accountability for workers that emerge from employers' expectations for literacy in 21st-century workplaces.

When most people think of workplace literacy, they generally think of how to write better business memos, read machine manuals, or create good PowerPoint presentations. But just as we saw in Chapter Four how economic issues can influence opportunities and limitations of literacy, these influences play an even more direct role when literacies are directly tied to the economic marketplace. Similarly, as we saw concerns of culture, capital, and power in the literacy practices of the groups we discussed in Chapter Three, we will see how groups within corporate and industry workplaces also negotiate, adapt, or resist literacy practices in response to their employers' expectations.

Literacy Sponsorship

At first look, the literacy issues playing out within today's corporate and factory workplaces may seem far apart. Even so, literacy scholar Deborah Brandt's (1998) concepts of *literacy sponsorship* and *economies of literacy learning* can help us see the economic and political forces in the larger global society that are driving these continual changes in the cubicles and on the shop floors. Brandt defines *sponsors of literacy* as "any agents, local or distant, concrete or abstract, who enable, support, teach, model, as well as recruit, regulate, suppress or withhold literacy, and gain advantage in some way" (p. 166). So we can certainly count most teachers and schools as literacy sponsors, but consider also churches, community organizations, and government programs as well. Equally important, we need to think of literacy sponsorship at the macro level of institutions—such as, in this case, multinational corporations—as well as individuals who influence how, what, and when we read and write various kinds of texts.

Definition
Literacy Sponsors
Any group, institution, or corporation that enables, regulates, or withholds literacy learning for individuals
Economies of Literacy Learning
The economic forces that influence institutions and companies to sponsor particular goals of literacy learning

Brandt's research seeks to understand the multiple effects of large-scale literacy sponsors on individuals' uses of literacy in their everyday lives. To this end, Brandt talks about economies of literacy development where large-scale literacy sponsors, like the Protestant Church in England before the formation of public schools or the U.S. Army in World War II, "are engaged in ceaseless processes of positioning and repositioning, seizing and relinquishing control over meanings and materials of literacy as part of their participation in economic and political competition" (p. 173).

In the case of Protestant Sunday schools, they offered basic reading to teach the working classes to read their bibles, but the working classes often demanded further schooling in an

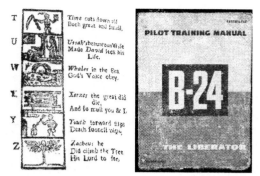

University of Missouri Library, Rare Books and Special Collections

effort to gain upward mobility. In the case of World War II, the new technologies of warfare required more complex literacy skills, so the army created the largest ever adult literacy program to meet this immediate need. But consider also how nation-states may sponsor literacy learning to compete for political and economic power. For instance, in the 1960s, the United States heavily funded new opportunities for scientific education in an effort to beat the "space race" after the Soviets launched *Sputnik* in 1957.

In this first decade of the 21st century, consider how often schools organize student projects and activities as collaborative teamwork in preparation for the kinds of teamwork expected now by corporations to meet demands of global competition. Very often businesses and business-supported organizations are the co-sponsors of these approaches to school curriculum, whether through public advocacy or grant monies. Brandt points out that large-scale literacy sponsors "lend their resources or credibility to the sponsored" in an effort "to gain benefits" from the sponsored's success (p. 167). From this view we can see how literacy practices and behaviors act as commodities to trade, buy, or sell. This view of literacy as an economic commodity takes on more importance in the knowledge economy, where a person's acts of literacy make knowledge-making a tangible economic property (as we will see later on).

Through her interviews with 80 people about their literacy histories in the 20th century, Brandt concluded that the economic and social structures of literacy sponsorship influence: class and race stratification, economic and ideological competition, and reappropriation of literacy practices by the sponsored.

Class and Race Stratification

When Brandt analyzed these people's patterns of literacy sponsorship, she found that people from higher social class positions and more privileged racial backgrounds had repeated access to many and various kinds of literacy sponsors. People from poorer and less socially and economically privileged racial backgrounds often had "less consistent, less politically secured access to literacy sponsors, especially to the ones that can grease their way to academic and economic success" (1998, p. 170).

> **Key Idea**
> *Literacy Sponsorship Influences*
> • class and race stratification
> • economic and social competition
> • reappropriation of literacy skills

As an example, Brandt contrasts the patterns of literacy sponsorship of two students who attended the same midwestern university. Raymond Branch is a White student with a professor father and a real-estate-executive mother. Dora Lopez is a Mexican American student whose father worked as a university shipping clerk and whose mother worked part-time in a bookstore. Raymond had access to the university's computer technologies through his father's job long before going to college. He also enjoyed access to the emerging market of computer stores supporting the university and growing local high-tech market.

In contrast, Dora encountered difficulties nurturing her interest in biliteracy, as there were few Spanish speakers and scarce Spanish print media available to her growing up in this university town. At age 13, she began to learn some computer skills through a teaching assistantship in a summer school program for children of migrant workers. Compared to Raymond, whose parents gave him his own computer when he was 12, Dora received a used word-processing machine from her father when she went to college.

Brandt concludes that Raymond's "literacy skills were underwritten by late century transformations in communication technology that created a boomtown need for programmers" (1998, p. 172). But Dora's "biliterate skills [that she uses in her job with a cleaning company while finishing school at a technical college] developed and paid off much further down the economic reward ladder in government-sponsored youth programs and commercial enterprises that, in the 1990s, were absorbing surplus migrant workers into a low wage, urban service economy."

Economic and Ideological Competition

Brandt's research reveals how forms of literacy, and individuals' experiences with these forms, "are created out of competition between institutions" (1998, p. 173). To detail this claim, Brandt describes how the expectations of literacy at work changed for Dwayne Lowery, an auto worker and water meter reader turned public employee's union representative. In the early 1970s, Lowery received training (sponsorship) from the union to learn contract negotiation. At first, he negotiated primarily with part-time public officials who were not as well trained as the union negotiators. But as the power of the public employee's unions grew in the 1980s, due also to the rise of the information and service economy, the municipal government officers brought in lawyers to take their place at the bargaining table.

Where once Lowery used his oral negotiating skills as much as his writing abilities, now all procedures were conducted in writing and legal discourse. Consequently, Lowery had to continually take training courses to keep up with the government lawyers. "Lowery saw his value to the union bureaucracy subside as power shifted to younger, university trained staffers whose literacy credentials better matched the specialized forms of escalating pressure coming from the other side" (Brandt, 1998, p. 176). As Brandt points out, Lowery was swept up in the rise of what political scientists call an "advanced contractarian society" at the latter half of the 20th century, particularly in labor relations following the civil rights period "when a flurry of federal and state civil rights legislation curtailed the previously unregulated hiring and firing power of management" (p. 177). This case study suggests how new standards of literacy arise from the struggles of competition, as here between unions and management.

Reappropriation of Literacy Practices by the Sponsored

As our discussion of how market-driven literacy sponsorship can exacerbate social inequities and economic competition suggests, many literacy sponsors may seek to control or channel the literacy practices they promote within workplaces and other institutional settings. Nonetheless, very little prevents the recipients of that sponsorship, the workers, from using some of that sponsored literacy learning in other parts of their lives. In other words, workers can often find ways to divert the resources of the sponsored literacy practices to their own needs outside the office doors.

To illustrate this concept of reappropriation of learned literacy practices, Brandt focuses on two examples of female secretaries, a job role historically with little economic or official power. Carol White borrowed what she learned about persuasive skills in writing from her boss, a vice-president of a company that produced Catholic missionary films. Outside of work, Carol used these persuasive techniques to craft convincing stories for her own missionary work as a Jehovah's Witness. Later in her job as a municipal revenue clerk, she also enrolled in a sponsored training course in persuasive communication, which she then used to further augment her evangelical work.

Similarly, Sarah Steele picked up the principles of budgeting from her employer's law firm and learned to apply those principles to the management of her lower-middle-class family household. She also learned much about the genre of the credit report to help her family with financing, and learned from typing documents of civil suits what local businesses not to hire for house repairs. Sarah's comment to Brandt suggests the sense of regained social power when the sponsored take their literacy gains out of the institutions: " 'It just changes the way you think,' she observed about the reading and writing she did on her job, 'You're not a pushover after you learn how business operates' " (Brandt, 1998, p. 181). In fact, it is precisely the reappropriation of literacy practices learned in the workplace that concerns executive management in the marketplace of the knowledge economy, as we shall discuss more fully later in this chapter.

What's Changed in Our Economy and Ways of Doing Business?

The Role of Corporate Memos in the 1980s

Brandt's concept of literacy sponsorship can help us better see what's at stake for worker literacies in the emergence of the knowledge economy. We can observe an element of this transformation to a knowledge economy in a scene from *The Secret of My Success* (1987) and then in the movie *Office Space* (1999). In the contrast between these two movies, we can see how the meaning and purposes of office memos changed in just over a decade. *The Secret of My Success* depicts the time when the world was shifting from a manufacturing economy to an information economy. Ten years later, *Office Space* satirizes the deep effects of that economic shift for the average cubicle worker, as we shall soon examine.

© The New Yorker Collection 2005 Mick Stevens from cartoonbank.com

In *The Secret of My Success*, Brantley (Michael J. Fox) is a business college graduate stuck in a mailroom job trying to work his way up the corporate ladder. In the decade before email, he soon learns which office mail items are executive memos intended only for other executives. As his friend in the mailroom tells him, "all the white ones are a bunch of suits talking to themselves." Secretly reading over these memos intended only for the "suits," Brantley finds all the problems within the chain of command. He comments that the memos list the right job titles but "the job assignments and objectives are all screwed up." Armed with the information from the memos, he covertly masquerades as an executive to develop his plan that ultimately saves the company from a hostile takeover. When Brantley is confronted along the way by a higher executive who doesn't recognize him, the executive chastises someone who is one rung down on the command chain for not informing him about this new executive hire:

> **Executive:** (to his underling) I didn't get a memo on that.
> **Brantley:** (quickly replying) Oh, you will.
> **Executive:** Well, alright. As long as I get the memo.

In the next scene, Brantley proceeds to send another memo out from the mailroom to make his role official.

This importance of the memos as the key to corporate control shows how office writing helped maintain the social hierarchy of corporations in the period after World War II up to the mid-1980s. The social hierarchy of management and power in large corporations, like General Motors or Proctor and Gamble, tended toward a highly gradated pyramid with several layers of middle management before reaching the executive elite at the top of the pyramid. Consequently, chains of command and accountability were more rigid and openly acknowledged.

Management and Workplace Writing Before the Information Economy

Employees were more likely to write memos, reports, and proposals as individuals within their particular rank and section of the company, and then hand the drafts to managers above them. Most companies focused on the manufacturing of a mass-market product, such as a general brand of soap or an insurance policy, rather than on the process of developing and serving niche markets of specific kinds of customers. Because there was more standardization of mass-market products, workplace writing tended to be far less regulated by government agencies or associations representing the corporations' legal interests. Overall, companies viewed workers' loyalties to their corporations as vital to each company's growth and sought to maintain those loyalties through benefits packages and other improvements to the workers' quality of life. In return, workers generally reciprocated this loyalty to their workplaces.

> **Key Idea**
> *The Transformation from Manufacturing Economy to Knowledge Economy*
> - pyramid hierarchies of management to flattened hierarchies
> - mass product to niche markets
> - standardization to quality of production processes
> - individual work to working in teams
>
> All of these are changes requiring *more* writing and documentation.

Within the blue-collar work of manufacturing in this same time period, most factories micromanaged the division of labor among workers. The assembly line model of work associated with Henry Ford required each worker to repeatedly perform his or her same individual task along the production line. The movie *Gung Ho* (1986) depicts the change that occurred in manufacturing styles and distribution of labor in American auto manufacturing that came with the global economy that began in the 1980s. At the beginning of the movie, we see auto workers in a Pennsylvania automotive factory each doing their individual job on the line, never needing to read and write anything on the job. As a Japanese company buys out the factory, however, we see the autoworkers' jobs change and require more documentation of manufacturing processes.

In most factory settings before the late 1980s and early 1990s, management and the foremen beneath them only demanded high quotas of production—such as how many razors or shaving cream cans per hour. Consequently, workers did not need to concern themselves with the quality or process of the mass commodity the factory churned out—there was little need to continually modify that razor or shaving cream can for changing consumer markets. And so there was little need for the workers to document their work or to use literacy skills to improve the process of production. In addition, the workers understood clear lines of authority and management, and often lines of power between unions and management. The managers, engineers, and designers in their separate hall of offices thought about the production processes and the foremen on the factory floor pushed the workers to put the product out.

Memos Today in the Information Economy: It's Everybody's Business

So what changed since the 1970s, and why have those changes produced such a profound impact on demands for different literacy practices in workplaces? To examine these changes, let's now compare the hierarchical distribution of memos in *The Secret of My Success* to the 1990s, film *Office Space*. In the first scenes of the movie, Peter Gibbons (Ron Livingston), who works in a cubicle at Initech, a software company, is bugged by three different bosses and some of his co-workers about the TPS memo.

First

Lumbergh: Hello, Peter. What's happening?

(Lumbergh doesn't wait for Peter to respond)

We have sort of a problem. You didn't put one of the new cover sheets on your TPS reports.

Peter: Yeah. I'm sorry about that. I forgot.

Lumbergh: We're putting the cover sheets on all TPS reports before they go out. Did you see the memo about this?

Peter: Yeah. I have the memo right here. I just forgot. But it's not going out till tomorrow, so there's no problem.

Lumbergh: Yeah, if you could just make sure . . . you do that from now on, that would be great. I'll make sure you get another copy of that memo, okay?

Peter: No I have the memo right here. (Lumbergh moves off talk to another employee)

Later again another one of Peter's bosses approaches his cubicle

Dom: Hi Peter, what's happening? We need to talk about your TPS reports.

Peter: I know. I know. Bill talked to me about it.

Dom: Did you get that memo?

Peter: Yeah, I got it. I understand the policy. The problem is that I just forgot one time. I took care of it, so end of problem.

Dom: It's just that we're putting new cover sheets on all the TPS reports before they go out so if you could just remember that from now on, that would be great.

(Dom exits as Peter reacts with irritation—his phone rings)

Peter: Peter Gibbons (Peter listens, then reacts) Yes. I have the memo.

And finally with his buddies Michael and Samir

Michael: Speaking of problems, what happened with your TPS reports?

Samir: Yeah, didn't you get the memo?

Compared to the hierarchical distribution of writing in *The Secret of My Success*, *Office Space* parodies the circulation of writing in teams. Here, the cultural assumption is that *everyone* must read the memo and be reminded about it several times over. When it comes to the circulation of writing, there is no clear hierarchy, and many people can be your boss.

The Effects of Total Quality Management on Workplace Literacies

We can find the origins of these changes in our economy of literacy labor starting in the 1970s. At that time, mass-produced consumer goods from mainly U.S. manufacturers were saturating the markets in industrialized nations. Meanwhile, Japanese companies were successfully competing for unprecedented portions of these consumer markets though management styles focused on the quality of the production process. Ironically, it was an American, W. Edwards Deming, when working with Japanese industries in the 1950s, who created the business approach of "Total Quality Management" that set the stage for the global hyper-competition that workers often face today.

Deming argued that the most important aim of any business is the customer's continuing satisfaction. Seeing business from this view, companies should emphasize continually improving the various processes of design and manufacturing that add value to the customer's satisfaction. In theory, this approach then assumes that workers closer to the actual production of the product or service, rather than the middle management, may know best how to repeatedly improve the quality of the manufacturing or service process because they deal the most with these everyday concerns. This is why Peter is repeatedly asked about the memo. Management assumes his and his coworkers' input is necessary to maintain quality management. In practice, however, whether the management of a business will fully act on this assumption and carry it through in an ethical manner with workers depends on the social contexts and power dynamics of each individual workplace, as the examples of workplace studies in this chapter will show.

If we turn again from corporate employees to the factory workers, we can see how the "total quality" approach also favors teams of workers involved in whole processes of manufacturing rather than the individual, isolated tasks of the assembly line. In the movie *Gung Ho*, the owners of the automotive factory are about to close the plant due to global competition. Later, after a Japanese auto firm buys the factory, everyone is carrying around clipboards, constantly reading and writing. Through these literacy efforts on the job they are supposed to keep track of each step of their team's production in order to repeatedly improve their team's process of work. In the movie, tensions emerge between the pride of the American workers who perform their individual jobs well and the Japanese expectations for working in teams.

The team approach assumes that when workers understand a whole system within the production or service, they will be better prepared to "add value" for the customers. For this reason, management in many companies today emphasizes teams of workers to continually evaluate

Activity: Perusing the Job Ads

How much can we see these trends in classified ads for jobs and career positions today? In groups, look at classified ads online. For more corporate positions, go to an online resume service, such as CareerBuilder.com, and look at several categories of jobs, particularly ones that call for various kinds of writing. For more factory-related jobs, you can look in online newspapers.

As you look and discuss, what does the information you find or don't find suggest about:

- transformations of the knowledge economy?
- the kinds of literacy you need to get the jobs?
- aspects of workplace literacy in the job that are explicitly stated and what is unsaid (what the worker would probably only learn when working in the job)?

and improve the set of processes assigned to them, whether they be keeping track of circuit board assembly or revising company documents to meet ever-changing standards and regulations in a global economy.

Since 1985 when *Gung Ho* was made, many companies have replaced the clipboards with electronic spreadsheets on computer terminals. This shift in literacy technologies within manufacturing and service has led many adult literacy experts in government and education to cry for new training in computer literacy skills. In contrast, ethnographic studies of literacy within these work settings have shown that success with these new literacy expectations has more to do with the social dynamics of the workplace than with retraining for a discrete set of skills, regardless of particular contexts or functions.

Implications for Work and Literacy in the Knowledge Economy

Competition Among Teams and Too Many Bosses

For corporations that adhere to this language of quality management, the identity of "customer" should not only apply to the end user of any product, but also to any others involved in another part of the production in the same company. For example, in Geoffrey Cross' study of Montmache Industries (2000), a financial services company, the technical services department had to develop documents called service level agreements that would act as contracts with the 22 other branches of their company. The top management forced the company's technical services department to compete with tech service providers outside the corporation by creating a bid for the services with the company's branches or risk having their services outsourced to another company and their jobs eliminated. The technical services department needed to produce the service level agreements to show in writing what services would be provided for each unit inside the company. To develop these service level agreement contracts, and to keep their jobs, the technical services department had to view the employees of these other branches as their "customers" more than their colleagues, and they needed to compete for company resources with these other units of their company.

As this example from Cross' research suggests, through this language of customers in the global marketplace, executive management of companies often seek to foster internal competition among teams of workers in the same company responsible for different production processes in the name of "adding value" to all these customers' satisfaction. These kinds of tensions often complicate collaborative literacy practices in the workplace as we will later discuss. The movie *Office Space* makes fun of corporations that foster the competition of teams within the same company. A large banner hangs over the cubicles of the software firm Initech asking "Is This Good for the Company?," falsely implying everyone's value as a team player. But when Peter talks to outside consultants hired to reduce the work staff, he speaks the greater truth about work teams where many people can be your boss:

> **Peter:** Here's something else. I have eight different bosses right now.
>
> **Bob Sydell:** Excuse me? Eight?
>
> **Peter:** Eight, Bob.
>
> **Peter:** That means when I make a mistake . . . eight different people come to tell me about it. My only real motivation is not to be hassled. And fear of losing my job. But that only makes someone work just hard enough not to get fired.

Writing for Work in the Age of Lean and Flexible Companies

Changes in technology and information systems have further promoted an emphasis on the customer and the quality of the product. Technologies of the past two decades have helped smaller companies to create niche markets produced for specific consumer identities. These niche markets in turn work to produce these identities that require these particular niche products. As various technologies allow more goods to be customized for particular markets, making more consumer choices available, companies assume they must forever innovate their products and services to appeal to changing customer desires. Information technologies, such as the Internet, also compress space and time, allowing for the creation of many products and services anywhere on the planet where the needed resources are available and the labor is cheaper. This global competition for smaller and smaller niche markets has promoted the disintegration of company loyalties to workers in the wake of management practices such as outsourcing and off-shoring labor. In a 1996 *New York Times* poll, 75% of those polled felt companies were less loyal to workers than 10 years earlier, and 64% believed workers were now less loyal to companies.

-- a radical *realignment* of industrialized *economies* --

Reinventing Comics by Scott McCloud © 2000 Scott McCloud. Reprinted by Permission of HarperCollins Publishers.

Key Idea

Flexible Capitalism

- working in temporary teams on companies' projects
- expectations of continual innovation
- no loyalties to worker or company

Global competition and assumptions of customer desires have led companies to assume they must remain flexible and lean, ready to innovate quickly as deemed necessary. In *Office Space*, the threat of downsizing hangs over the employees of Initech as consultants come in to assess how much "value" each worker's job adds to the company's supposed quality. One of the workers at Initech complains in fear and anger that the consultants are called efficiency experts but that they're actually making everyone interview again for their own job.

In this view of the corporate workplace, top-management demands, many people will need to move in and out of teams, different projects, and sometimes jobs. Some management books on this brand of *flexible capitalism* suggest the analogy of a movie studio, where people assemble for a project, disband when no longer needed, and then seek work again with another project, possibly with a different company.

As this overview of work situations today indicates, these changes often require people to change their literacy practices and behaviors in many corporate and manufacturing settings. In terms of literacy practices, the assumptions of flexible capitalism require more amounts and kinds of writing than before. In general, every company and factory working under a process-centered model of management and global hyper-competition must use various forms of writing to constantly:

- identify customers, their needs, and the processes that deliver greatest customer satisfaction,

- design improvements to those processes of production (often through team management that then requires greater abilities in collaborative writing), and

- implement the recommended changes in these processes.

Workers' Literacy Identities in Flexible Capitalism

The promoters of flexible capitalism also expect workers take on new literacy behaviors that, as literacy scholars James Gee, Glynda Hull, and Colin Lankshear (1996) argue, also require a different social identity kit associated with these literacy behaviors. Although the degree of demand for these behaviors may vary between different corporate and manufacturing settings, upper management often requires workers to behave in the following rules.

- **Both entrepreneur and collaborator.** On the one hand, flexible capitalism requires corporate workers to assume they are independent employees who contract out their work to companies. As branches of companies seek to remain lean to meet changing demands in the marketplace, the worker cannot assume any loyalty from these companies beyond the end of each major project required by the company. Consequently, he must draw on his workplace literacy practices to repeatedly market his abilities as necessary. On the other hand, even as the worker must act as her own independent agent, employers expect her to deftly ease into the collaborations needed for each new project, often with new players. As many management books on flexible capitalism state, companies need workers who are "eager to stay, but ready to go," clearly a contradictory state of mind that calls for a complex balance of literacy behaviors.

- **An endlessly flexible team player.** Given the expectation of flexible team projects within lean companies with supposedly flattened hierarchies of management, business and education officials stress the need for workers in the 21st century to develop strong interpersonal skills and oral and written communications to serve them well in ever-changing collaborative contexts. Furthermore, some educators of adult literacy point out that workers' tolerance of other cultures has also become necessary in an increasingly ethnically diverse workforce in service and manufacturing jobs.

- **A perpetual learner, always eager for retraining.** According to the *New York Times* in 1996, a young American with at least 2 years of college could expect to change jobs at least 11 times and change their skill base at least 3 times in 40 years of labor. With the rapid continuous demand for greater efficiency, technological innovations, and higher quality for niche markets, many workers are forced by their employers or their job situation to continually learn new literacy skills for different social and technological contexts. For these reasons, educational policymakers, particularly those aligned with business interests, stress that elementary and secondary schools must teach students how to learn for themselves. They assume technological and social innovations will eventually make obsolete the *content* of current knowledge used in workplace settings. Deborah Brandt (2005) notes this expectation of continual retraining in her recent study of the changes for professionals who often write for their jobs in the knowledge economy. All the workers she interviewed who were not self-employed "attended work-related training ranging from several weeks at special institutes to day-long in-house classes. In addition, several pursued self-education via career-related reading during leisure hours" (p. 186).

So What Happens to Workers' Knowledge in a Knowledge Economy?

Although *The Secret of My Success* depicted the older hierarchical structure of American corporations, the movie also satirized the problems of knowledge distribution within the emergence of a more global economy. In the first scene Brantley loses his first corporate job on the first day of work due to a "hostile takeover" by a larger company. When Brantley goes to another company's personnel department, he's told he doesn't have experience for a job in that company. When he asks how he can get the experience if he doesn't have a job, the personnel guy says:

Personnel: If we gave you a job to just give you experience, you would take that experience to get a better job. And that experience would benefit someone else.

Brantley: Yeah, but I was trained in college to handle a job like this, so in a sense I already have experience.

Personnel: What you've got is college experience, not the practical hardnosed business experience we're looking for. If you joined our training program out of high school, you would be qualified for this job now.

Brantley: So then why did I go to college?

Personnel: You had fun, didn't you?

This paradox of job experience suggests the corporations' fear that their workers' knowledge cannot be wholly contained as the property of the company. When companies and manufacturers emphasize the quality of goods and services to highly targeted markets, the ideas of the employees become the necessary commodity to meet global competition. And, as Deborah Brandt (2005) puts it, "The human skills of literacy make the knowledge economy viable. Writers put knowledge in tangible, and thereby transactional, form" (p. 167). Once workers write down their ideas in the various forms of business writing (such as reports, proposals, and process manuals), the writing itself can become a marketable commodity. As management recognizes the employees' writing as a commodity with economic value for trade and profit, they will likely seek to contain the writing and the employees' ideas within the company. Similarly, since writing as a commodity can promote profit, outside organizations, such as government agencies and corporate trade associations, may seek to regulate forms of writing to prevent unethical behaviors by companies. For these reasons, the knowledge economy represents a major shift from an economy of material production (where the product you produced is what counted) to information processing (where the knowledge for how to continually improve the quality of the process and product will keep the company competitive).

> **Key Idea**
> *Managing Workers'*
> *Knowledge in the*
> *Knowledge Economy*
> 1. focus shifts from material production to information processing
> 2. ideas of employees become the necessary commodity for profit
> 3. workers' literacy practices become crucial human capital for corporations
> 4. corporations become vulnerable to leaky property of workers' literacy

Workers' Literacy Gains and Companies' Knowledge Drains

In this way, workers' literacy practices become the human capital of the 21st century that fuels greater economic success more than physical labor or the money of the stockholders. But when companies rely on people's continually expanding literacy practices as necessary human capital, they also become vulnerable to the "leaky property" of workers' knowledge-making. Brandt writes, "When the assets are human, companies can't own them, but they can grow them and try to control them" (2005, p. 188), as we saw in this moment from *The Secret of My Success.*

This vulnerability of knowledge drain from companies further explains the importance of team processes and the strategies of "just-in-time" learning in today's workplace literacy. Management experts talk about guiding "knowledge flows" within companies and organizations. As Brandt points out: "The aim [of these managers] is to embed knowledge deeply within the organizational routines and structures, so that it does not belong to any one person" (2005, p. 189) who might be able to take that knowledge with him.

> **Definition**
>
> **Distributed Knowledge**
> Organization of worker teams in which no single worker manages the full knowledge of a corporate system or structure.

The corporate model of team organization serves these contradictory goals of *distributed knowledge* where each worker's contributions help create a smart system, but each worker is less likely to benefit individually from the knowledge created by the whole team. From the management's view, they want to organize the corporate workplace to make communication and learning of new systems easier among co-workers, yet more difficult to identify for competitors.

The corporate need to contain and channel "knowledge flows," so they most benefit the company, also explains many managers' great interest in the strategy of just-in-time learning. On the one hand, businesses assume that the evolving changes in customer markets require a flexibility to learn new skills as the needs emerge for a given work project. For instance, a team may need to learn how to manage new software, run new machinery, or write different kinds of documents, challenges that will likely require building upon their previous set of literacy practices and behaviors to manage this new learning. On the other hand, the corporate strategy of just-in-time learning can also serve the company by better preserving competencies within the business rather than with individual workers who may leave the company or be laid off.

Power and Social Dynamics of Literacy Teamwork in the Knowledge Economy

So what are the challenges that workers face when collaborating in teams within the new work order of flexible capitalism? In this section, we will discuss what factors can complicate and motivate collaborative literacy work in corporations, highly regulated industries, and in manufacturing. Having identified these factors, you will be better prepared to look for them, or patterns of social dynamics related to these factors, in any workplace settings you might research or encounter in your own future work situations.

Challenges of Collaborative Literacy in Corporations

In the case of corporate settings, Geoffrey Cross's ethnography of Montmache Technical Services shows how a company's expectations of total quality management can demand collaboration across many branches of a business. As mentioned earlier, the technical services branch of Montmache Financial Services had to quickly learn how to be more responsive to the different information technology needs of 22 other units of the company to prevent the

> **Key Idea**
> *Three Factors Involved in Large-Scale Collaborative Writing*
> - choosing consensus vs. hierarchical model of collaboration
> - balancing oral culture with written communications
> - collaborating within an environment of constant change

outsourcing of their jobs. To develop customer-designed service level agreement contracts with the other branches of Montmache, the technical services department needed to collaborate on writing these documents with branch representatives from all over the company. Cross identified several major factors that challenged this large-scale collaborative project. We will discuss three of these factors that would likely emerge in most large corporate work situations.

■ *Choosing between a consensus vs. a hierarchical model of collaboration*

Drawing from earlier studies of collaborative work, Cross asserts that the goal of large-group collaboration is to develop a "collective mind." Weick and Roberts (1993) identify a collective mind as when members of a large group (or set of groups) maintain "heedful interrelation of group members" (Cross, 2000, p. 9). The members of the group(s) work toward this heedful interrelation by carefully listening to the concerns of the other members and the groups involved as they relate to the goals of the project. To achieve these goals, a group can employ a consensus model of collaboration, where all, or most, members involved take part in decision making, the planning of tasks, and the writing of documents. Or group leaders can choose a more hierarchical model of collaboration, where leaders make the decisions and assign communication and writing tasks to smaller groups.

The technical services people at Montmache first attempted a consensual model in the form of large-scale planning meetings to design the format of the service level agreements and their strategies for collaborating with the 22 other branches of the company. This approach, however, proved a dismal failure, particularly because many of the staff were already over-booked with other duties and were not prepared to take on a collaborative decision-making process. Cross also points out that research on organizational behavior indicates that as groups grow larger than five members, "the gap widens between productivity and potential" (2000, p. 5). Just remember how difficult you found collaborative projects that included more than five people. There were just too many staff members in the technical services department for collaboration by consensus.

In the end, the two leaders of the service level agreements project opted for a hierarchical approach in which they first created and carried through a model of collaboration with one other branch of the company. Once the leaders could present a proven model for interacting with representatives of another branch of the company through surveying, communicating, and finally documenting the specific technical needs of that department, they were better able to motivate the other staff members in technical services working in pairs to follow their lead. To further prompt this motivation, the leaders created "the war room" as their base of operations. The war room was a highly visible meeting room, nearby the physical center of power in the office embodied by the workspace of three senior managers. In the room, the leaders also kept a large grid publicly displaying the progress of each team, which all employees could easily see from the main elevators. Cross believes this strategy also served to enhance the internal competition among the teams on the project.

- *Balancing a corporate oral culture with the need for written communications*

As mentioned earlier, many corporations in the knowledge economy seek to channel distribution of their workers' knowledge to promote continual innovation among workers and the containment of company knowledge. Cross found this same trend in the physical design of the technical services floor of Montmache Financial. To develop a collaborative information culture, the management had replaced the more private cubicles with carrels each divided only by a 3-foot wall to encourage conversation and problem solving among the technical staff. This design supported the sharing of ideas among nearby staff and the multitasking of problems that arose with the information technology services they provided to the company's other departments. But this office configuration made it harder for some of the key players in the service level agreements project to concentrate on the great amounts of reading and writing they needed to do for this large-scale collaboration.

Cross also claims management's promotion of oral corporate culture hindered the success of a consensual approach to the project because most staff members had not read, or read too quickly, the necessary drafts of the documents before the meetings. Similarly, the project managers did not think to bring copies to help keep everyone on task during the meetings. Moreover, due to less experience with collaborative writing, the project managers had difficulty putting the project's tasks in writing during the attempted large-scale staff meetings.

Over the course of the project, however, many of the technical services staff came to appreciate how processes of writing can help maintain such large-scale collaboration across departments. Based on the employees' experiences and their own comments, Cross argues that the various stages of writing in the project acted as a necessary pretext for the organizing of group process, to get people across departments to talk with each other on the same page. Near the end of the project, the vice president of technology services came to value the writing in this way, "It's almost like this document really is a stimulus or a trick to cause people to really stop and think and interact, so the real benefit has been people reaching at a higher level or deeper level of understanding regarding service level agreements" (Cross, 2000, p. 163).

So the project required continual interaction between written and oral communications to ensure "heedful interrelation" of all the workers and departments involved. The initial writing involved in the surveys of each branch department's needs helped to identify the particular issues of technical service for each department. The face-to-face interviews with representatives from each department in response to the surveys helped ensure people listened, negotiated, and further clarified the department's concerns. And each department's oral feedback on drafts of their particular service level agreement helped the technical services staff focus more on the needs that emerged from the earlier interviews. Cross's research of this large-scale collaborative process shows us that continued documentation of all changing production practices (technical and otherwise) is essential for such "large scale transformation of technological practices" in the new work order of flexible capitalism (2000, p. 192).

■ *Collaborating within an environment of fear, distrust, and constant change*

As Gee, Hull, and Lankshear (1996) show, managers in the information economy tend to rely on technological solutions to meet global competition. Therefore, managers often also apply this technological view to their employees. They believe the continual "social reengineering" of their workforce will help them maintain a competitive edge when the information technologies continue to change. Social reengineering can take the form of continuous reorganizing of departments in response to project and customer needs. Or it may take more extreme forms such as downsizing, outsourcing, and off-shoring. For workers, however, all of these management solutions tend to create an unstable work environment that can foster fear and distrust among co-workers.

"How soon can you start?"

© *The New Yorker Collection 2006 Tom Cheney from cartoonbank.com*

This lack of security plagued the technical services people at Montmache Financial. By agreeing to develop the service level agreements with the 22 other branches of the company, they had won the bid against other outside information technology services, and they had prevented the company from outsourcing their department. But part of their winning bid included a promise to downsize their workforce by 30% (40 people) over the next 4 years, and to create software that would replace the account managers in their department. So even though the promise of the service level agreements saved the technical services department from the outsourcing axe, their collaborations with other departments on the project mainly served to find out where they could cut costs and employees.

Consequently, it's not surprising that Cross found many people feeling too insecure "to engage in the broad-ranging, time-consuming and creative tasks" of inter-departmental collaborations needed for the project's success (2000, p. 75). Cross relates the employees' sense of distrust and fear that hindered full collaboration:

> It was hard to work together because employees were afraid that if they gave out information, someone would learn enough about their

job to replace them. It is difficult to collaborate if an individual feels that forfeiting any part of his or her territory might result in job loss. Another participant said that people in this atmosphere often said one thing, but their actions indicated something else. (p. 75)

In addition, there was the threat that the service level agreements themselves would be used for future downsizing decisions. Cross's research clarifies the stakes involved when workers must collaborate within an unstable work environment.

The workers' apprehension throughout the company also hindered the technical services department's collaboration with representatives from other departments. The continual restructuring of units in other departments made it difficult for people to document the specific needs they would require in the future from the technical services branch. The goal of the service level agreements was to clarify information technology services needed by the other departments. But the continual cost-cutting measures instigated by higher management pressed representatives from some of these departments to seek negotiations for cheaper services, rather than agree on current levels of service. Finally, other departments were reluctant to cooperate on the project because they feared the technical services branch would use the service level agreement to inflate the price of services.

Literacy research in corporate workplaces today illuminates a paradox of collaborative work in the information economy. In many work settings, the pressures of global competition and higher management's demands for total quality management push toward collaboration in management and production. But several outcomes of this flexible capitalism, such as those we have detailed here, tend to complicate these collaborative efforts in the short run.

Political Factors That Influence Collaborative Writing in Regulated Industries

Yet hyper-competition in the knowledge economy isn't the only reason for more collaborative writing in the workplace. Researchers Carolyn Boiarsky and Sarah Liggett illustrate how the "heightened public awareness of environmental and social issues" since the 1970s has required a hierarchical chain of writers and readers for industries that are regulated by government agencies and are often monitored by public watch groups. In industries that could pose threats to public health, such as the nuclear, chemical, or waste management industries, writers need to be aware of the political consequences of their choice of language in reports and other publicly available documents. The stakes involved in monitoring the political nuances of a company's reports require these documents to be read and revised by managers throughout the organizational hierarchy.

Boiarsky and Liggett's research shows how these potential political conflicts lead to the necessity for collaborative writing within a nuclear power plant. The nuclear industry is required by the Nuclear Regulatory Commission (NRC) to write a "licensee event report" (LER) whenever unexpected events occur at a plant. While the primary audience for these reports is the NRC, they have two other audiences: the plant's stockbrokers and the general public (including the news media). The plant is required by law to fully disclose to the NRC the consequences of the problem stated in the LER. But since the NRC uses the LERs to determine whether a plant should be fined or closed, the management wants to avoid stating anything that would alarm its stockholders or the public (who by law can have access to these reports).

For these reasons, LERs are reviewed, and often revised, by at least five people (from the original writer to the power company's CEO). First, the operators and technicians who witnessed the event write up their version of the problem and its longer-term consequences. Then an engineer researches the technician's version of the problem, often consulting others involved in any aspect of the event as well as documents and manuals. Once the engineer has written the LER to the specifications required by the NRC, it then goes up a chain of ever higher management, who each may revise sections or send it back down the chain for revision. Boiarsky and Liggett explain why upper management must be involved in this hierarchical collaboration:

> The higher up the organizational hierarchy, the more reviewers are aware of the political situation in which a document will be read [by these various audiences], the more concerned they are with the nuances of a word or phrase, with the overall tone of a report, and with misleading or obligatory statements. Because writers at lower levels lack this knowledge, they must expect collaboration and changes at each level of the review process. (1998, p. 127)

Activity: What Have Been the Tradeoffs of Team Projects?
As someone who has grown up during the rise of the knowledge economy, you have probably worked on several team projects for classes since high school, and maybe back to elementary grades.
Write about what have been the tradeoffs, the pros and cons, for you working on a few of these group projects.
Compare your list and descriptions of tradeoffs in small groups. How much do your group's common tradeoffs resemble some of the benefits and drawbacks of teamwork addressed in this chapter? Among several possibilities, does your group notice any common patterns of:

- tensions that writers might face when they must collaborate?

- power dynamics between collaborators?

- authority figures controlling aspects of the collaboration?

Boiarsky and Liggett also point out that several other kinds of documents intended only for workers within the plant can nonetheless be as politically sensitive as the LERs may be for readers outside the industry. In-house audit reports written by quality assurance workers where one unit of the plant reports on the performance of another are a prime example. Consequently, these reports require strict guidelines for content and format in order to clearly distinguish the auditors' recommended corrective actions from accusations of blame. Similarly, Brandt's (2005) research with corporate writers identifies the rise of regulations for writing in many industries competing in the 21st-century knowledge economy. Writing in businesses has become a major commodity of economic industries, so federal and state governments, as well as professional licensing organizations representing the interest of their industries, have stepped in to prevent unethical behaviors and expensive errors. Brandt's interviewees describe complicated processes of approval and compliance with in-house lawyers and various managers when they are revising letters and reports. Clearly the deep regulation of corporate writing has changed the frequency and methods of collaborative writing in workplaces.

Literacy and Teamwork on the Factory Shop Floor

Many manufacturing industries have also shifted to a teamwork model in their focus on the continuous quality of processing their products. These teamwork models of factory work often require more complex written and oral communications skills for all the workers. The majority of business and adult education experts claim that most workers in America do not have the skills necessary for teams to monitor, document, and evaluate their own processes of manufacturing for the goals of "total quality management." In contrast, researchers in workplace literacy often demonstrate how the social dynamics and power structures of a workplace, rather than a worker's knowledge of a discrete set of skills, tend to determine the success or failure of workers' team efforts requiring written and oral communications.

To examine some of the social dynamics involved in these manufacturing teams, let's look at two computer assembly plants, called Kramden Computers and Teamco by the literacy researchers who studied them. In both factories, management linked team performance to pay compensation, seeking to generate competition among the teams. At the same time, the management in both factories wanted teams to cooperate with each other when necessary for the good of the company.

Charles Darrah's research (1997) identifies the tensions this contradiction of expected cooperation and competition created for the workers at Kramden Computers. He describes a situation in which a supervisor wanted a team to temporarily "loan" its circuit board technician to another team because that technician knew the other team's model of board circuitry very well. Previously management had told the workers they should consider each team its own company with everyone acting as its vice-president empowered to make decisions for the good of the team. Based on this statement, the team ultimately rejected the supervisor's request for the technician because it would have affected their team's production quota—and that quota depended on competition between teams and influenced pay compensation. Incensed by the team's show of power, the supervisor permanently removed the technician from the team. As Darrah's interviews with the workers suggest, the supervisor's actions convinced all the worker teams that the company had not granted them decision-making power. To avoid the dangers of this contradiction, most of the teams "retreated immediately from opportunities to make decisions presented by management" (p. 258).

Glynda Hull and her co-researchers (1996) observed similar frustrations for most teams of circuit board assembly workers at Teamco. For instance, upper management at Teamco offered pay bonuses to worker teams that could best present to management their ideas for improving their teams' labor processes. The preparation for these presentations required abilities with computers, graphs, writing, and oral communications. As few of the workers at Teamco spoke English as their first language, the teams' presentations, as an added task to their assembly work, were no small feat. Hull documents the critical thinking involved in one team's evaluation of and recommendations for improving their assembly processes. Yet because this team's presentation skills and materials, in English, were not as polished as those of a team who presented the same surface ideas management liked the year before, this team that took greater analytical care was not rewarded. From experiences of bad faith like this, many workers choose not to fully participate in the team efforts of their companies.

At both Kramden and Teamco, often circumstances beyond the control of the worker teams prevented their efforts. At Kramden Computers, the senior managers told Darrah that the worker teams would not initiate inventories and calculations needed to plan for faster assembly of various computer models to improve monthly production quotas. Managers and supervisors assumed workers were lazy or did not possess the needed literacy and numeracy skills to learn as a team how to improve the whole manufacturing process. But Darrah's observations show how circumstances beyond the workers' control (such as the tendency of the wholesale customers to delay orders and the company's vendors to insufficiently supply parts on a regular basis) worked to constrain advance planning by worker teams. At Teamco, Hull found that the company's rigid demands to document and routinely quantify every step of the teams' assembly processes left little room for teams to negotiate options in the way that management claimed they wanted.

Tensions of Workplace Literacy Today: Opportunities and Accountability

Over the past 10 years, literacy research in workplaces has identified some common tensions related to assumptions and practices of literacy caused by the technological and social changes forced by the knowledge

Activity: What Have You Noticed About Literacy in Service and Industry Workplaces?

Most of you have probably worked in service and industry jobs, whether as part-time or full-time work. As you read through these analyses of often unexpected literacy issues in service and industry settings, try to recall with some short writing what kinds of literacy were required of people in your job experiences. It may not have been your job but those of others around you.

What can you remember observing?

Discuss in groups how the experiences of these workplaces compare to the tensions addressed in the next section of this chapter.

economy. By using the term *tensions,* we do not mean always negative tensions for workers and managers, although workers feel these tensions more. Rather we are referring to both the opportunities and the problems that the knowledge economy brings for workers involved. As we have already seen in our discussion of teamwork and continuous "just-in-time" on-the-job

Key Idea
Two Major Workplace Literacy Tensions in the Knowledge Economy
-documentation vs. production
-manuals vs. workers' knowledge

learning, what happens with these tensions depends on the social dynamics of each workplace.

Here we will discuss two major tensions that emerge from the changing expectations for reading, writing, and thinking at work in the knowledge economy. The first tension deals with the need for greater documentation of work production due to the demands for quality control and regulation. The second centers on the increase of manuals at workplaces, due to rapid technological changes along with the calls for greater quality control. What's important here is how workers actually use or don't use these manuals and why. Understanding these common tensions of workplace literacy will help you to research, or simply manage, the specific situations you might find in many industry or corporate settings today.

Documentation vs. Production: "Damned If You Do, Damned If You Don't"

At Texco, a Canadian textile manufacturer researched by Sue Folinsbee (Bellifore et al., 2004), the management expects the machine operators to keep strict documentation of their production processes in order to maintain quality of the company's products. In the knowledge economy of global competition, upper managers view improvements of quality in the production processes as just as important for profits as the product itself. Consequently, competition in many industries and companies today often requires adherence to the quality controls for production and service set by national and international government organizations and trade associations. So manufacturers strive to maintain standard operating procedures that are dictated by organizations like ISO (International Organization of Standards) or HACCP (Hazard Analysis and Critical Control Point), a program that certifies consumers' food safety in manufacturing. Industries and businesses that seek these certifications within the global market must keep strict documentation of "product identification and traceability during all stages of production" (Bellifore et al., 2004) to demonstrate their accountability to these standards programs and to the larger customers these programs serve.

But Folinsbee's research shows how Texco machine operators were also held responsible for documenting and analyzing the production of experimental textiles for their research and development unit of the plant. These expectations to analyze the experimental textiles conflicted with the documenting of the regular product line. The knowledge economy's focus on continuous improvement, as seen at the Texco plant with the continual experimentation of new lines of textile products, requires documentation. Managers call for reports, graphs, and charts at all stages of production to help eliminate inefficiencies, improve quality, and remain flexible to new customers' needs. Because the data for quality assurance and improvement must come from all phases of a company's production processes, managers view plant floor workers, such as machine operators, as equally responsible as supervisors and quality assurance technicians for collecting this data throughout their work. Yet floor workers have to do all this documenting while still maintaining their production quotas. When workers need to document the regular production, this data collection requires strict, regularly timed record keeping.

But in the cases of experimental products, workers are expected to analyze and comment on problems in production.

Folinsbee saw this conflict for Texco machine operators between the documentation expected for their regular production and the expectations of written analysis for research and development's (R&D) experimental products. She examines several incidents regarding documentation between the plant's machine operators, research and development technicians, and plant supervisors. When these R&D products were run through production, the R&D technicians would require the machine operators to give more extensive written feedback and ideas on the production processes for these potential products. In contrast to these experimental products, the regular lines of production required the operators to follow all the standard operating procedures and documentation. Sometimes these two lines of production would be going at the same time, requiring the operators to continually shift gears in their literacy practices while keeping up with the production quotas. Although the operators' supervisors often claimed they would protect the workers from blame if they did not produce the analytical feedback sufficient for the R&D division, Folinsbee rarely found this to be the case. As one worker put it, "They say paperwork is more important than production, but when it comes to the crunch, no" (Bellifore et al., 2004, p. 87).

The Power Dynamics of Filling out NCR Forms

As in the case of Texco, many workers in various industries see themselves having to do the literacy work of technicians for less money and status. Often managers complain that workers don't understand the forms, the company's expectations, or the necessity for documenting precise times and information needed for technicians to trace and solve the problems that occur in production. But for many workers in these industries, what looks like a simple form is a potential landmine of power dynamics and job risks, as *Reading Work: Literacies in the New Workplace* (Bellifore et al., 2004), a collection of workplace ethnographies of manufacturing and service industries in Canada, so well illustrates.

From the perspective of most workers, the standards requirements force them to document their mistakes when they occur or they face being disciplined for not documenting. As many workers have told literacy researchers, "you're damned if you, and damned if you don't." Seen from this view, it's not surprising that managers may receive, and complain about, incomplete data and half-formed sentences of a worker's unclear analysis of a problem in a production process. The research in *Reading Work* describes some situations where the demands of the workers' production prevented them from fully completing the data at the required times during production, as in the case of the Texco workers. In other instances, however, some workers made conscious choices to fudge the information required, particularly when it called for analysis and comments on production processes. Through their responses to these literacy expectations of upper management, these workers chose to protect other workers or themselves from the discipline of supervisors whose bottom line required high production quotas.

These ethnographies reveal the complex power dynamics involved in filling out forms during the processes of production. For instance, Folinsbee's research of the Texco employees' use of non-conformance reports (NCRs) serves as a strong case in point. Workers are supposed to fill out NCRs to document any deviations from the ISO standard procedures of production the company must maintain to keep its quality certification. From the workers' view, however, the NCR reinforces some of the inevitable contradictions between documentation and production at Texco. Managers state they want people to document the problems with quality production, but the company also sponsors a reward system for having no NCRs for the month. Moreover, some jobs, such as those in the weave room, lent themselves much more to non-conformance problems than other jobs at the plant.

Despite these contradictions, Folinsbee found workers using the writing, or not writing, of NCRs in very different ways depending on their position and power in the company. Ted, who worked in shipping and receiving and had greater seniority status, would use NCRs to get things done in the production rooms in order to make room for new shipments. Karen, who worked in the weave room, avoided writing up NCRs in several instances to keep any of her coworkers who worked different shifts out of trouble. Barb, who worked in finishing and inspection, would write very clear comments on NCRs to protect herself from possible customer complaints later on. In contrast, Mary, who also worked in the same department as Barb, wrote up an NCR on the mistakes of Wendy, a higher-status lab worker who looked down on her. Through these examples, Folinsbee pinpoints the complex tensions of documentation and social power that can arise in today's workplaces.

The Authority of Industry Manuals vs. the Knowledge of the Workers

Both the rapid changes in technologies and the certifying of industry standards in production and service have promoted the increase of training and operation manuals. Here again, many business and adult education experts call for more advanced literacy skills to help the average worker understand and use the kinds of technology manuals that require complicated language and data. These experts tend to assume the solution is training workers in more advanced reading skills. Several workplace studies address workers' frustrations with manuals required for their jobs. These frustrations, however, most often grow from the difference between the worker's own knowledge of the job and the required instructions that the manuals dictate in order for the company to maintain its quality certifications.

A number of workplace studies show how some workers keep notebooks to better accomplish their jobs. In effect, they are creating their own manuals based on their experiences in the job. To return to Folinsbee's study of Texco, she documents how some of the mechanics at Texco who work with the weave machines keep notebooks to make their jobs safer and more efficient. These notebooks include diagrams, calculations, and instructions drawn from the manuals and the knowledge of their coworkers. It's not that the official company manuals are all wrong, but rather they lean toward excessive detail and jargon that rarely apply to the mechanic's own job situation. Nor do the manuals take into account the various situations that can arise with the machines, as well as the differences of calculations and calibrations of the machinery necessary for production of different textile products. This extensive and flexible knowledge recorded and analyzed in their notebooks can only come from what the mechanics have learned from experiences and their coworkers' collective knowledge.

Yet the required certification standards of the industry mark the mechanics' use of literacy as uncontrolled nonstandard documentation because it does not conform to the industry standards of operation. In fact, workers can be disciplined for using their notebooks rather than the manuals. Folinsbee describes an internal audit (an inspection by the company of its processing standards) where the auditors felt compelled to advise the mechanics to hide away their notebooks or they would be written up for non-conformance.

In the service industries, sometimes the manuals' written standards for interactions with customers do not fit the particular situations encountered by the workers. Judy Hunter's study of workers at Urban Hotel (Bellifore et al., 2004) shows how the company supplies standard scripts meant to control the quality of interactions with hotel guests. Yet Hunter describes several instances that the scripts do not account for where workers require a level of spontaneity to display courtesy in meeting unexpected needs for guests.

Trust the Written Documentation or Workers' Knowledge?

In some cases, workers' fear of their supervisors' and managers' power pushes them to bow to the authority of the industry texts even when they know them to be wrong. This fear can also be tied to the authority of the written English language for workers not comfortable with English. Glynda Hull describes the responses of two worker teams at Teamco, the circuit board assembly plant we discussed earlier, when they discovered a significant error in the manufacturing process instructions for a particular board. Company engineers write these instructions to dictate the worker teams' exact process of assembly for each board model. The engineers designed the specific instructions for each board model on their calculations for the most efficient method of assembly.

One of the team workers, Xuan, recognized that an engineer had miswritten a "1 when an 11 should have been in the column listing the number of components" (Gee, Hull, and Lankshear, 1996, p. 123) required in a step of the instructions. This error made a big difference in assumed assembly time, and so production quotas, since the engineers would assume the board could be assembled faster than it could be. Yet when another team member tried to change the document, Xuan would not allow her, saying no one could change the manufacture process instructions. Instead, the team assembled the boards correctly and suffered the company's assumed lower production quotas. Another team, however, obeyed the inaccurate instructions to the letter, assembling the boards incorrectly even though an engineer had verbally permitted them to change the instructions. " 'Don't go verbal, go by written,' Mr. Marcos (the team leader) warned his group again and again, having been burnt once too often" (p. 123).

In each of these instances from the manufacturing sector, we see how the growth of technologies, along with rising global standards of quality control, promotes the enforcement of manuals on the job. Finally, Deborah Brandt chronicles a similar trend in the professional world. She writes how the forms and expectations of various information technologies, such as websites, PowerPoint, and email, have forced many professionals in business to adapt to different genres of writing that rely on these technologies. Ed Halloran, an educational materials designer whom Brandt interviewed, claims it's "a whole culture that now revolves around the computer rather than typed words on paper" (2005, 187). The professionals' need to adapt to new genres of writing and communication within these digital environments suggests how today's issues of literacy and the workplace are closely linked to our final site of literacy and technology.

ACTIVITIES AND PROJECTS

1. **Participant/Observation of Workplace Literacy Practices.** Using the Project Appendix on conducting observations, observe (and if you work there, participate in) an office setting where you have access. Observe how, when, and where workers engage in various literacy practices, either for work or for their own purposes on work time. Focus on what cultural patterns of group behaviors you see emerging in your data. Develop an ethnographic analysis paper about what these patterns might suggest about:

   - the power dynamics of work members regarding issues related to workers' literacy practices.
   - larger social contexts of literacy sponsorship today.
   - the effects of the knowledge economy (as we have discussed it in this chapter) on the local context of this workplace.

   (This project can also be adapted to be a team collaboration of observations in different workplaces, similar to the collaborative interview project, the fourth project listed below.)

2. **Research Project: How Does the Workplace Literacy of Academia Compare to That of Corporations?** Some scholars who study academic workplaces have argued that the knowledge economy has changed the way literacy work is done within universities. They also often claim that universities have become more like corporations.

   For this project, you will research and test this claim. In what ways do corporate and academic literacy practices seem to resemble each other, and where can you find sharp differences?

   Your methods of research will be analysis of several sections of your university website and an interview with a professor.

   Web Analysis

   As you look at various parts of your university website, look for language (and possibly images) that fits more of a corporate model based on this chapter's discussion of corporate structures and concerns in the knowledge economy. How does the website's claims about work and knowledge distribution relate to today's corporate managers? You might want to compare your university website to the websites of a few corporations. Consider as well what aspects of the site seem to encourage more academic forms of literacy. Which model, corporate or academic, seems more featured? In what ways?

Interview a Professor

Choosing a professor who has been working in a university setting for at least 10 years, interview the professor about the changes of workplace literacy he or she has seen in the course of his or her college career.

To develop your interview questions, look closely at the template of interview questions in the Project Appendix and adapt it to research some of the themes of literacy in the knowledge economy that you find in this chapter. In addition, we suggest you ask the professors questions about:

- new reading and writing activities they now do in their jobs,
- new team activities they now participate in,
- changes in technology that have affected their workload and the ways they structure their work, and
- changes in the ways knowledge in their field or in the university are produced, circulated, and distributed.

Synthesis and Analysis

To write your paper, look for common patterns between what you found in the interview and your web analysis. How much do these patterns relate to:

- corporate models we discussed in this chapter?
- tensions and changes fostered by the knowledge economy?

And finally, in what ways does the academic workplace seem to resist the corporate model?

Based on your analysis, how much influence of corporate ideas of workplace literacy do you see within these aspects of the university that you researched?

3. **Collaborative Dramatization.** At the beginning of this chapter, we offered a short dramatization of some of the issues of workplace literacy that can occur in corporations and manufacturing industries. For this project, you will work as a team to create a 10-minute sketch (several

pages of developed dialogue using several characters) to perform for your class that dramatizes some issue(s) discussed in the chapter.

Dramatizing a Problem

In your sketch, your characters need to have a problem related to workplace literacy they must work to solve. For instance, it might be tensions in a meeting or conflict over a proposal when people are under the threat of the latest round of "social engineering." Or if the setting is a factory, it might be about problems with documentation and training between workers, management, and lab technicians.

Realism or Parody

Your team can decide to make the play realistic, showing what people face today in these situations of workplace literacy. Or your team can develop the sketch as a parody, using the exaggerated style of *Office Space* and *The Secret of My Success* as models.

Setting and Characters

Choose a workplace setting (whether corporate or industrial) and context of that company that will bring out the problem that the characters need to address. Develop as much specific context as we presented in the chapter about Montmache Financial or Texco, which will then help you develop the situation the characters will face. Your team might even do some brief web searches to find appropriate companies for your sketch.

Consider how your characters could represent different positions within the company and/or different positions toward the problem they face.

Collaboration and Brief Analysis of Collaborative Process

To research, write, rehearse, and perform your team sketch, you will have to collaborate on the writing and performing. You need to keep notes about the team processes, as you will write a brief analysis of your creative collaborations. How did the creative aspects of collaboration for this project compare to other collaborative projects you have done in school or for work? In what ways did it compare to some of the teamwork concerns about workplace literacies raised in the chapter?

4. **Collaborative Interview Project.** It's one thing to read about situations of workplace literacy and another thing entirely to hear about them in detail from those who are negotiating the concerns of the knowledge economy on a daily basis. For this project, you will work as a team of researchers using interviews as your method and source of data. As a team, you should decide if your project will compare the workplace literacy experiences of people:

- in the same jobs, professions, or careers (leading to comparative analysis of situations in the same job world), or
- in different jobs, professions, or careers (leading to an analysis of commonalities and significant differences across job situations).

   1. Your team must collect interviews from five or more people about workplace literacy in their jobs. As a team, you must decide to do separate interviews or work in pairs.
   2. To develop your interview questions, look closely at the template of interview questions in the Project Appendix and adapt it to research some of the themes of literacy in the knowledge economy that you find in this chapter.
   3. Once your team has collected the interviews, you will need to compile your "data" together, deciding through collaboration what themes you want to feature in your analysis paper.
   4. Depending on your teacher's goals, you may also need to collaborate on researching secondary sources and using them to support and develop your claims for the analysis.
   5. Along with your interview analysis, your team will need to write a brief analysis of the team's collaborative process. So you should keep notes of your team's process along the way. In what ways did it compare to some of the teamwork concerns about workplace literacies raised in the chapter?

5. **Collaborative Proposal and Process Report.** Congratulations, your group has made the cut for a remake of *The Apprentice*.
   1. Here's your general task to accomplish as a business team. You are to research possible solutions to a problem on your campus and write a proposal document or presentation using text and images weighing the best solutions. Your proposal must also include analysis of those individuals or groups most likely to help produce the changes to the problem you have identified. In

other words, the team must also identify the strongest points of intervention.

2. As with *The Apprentice*, your team decides how to organize and carry out the project. For your project, you will need to consider how your team will:

- establish your team's decision-making process (what role will each person take?),
- divide the labor among the team,
- access the knowledge needed (such as local and secondary research, brief interviews, technology)—to consider best solutions—where is the distributed knowledge?
- identify those people most likely to produce change and what would be the arguments used to persuade these people.

3. Unlike the show, we want you also to keep notes about your process and provide a report of your team's collaboration.

    Using the team concerns just listed, develop a report about your team's experience of collaborative research and writing. In your report, be sure to compare your team's experiences over the course of this project to specific concepts and situations about teamwork in the knowledge economy featured in this chapter.

- In what ways did your team's experiences encounter some of the issues discussed in the chapter?
- What might have been different if your team were dealing with an actual "flexible company" for this project?

FOR FURTHER READING

Bellifore, Mary Ellen, Defoe, Tracy A., Folinsbee, Sue, Hunter, Judy, & Jackson, Nancy. (2004). *Reading work: Literacies in the new workplace.* Mawah, NJ: Lawrence Earlbaum.

Bernhardt, Stephen A., & Garay, Mary Sue. (Eds.). (1998). *Expanding literacies: English teaching and the new workplace.* Albany, NY: SUNY Press.

Brandt, Deborah. (1998). Sponsors of Literacy. *College composition and communication, 49*(2), 165–185.

_____. (2001). *Literacy in American lives.* Cambridge, UK: Cambridge University Press.

_____. (2005). Writing for a living: Literacy and the knowledge economy. *Written Communication, 22*(2), 166–197.

Cross, Geoffrey. (2000). *Forming the collective mind: A contextual exploration of large scale collaborative writing in industry.* Cresskill, NJ: Hampton Press.

Gee, James, Hull, Glynda, & Lankshear, Colin. (1996). *The new work order: Behind the language of the new capitalism.* Boulder, CO: Westview Press.

Hull, Glynda. (Ed.). (1997). *Changing work, changing workers: Critical perspectives on language, literacy and skills.* Albany, NY: SUNY Press.

LiteracyOnline.org/workplace. (8/14/07). National Center on Adult Literacy at the University of Pennsylvania Graduate School of Education. Available online at http:www.literacyonline.org/ask/workplace.html.

6

Literacy and Technology

Before You Read. Consider your educational experiences and home life. What technologies relating to literacy (such as visual media and computer mediations—email, IM, websites) have you seen change in your lifetime? Who might have been competing literacy sponsors involved in those changes? What assumptions about literacy have remained the same since those changes, and which ones have been disrupted? How have definitions of literacy changed over the course of your education? How much do these changes relate to the sponsorship of particular technologies? Who stands to gain from their sponsorship?

Crisis and Opportunity

In 1985, if you wanted to find a job as a writer and editor who produces proposals, newsletters, and various public relations materials, typical classified ads in the *New York Times* would require qualifications such as "write with clarity and speed" and "able to manage a challenging workload." These companies would expect job candidates to have a degree in journalism or English plus a year experience as a reporter on an in-house writing staff, but these jobs did not require any special technical skills other than typing. In 1985, the graphic user interface for personal computers, other than the Macintosh, required special knowledge of DOS commands for the operating system, and word processing looked and operated on the screen nothing like typing on a page of paper.

In 2007, however, typical job ads for writer and editor positions roughly equivalent to the jobs of 20 years ago often required a working knowledge of several digital design programs. A typical job as a proposal writer and marketing associate for an international firm demanded not only experience in Microsoft Office programs but also design programs like Photoshop, Illustrator, and Quark Express. Similarly jobs as online editors that develop written content material for websites required knowledge of HTML and several page design programs like DreamWeaver and Cyberstudio.

What's evident here is how much writing for organizations and companies now also requires various work in *design*, calling for knowledge of different kinds of software for print and digital formats. As digital technologies have made it easier to manipulate elements of design using desktop publishing software and editing programs for web authorship, the expectations for writing have also shifted. Moreover, as the avenues for digital networks, such as email and interactive web spaces, have grown, producers of digital texts require more knowledge of software packages related to these interactive networks. Through this comparison of job ads from 1985 and 20 years later, we can see how new literacy technologies heighten tensions of change and continuity. For those who have difficulty adapting to these changes, the situation creates a crisis that fosters nostalgia for simpler or more meaningful eras of literacy. These people yearn for a bygone era of books and they fear the rise of an increasingly mechanized society. But those who stand to gain from these technologies view these changes as new opportunities, fostering a more utopian vision of future literacies. These people envision a digital world of greater interactivity and control of texts.

Arguing for Technocritical Literacy

Some scholars of literacy and technology would argue that both of these perspectives rely too much on *technological determinism*. In earlier chapters, we questioned the assumption that literacy by itself, regardless of other social and economic factors, determines the creation of civilization or an individual's opportunities in life. Similarly, we cannot assume that technology by itself determines the ways people end up using it and the social results of that use. In contrast to the view of technological determinism that breeds utopian or dystopian assumptions, the literacy and technology scholars we will feature in this chapter argue instead for the perspective of *technocritical literacy.* These scholars critically analyze the *social uses* of technologies of literacy. The social effects of these literacy technologies all depend on how they are used and the contexts in which people use them.

> **Definition**
>
> *Technological Determinism*
> Assuming that technology by itself determines social change
>
> *Technocritical Literacy*
> Assuming that the effects of technology on people's literacy depend on people's social uses for the technology

For instance, since the mid-1980s some scholars of technology have worried about a digital divide where only people with higher socioeconomic status would be able to afford the technology needed to function effectively in the information age. While these arguments about technological access and income are important, they assume that access to the technology is all one needs. From this view, once everyone has that access, whether at home or in a public library, the problem of digital inequities is solved. In contrast to these arguments of technological determinism, scholars since 2000, like Jan van Dijk (2004), contend that the digital divide may be more about unequal access to technological skills, continued training in various digital mediums, and technical support rather than solely access to the hardware. In particular, Van Dijk addresses access to strategic skills as an issue of usage access for digital environments. He defines strategic skills as "the ability to use digital means to improve one's position in society" through the use of ever-changing software applications like those called for in the job ads shown earlier (p. 248). Through studies of census data, Van Dijk asserts that these issues of skills and usage access also correlate with factors of socioeconomic status such as race, education, and income.

Technocritical scholars of literacy also recognize that while our social uses of literacy technologies do disrupt our assumptions about literacy, we can also see continuity in the historical responses to these disruptions.

In this chapter, you will learn how the social and economic uses of literacy using digital technologies are shifting our assumptions of what counts as authorship, text, and acts of writing and reading. But you will also see how these changes in assumptions recall previous social responses to moments of change in technologies of literacy.

Drawing on literacy research that analyzes the social uses and implications of digital networks, texts as databases, and various kinds of design in digital media, you will learn to:

- Consider the claims for utopian and dystopian visions of change in technologies of literacy.
- Explore how literacy practices in digital environments change writing processes and ideas of authorship.
- Understand how literacy practices are changing in the context of technologies fostered by the information economy and copyright culture.
- Examine the cultural and educational significance of emerging new media literacies: digital, visual, and gaming literacies.
- Investigate how new literacy technologies push us to reconsider what we know about oral and literate modes of communication.

Stages of Literacy Technologies

Everyone can recognize the tensions in the job market enabled by newer digital technologies, such as those the employers call for in the job ads from 2007 shown earlier. Dennis Baron (1999), however, shows us how these tensions are part of a repeating historical cycle in the stages of every new literacy technology. Baron outlines four overlapping stages for all literacy technologies, from pencils to pixels, and indeed the creation of writing itself. To better comprehend the cyclical nature of these historical stages of literacy technologies, let's compare Baron's discussion of stages for the oldest literacy technology, writing, to similar stages he sees in the evolving use of the computer.

But before we discuss Baron's scholarship on these stages of literacy technologies, we want to qualify some of his claims. To a degree, Baron's focus on the computer does suggest a kind of technological determinism—implying that the existence of the computer itself brought these changes. In the long run, the ways the information economy is shaping the social uses of digital networks may be creating greater tensions of crisis and opportunity than the computer itself.

> **Key Idea**
> *Stages of Literacy Technologies*
>
> 1. Restricted communication function
> 2. Adaptation to familiar functions
> 3. Creation of new forms and functions
> 4. Nostalgia and anxiety over new literacy technologies

Stage 1: Restricted Communication Function

As Baron and others point out, our first historical examples of writing in ancient Sumaria from ca. 3500 B.C.E were not used to approximate speech, but to keep records of more complex business transactions and land sales. They were markings on stones as a "tool of the bean counters" (Baron, 2001, p. 75). Similarly, mainframe computers, the historical precursor of the PC, were created for numerical calculations too vast for human memory. The earliest computer programmers often preferred to use pencil and paper to write their computer code because the mainframe line editors were so clunky. So, as Baron points out, just as the first users of computers were labeled geeks because their work seemed so foreign from everyday use, the early Sumerians saw the rise of "cuneiform geeks . . . who walked around all day with a bunch of sharp styluses sticking out of their pocket protectors and talked of nothing but new ways of making marks on stones" (p. 74).

At this earliest stage, only a small number of people use the literacy technology because the restricted communicative function of the technology cannot serve a larger population. Further, the economic costs of the materials and the awkwardness of the initial technology restrict many from creating other uses for it. In the history of writing, certainly before the invention of the printing press, scribes were often part of the aristocratic or priestly class. By comparison, the early days of computer word processing saw the rise of the late-20th-century's priestly class—the computer guru who could understand all the formatting commands before computers could be programmed to act more like typewriters.

In the history of literacy technologies, after the printing press, the priestly scribes of old dwindled away in importance and numbers. Today's priestly class of technical support in many offices, however, has not dwindled in numbers since word processing grew in popularity in the 1980s. They remain important because digital literacy technologies continue to change and accumulate at such a rapid rate—from word processing and databases to desktop publishing to Internet communications to multimedia on the web. The people working in information-rich environments of the knowledge economy continually require the support of those who can maintain the increasingly more complex technical infrastructures—of servers, software, hardware—necessary to keep up with these changes and opportunities.

Stage 2: Adaptation to Familiar Functions

The literacy technology only begins to gain wider acceptance when gradually the small numbers of first users begin to "mediate the technology for the general public" and learn to adapt the technology to "earlier accepted forms of communication" (Baron, 2001, p. 71). Writing only grew in acceptance as its function and structure better mimicked the structures of spoken language. In our age of digital literacy, word processing did not really expand beyond the use of a small cadre in offices until the software could visually mimic the typewritten page. The early word processing could not visually show pages, paragraphing, capitals, indentation, and other markers of written communication on the screen.

THE FACE OF COMPUTING IN THOSE DAYS -- THE "INTERFACE" BETWEEN MACHINE AND USER -- WAS A STARK ARRAY OF WRITTEN COMMANDS, OFTEN IN AN ARCANE LANGUAGE REQUIRING SPECIA --

> WARNING: ERROR LINE 47.

-- LIZED KNOWLEDGE TO ACCOMPLISH EVEN THE SIMPLEST OF TAS --

> ILLEGAL COMMAND: 132452 SYS/D4038
> SYS STAT/MEM CONF837-97 A:&)%

-- KS. (OH, NEVER MIND...)

> ABORT?■

Reinventing Comics by Scott McCloud © 2000 Scott McCloud. Reprinted by Permission of HarperCollins Publishers

As Baron points out, only with the creation of WYSIWYG (what you see is what you get) software and its decreasing cost did the functional literacy of word processing begin to spread across populations.

Stage 3: Creation of New Forms and Functions

As more people take on the literacy technology, gradually others develop innovations. So even though writing does not allow for the intonations and gestures of face-to-face communication, the written form "takes on a life of its own," developing new ways for people to communicate in ways that speech does not (Baron, 2001, p. 75). Writing, in the forms of letters, books, legal documents, and so forth, creates new ways to bridge space and time unimaginable before its creation.

As for the medium of writing using a computer, we have seen innovations that expand beyond the imitation of the 8½-by-11 sheet of typing paper. Just as medieval monks would design and adorn the margins of the handwritten page with illustration and color, people now design print documents with color and graphics and create web pages using other nonprint modes of sound, video, and animation.

To see how contemporary American society represents these changes in popular culture, consider how movies over time have depicted the tools for writing. In movies two decades ago, we might have seen an aspiring writer jotting down her thoughts in a journal or diary. In the 2005 movie *The Upside of Anger*, the youngest daughter in an upper-middle-class family keeps a multimedia journal on her laptop. She dubs in her voice track over clips of old silent movies and early black-and-white animation she has presumably collected from all over the Internet. While the track of her voice offers abstract comments on the themes of her family's troubles, the silent images on her laptop create a counterperspective to the spoken words.

Baron's essay attributes these kinds of innovations of literacy to the computer. Yet we also must acknowledge the larger social changes in written communication, including changing experiences of space and time, generated by the wider impact of Internet technology. We will return to these issues of change later in this chapter.

Stage 4: Nostalgia and Anxiety over New Literacy Technologies

As people begin to create new forms and functions for a literacy technology, others begin to grow nostalgic for earlier literacy technologies and anxious about authentication of these new forms. In Chapter Two, we discussed Socrates' nostalgia for the interactive dialogue of face-to-face communications in contrast to his view of the silent written page. In our digital age, advertisers and graphic designers often use the image of the typewriter, particularly a manual one, to evoke a simpler, grittier, and somehow more authentic time of writing newspapers and novels. Rarely do these images of typewriters serve to evoke the major historical context of the typewriter—the secretarial typing pool, the former place of manual reproduction and women's repetitive labor. Yet in 1938, people viewed the typewriter with the same anxiety we see today for computers. Editorials from the *New York Times* feared that the typewriter "depersonalized handwriting, usurping the place of 'writing with one's own hand'" (Baron, 2001, p. 74).

Baron claims that each new major technological and cultural shift in literacy also provokes anxieties over issues of fraud and authentication. Sometimes these fears of fraud can be well founded, as the example of recording land transfers in 11th-century England demonstrates. Before the common use of written documentation, literacy historian Michael Clanchy explains, the Anglo Saxons trusted exclusively face-to-face interactions in a court to determine the authenticity of a landowner's claims. But as the Normans sought to claim land from the Saxons, some Normans would enlist monks, the ones in control of the writing technology at the time, to forge documents. Without the human interaction of testimony and witnesses, the courts and landowners had to create ways for documents to show authenticity of ownership. Initially, people attached items, such as knives or wax seals, to the documents to proclaim their identity. Over centuries, people developed systems to personalize signatures and later read the idiosyncrasies of one's handwriting to prevent major forgeries. For the most part, these methods helped to ensure people's belief in the authentication and reliability of written documents.

Similarly, in these early years of the digital age we now face all manners of fraud using the new literacy technologies. We see the rising need for Internet security systems and the public anxiety over identity theft and increasing plagiarism using the Internet. Baron, writing in 1999, comments on how easily people can alter digitized texts as well as images, and he suggests Internet users increasingly need to find ways to evaluate the claims and credibility of various websites found through search engines. Recently, academics and public critics have debated the informational value and credibility of Wikipedia, the user-created online encyclopedia. In a fake news commentary, Stephen Colbert of the *Colbert Report* pretended to alter an historical entry in Wikipedia. Arguing that since anyone can edit and revise the encyclopedic entries in Wikipedia, Colbert stated that "together we can create a reality we can all agree on—the reality we just agreed on" regardless of historical facts.

We can also extend Baron's claims about anxieties over digital fraud to copyright and intellectual property issues. As companies, artists in various media, and educators struggle over ownership and use of creative work circulating in the expanding networks of digital media, we encounter new twists to 11th-century England's concerns over authentic ownership and property rights, which we will address later in this chapter.

From Authorship to Network

Many of our digital society's concerns about fraud or intellectual property do not originate from the technology of the computer itself. More accurately, they come from the vast networks that we now create with

Activity: Comparing Authorship and Networks in Blogs

1. Using a search engine, such as Google, find several weblogs on whatever topics interest you for the moment.

2. As you read over the bloggers' texts and links to websites and possibly other blogs, consider:
   - How much do you see the writing of a single author?
   - How much do you see other authors or groups linked to this blog?
   - How much is the content about the individual blogger?
   - How much is the content about the wider public that uses blogs?

3. In groups, discuss your findings.
   - What do they suggest about how the assumption of a single author as a creator of ideas has changed?
   - If you have read Chapter Five, consider in what ways the effects of the knowledge economy may influence this view of authorship as a network.

digital technologies everyday. As a case in point, we offer this activity to focus your reading of this section.

For decades now, cultural and literary theorists have argued that any person's speech and writing is made up of many voices—such as the voices of one's communities, institutions, family, and upbringing. At the same time, however, an older tradition of teaching the arts and sciences tended to favor a view of the artist and scientist as sole creator and individual author of his or her works. Despite these older teachings about individual authorship, much of the world living within the knowledge economy and the digital age tends to act otherwise. When we read, write, and use texts throughout our day, we tend to operate within social, and now digital, networks, whether we acknowledge these networks or not.

We can see people forming social networks to expand their literacy practices when we think about the concept of *distributed knowledge* in the workplace. As we discussed in Chapter Five, the socioeconomic forces of the knowledge economy lead many businesses to organize workers as teams where no one worker manages the full knowledge of a corporate system or structure. The rise of collaborative writing within the workplaces of the knowledge economy also provides evidence for the greater shift from the view of a single writer to that of a network of collaborators.

Social Networks Online

When we look at forms of computer-mediated communication (CMC), such as the blogs you examined in the last activity, we see how technology enables these social uses of networks promoted by larger socioeconomic forces. The act of linking one website to another, as is the practice in many CMC websites such as MySpace, Facebook, or various Wiki texts (web texts like Wikipedia that can be edited and revised by users), makes visible the social networks in our writing that literacy scholars assert have always been part of the act of speaking and writing. People's individual blogs particularly reveal this shift from authorship to network because weblogs are a hybrid genre of writing in digital spaces. As a log, they stretch back to the genre of journal and diary writing, but as a web text, they encourage the linking to other networks, both by the blog owner and users of the blog.

Some news articles further demonstrate this public nature of personal blogs in which the goal is to expand social and technological networks. A writer for the *Boston Globe* argued that specialized personal blogs related to one's career can help you in the job market. They make you more visible to other employers within the same field: "It's the new public relations." But the public nature of these networks created by blogs can also backfire on the blogger. In an article for the *Chronicle of Higher Education,* a professor writes that his colleagues' interest in several job candidates cooled down when they looked closely at the applicants' blogs. They found that one candidate's blog was more focused on technical minutiae of software than the academic scholarship. Another candidate's blog revealed far more personal information than would be asked for in a job interview, while another's blog misrepresented his research.

Whereas many personal blogs reveal these permeable boundaries between the private and the public, community blogs herald even more the shift from author to network. Johndan Johnson-Eilola (2004), a scholar of digital composition, identifies community blogs as a new form of writing, where collection, the choice of links by each participant author, makes up an ever-changing set of positions and content. In this respect, Johnson-Eilola views a community blog as a "fragmented database" in which the circulation of fragments of information (pieces of other websites, for instance) matters more than the "authorial voice" of any one blogger (2004, p. 202).

Text as Database, Writing as Remix

Just as the convergence of the information economy and digital technologies emphasizes the notion of authorship as a series of networks, it also highlights a view of the writing process as remixing samples of earlier texts and images. This view of writing as remixing also leads to the rise of the database as a form of textual composition. These two digitally based forms of writing, recombination, and database construction, have already had an enormous social and economic impact in America and other parts of the world. And they will continue to reshape our world's understanding of literacy and its social effects for years to come.

So how does the structure of digital technology lead to the emphasis on these writing processes and forms? And why do the values of the post-industrial information economy foster these social uses of the technology? To begin exploring these questions, let's look at the 2004 film *Eternal Sunshine of the Spotless Mind*, a movie we believe portrays the workings of the digital database in new forms of literacy and culture.

In the film, Joel (Jim Carrey) finds out that his girlfriend Clementine (Kate Winslett) has had the memories of their relationship digitally erased from her mind. In response, Joel also chooses to undergo the same procedure. He brings all the objects he owns that relate to her memory to the technicians at Lacuna (the Greek word for *absence*), a clearly low-budget company, who use them to make a digital mental map, so they know where to erase the memories in Joel's brain while he sleeps. Once the technicians visit Joel's apartment at night and begin the process of erasure, we enter Joel's mind and experience the erasing of his memories of Clementine. Although some memories are wholly wiped out, most are not erased as a whole block. Instead, we see bits and parts of memories disappear while other aspects of the scene remain intact.

At first, we just see Clementine disappear from the scene of each memory, but then in several scenes other elements in the movie frame vanish. When Joel gets up from a meal with Clementine at a

Chinese restaurant, he comes back to a vacant room except for his own now-empty table. In another scene outside a drive-in theater, the screen first disappears and then the fence of the theater pops away in fragments. At another point, Joel and Clementine are in bed, but then the background vanishes and changes to an earlier memory from the win-

The Kobal Collection/Focus Features/ David Lee

ter on Long Island with the bed from the earlier memory sitting on the frozen sand.

In each of these moments, we see the removal of some parts of Joel's memories while other elements of his memory stay within the database of Joel's reformatted memory. In this way, the movie invokes the modular structure of digital technology that is changing the literacy of the information age.

Multimodality and Design

Moreover, when the movie depicts Joel's memory as scenes made from separate components of images, voices, and sounds that can be individually manipulated, it also points to a literacy of *multimodality*. Multimodality refers to using several modes, such as language, images, music, sounds, voices, at the same time to create meaning, as you might when designing a website or a multimedia presentation. Whereas before digital technologies most people did not have the technological capability to use several modes at once, now a single writer can assume the role of designer of layout, visuals, sounds, and so forth as well. As literacy scholars argue, meaning-making has always been multimodal. When we write, we are also involved with visual design of text. When we speak, we are using the modes of language, the human voice, and probably the mode of physical gestures.

Digital technologies certainly enable a single computer user to work in several

> **Definition**
>
> *Multimodality*
> Using several modes at the same time to create meaning, such as combining language, images, color, sound, and/or music, as is often done for multimedia presentations

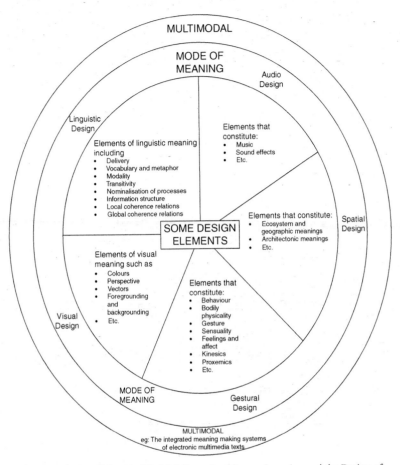

Bill Cope and Mary Kalantzis. Eds. Multiliteracies: Literacy Learning and the Design of Social Futures. *Routledge Press. 2000.*

modes on the same product of meaning. But a group of literacy scholars known as the New London Group (named for their meeting in New London, Connecticut, in the mid-1990s) suggests that the accumulating effects of globalization and the greater diversity of cultures and languages in many industrialized countries also necessitate more multimodal forms of communication. As people need to communicate ideas and messages across different cultures and languages, they are more likely to seek multiple modes of communication to make sure their meanings get across to diverse audiences.

And as communication becomes more multimodal for anyone using digital technologies, the term *writing* seems to cover only a small part of the picture of how people create meaning using various modes. For this reason, the scholars of the New London Group use the term *design* to indicate the deliberate creation of meaning using any mode. From this view of meaning-making as design, we see a much broader picture of literacy in the knowledge economy, as their diagram of the multiple modes for design indicates.

Later in this chapter we will return to the concerns of literacy as design and how our greater awareness of multimodality reveals previously unexplored political and cultural issues of literacy.

The Digital Logic of Modular Structures

This process of multimodality and design, as in the film *Eternal Sunshine* when the memory technicians reconfigure Joel's memories, comes from the logic of modular structure in digital technologies.

According to Lev Manovich (2001), a filmmaker and theorist of digital media, digital technology works by a modular structure in which a media composition, such as a PowerPoint presentation, a computer game, or a music CD, "consists of independent parts, each of which consists of smaller independent parts, and so on, down to the level of the smallest atom—pixels, 3D points, or text characters" (p. 31). Each of these elements can be repeatedly combined or deleted without "losing their independence," just as we see pieces of the scenes of Joel's memory disappear independently from the rest of the scene. A text document for the web may consist of verbal text, photos, charts, and even sound or movie clips. All of these module elements can be recombined or deleted without ruining the integrity of the document as a set of digital files.

Similarly, a computer user can add or replace multiple layers of color or visual effects to a picture produced in image software like Photoshop without destroying the set of files that makes up the final image. The same principle applies to multiple tracks of sound waves in digital audio compositions. In the modular structure of Photoshop, Joel and Clementine in bed are only one layer, or module, and we can change the layer from his bedroom to a beach in winter. In all earlier forms of processing media, once the media object (whether the typed page, edited film, or audiotapes) had been fully processed, we could not take it apart and recombine its pieces with others without changing or losing the whole form. Manovich traces two major reasons for the modularity of media in digital technology. First, all digital information is numerical representation, binary 1s and 0s, structured by algorithms, and these algorithms make up individually discrete samples of data that ultimately show up as the human computer interface of text characters, colors, animation, and so forth. In this way, media becomes programmable, subject to endless changes of algorithmic manipulations. Second, this digital logic of modularity began in part when programmers in the 1970s started creating modules of programming, such as subroutines, functions (as in the use of function keys), and macros, to help streamline their work.

Fluid Legos and Consumer Customization

Computer media scholars most often liken the modular nature of digital elements to building and rebuilding with Legos, but the plastic pieces of Legos don't capture the greater fluidity of digital elements. To accomplish that fluidity of modular digital design, you would have to melt the legos down and remold them. The process is much more like the erasing and recombining of multiple elements that we see in the movie *Eternal Sunshine*. Manovich defines the composing of digital media as "the construction of an interface to a database" of smaller and smaller module elements (2001, p. 226). The movie represents the brain as a database of differently shaped and constructed module elements. Each of these elements in the database can be digitally manipulated to revise the interface of Joel's identity. At several moments of crisis within Joel's mind, he and Clementine reappear in a darkened and haphazardly-lit bookstore where Clementine works. The bookstore functions as a dream image of the mind's database, as the camera pans over the rows of bookshelves.

Manovich and other scholars of technological culture assert that new digital media follow the logic of post-industrial "on-demand" individual customization of production. As we discussed in Chapter Five, this customization of production is also reshaping practices in today's workplaces. The production and distribution of media during the 19th and 20th centuries generally followed industrial factory logic, with a standardization of parts and identical copies produced from a master. In contrast to the dominant industrial era values of conformity through mass standardization, the knowledge economy values individual consumer choices through customization using the modular structure and programmability of digital technologies. The *mind* erasure company in *Eternal Sunshine* exemplifies this model of information age customization, as the company requires the individual memories of each customer in order to provide its service. Similarly, web page authors and designers create sites that can be customized within the site's social networks by other users. In comparison to other science fiction movies, such as *Total Recall* or *The Matrix*, that depict vast companies and institutions wielding digital technology, the Lacuna company in *Eternal Sunshine* works on the cheap, presumably able to adapt to whatever customization may be required.

The Design of Remix Culture

Manovich and others also claim that the greater flexibility of digital modular structures has also helped promote a remix culture both at the margins and the mainstream of the knowledge economy. Manovich and Anne Marie Boisvert (2007) trace the term *remix* to the audio innovations of disco djs and producers in the early 1970s. The creation of electronic multitrack mixers in this period, an analog precursor of digital modularity, allowed for the remixing of 16- or 24-track master tapes. Boisvert emphasizes that the disco culture of remixing began as one expression of the African American urban experience. From Boisvert's view, remixing often becomes a social act: cultures on the margins draw on what they can grab from the mainstream or each other to fashion new expressions and meanings.

Manovich, however, reminds us that "most human cultures developed by borrowing and reworking forms and styles from other cultures [. . .] Ancient Rome remixed Ancient Greece; Renaissance remixed antiquity" (2001). Working from this view, Manovich distinguishes these kinds of traditional cultural acts of remixing from the "vernacular remixing" enabled by digitally based production and distribution of modular samples by various networks and interfaces. At the beginning of the 21st century, we find tensions between the traditional or more authorized forms of recombination, particularly in the realm of commerce, as we address further in the next section, and the rise of the vernacular tradition of remixing, often in the form of parody, satire, or critique. For instance, in response to the U.S. and British decision to invade Iraq, someone (or some group) circulated over the net a music video with the soundtrack of the song "Endless Love" dubbed over digitally remixed stock footage of George W. Bush and prime minister Tony Blair. With the new soundtrack and the choice of footage, Bush and Blair now looked like they were singing of their endless love for each other and their foreign policies.

Remixing Can Make New Culture

As Boisvert points out, all the digital technologies of production, distribution, and Internet communication have become "household tools for selecting, cutting up, editing, and manipulating the tide of images and sounds." These tools foster "reinvention of expressive means," starting out "underground before being co-opted by mass culture [...] only to go on developing, mutating, and giving birth to new forms underground over and over again" (2007). We see this process of remixing as cultural subversion in the film *Eternal Sunshine*. When Joel in his mind resolves to preserve his relationship with Clementine, he subconsciously subverts the procedure of the mind erasure company by remixing his memories. While Stan, the Lacuna technician, is methodically hunting down and deleting all of Joel's memories of Clementine, Joel and Clementine try to hide out in his memories that have nothing to do with their relationship. In one scene from his childhood when he's harassed by bullies, Clementine appears as an 8-year-old girl (with Kate Winslet's adult voice) who befriends the child Joel (who appears as both a boy and Jim Carrey in the boy's clothing). In another memory, 4-year-old Joel hides crying under a kitchen table. In this scene, Clementine becomes a composite of Joel's mother's friend. She retains her own body and personality but also plays the role of this woman dressed in mod 1970s fashion complete with go-go boots. She tries to reassure the crying Joel, who has also become a composite of his present and childhood self,

The Kobal Collection/Focus Features/
David Lee

Activity: Remixing Collage

Working in pairs, try out some remixing of your own. Using images on the web, design a collage of images that remixes any of these elements:

- High art vs. popular culture
- Different time periods
- Different styles of imagery
- Different cultural groups

Once you have chosen what elements you want to remix, be sure to define a purpose and audience for your collage to better help focus your choices of design. As you work on selecting and placing images in your remix collage, consider the message you mean to convey with these choices. In light of Boisvert's and Manovich's discussions, what does your remixing show you? What implications of your initial choices of purpose and audience do you see now in the finished collage?

retaining his adult body within a child's pajamas. Underneath a comically oversized table, Joel cries for his mother (as the 4-year-old child) and for the loss of his sexual relationship with Clementine (as an adult).

Within each of these scenes, the film remixes the modular elements of soundtrack and images to invent new meanings within new contexts, just as many computer users are now doing. In Manovich's words, "remixability becomes practically a built-in feature of the digitally networked media universe" (2001).

Recombining Fragments for Profit

But remixing and recombining elements of digital information isn't only about reinventing cultural meaning. It's also big business in the 21st-century information economy, as this parody from the *Onion* suggests.

Google Announces Plan to Destroy All Information It Can't Index

August 31, 2005 | issue 41•35

MOUNTAIN VIEW, CA—Executives at Google, the rapidly growing on-line-search company that promises to "organize the world's information," announced Monday the latest step in their expansion effort: a far-reaching plan to destroy all the information it is unable to index.

"Our users want the world to be as simple, clean, and accessible as the Google home page itself," said Google CEO Eric Schmidt at a press conference held in their corporate offices. "Soon, it will be."

The new project, dubbed Google Purge, will join such popular services as Google Images, Google News, and Google Maps, which catalogs the entire surface of the Earth using high-resolution satellites.

As a part of Purge's first phase, executives will destroy all copyrighted materials that cannot be searched by Google.

"A year ago, Google offered to scan every book on the planet for its Google Print project. Now, they are promising to burn the rest," John Battelle wrote in his widely read "Searchblog." "Thanks to Google Purge, you'll never have to worry that your search has missed some obscure book, because that book will no longer exist. And the same goes for movies, art, and music."

"Book burning is just the beginning," said Google co-founder Larry Page. "This fall, we'll unveil Google Sound, which will record and index all the noise on Earth. Is your baby sleeping soundly? Does your high-school sweetheart still talk about you? Google will have the answers."

Page added: "And thanks to Google Purge, anything our global microphone network can't pick up will be silenced by noise-cancellation machines in low-Earth orbit."

As a part of Phase One operations, Google executives will permanently erase the hard drive of any computer that is not already indexed by the Google Desktop Search.

"We believe that Google Desktop Search is the best way to unlock the information hidden on your hard drive," Schmidt said. "If you haven't given it a try, now's the time. In one week, the deleting begins."

Although Google executives are keeping many details about Google Purge under wraps, some analysts speculate that the categories of information Google will eventually index or destroy include handwritten correspondence, buried fossils, and private thoughts and feelings.

The company's new directive may explain its recent acquisition of Celera Genomics, the company that mapped the human genome, and its buildup of a vast army of laser-equipped robots.

"Google finally has what it needs to catalog the DNA of every organism on Earth," said analyst Imran Kahn of J.P. Morgan Chase. "Of course, some people might not want their DNA indexed. Hence, the robot army. It's crazy, it's brilliant—typical Google."

Google's robot army is rumored to include some 4 million cybernetic search-and-destroy units, each capable of capturing and scanning up to 100 humans per day. Said co-founder Sergey Brin: "The scanning will be relatively painless. Hey, it's Google. It'll be fun to be scanned by a Googlebot. But in the event people resist, the robots are programmed to liquify the brain."

Markets responded favorably to the announcement of Google Purge, with traders bidding up Google's share price by $1.24, to $285.92, in late trading after the announcement. But some critics of the company have found cause for complaint.

"This announcement is a red flag," said Daniel Brandt, founder of Google-Watch.org. "I certainly don't want to accuse them of having bad intentions. But this campaign of destruction and genocide raises some potential privacy concerns."

Brandt also expressed reservations about the company's new motto. Until yesterday's news conference, the company's unofficial slogan had been "Don't be evil." The slogan has now been expanded to "Don't be evil, unless it's necessary for the greater good."

Co-founders Page and Brin dismiss their critics.

"A lot of companies are so worried about short-term reactions that they ignore the long view," Page said. "Not us. Our team is focused on something more than just making money. At Google, we're using technology to make dreams come true."

Google executives oversee the first stage of Google Purge

"Soon," Brin added, "we'll make dreams clickable, or destroy them forever."

"Google Announces Plan to Destroy All Information It Can't Index," *The Onion*, Volume 41, Issue 35. Copyright © 2008, by ONION, INC. Reprinted with permission of THE ONION, *http://www.theonion.com*

Here, the satiric concept of "Google Purge" expands from the Lacuna memory erasure company in *Eternal Sunshine* to the planned deletion of the (digital) world's collective memory, again aided by the modular structure of computer technologies. We think the *Onion* parody also mocks a real truth of our knowledge economy and the changes in literacy practices in a digital world. "Organizing the world's information" *is* the major cultural and economic power at the beginning of the 21st century. Like Google, many companies now make their living by sorting the world's information. More important, they profit by repeatedly *reorganizing* the world's information into customized databases, search engines, and various kinds of human–computer interfaces.

Writing in 1991, former U.S. labor secretary Robert Reich recognized the coming economic power of reorganizing (or, in the language of digital literacy scholars, remixing) information. Ironically, Reich's perspective sounds very much like the *Onion*'s Google CEO, who believes Google "users want the world to be as simple, clean, and accessible as the Google homepage." Reich writes that "[R]eality must be simplified so that it can be understood and manipulated in new ways" (quoted in Johnson-Eilola (2004), p. 229). Reich's reference to reality, however, refers to "the chaos of data that are already swirling around us" in the information age, rather than the reality of the natural world. Reich and others predicted the rise of a particular kind of worker connected to technological networks: the symbolic analyst. In Reich's words, this kind of worker "wields equations, formulae, analogies, models, [and] constructs categories and metaphors in order to create possibilities for reinterpreting and rearranging" the deluge of possible data.

The Business of Moving Around Data

Johnson-Eilola points out how much the symbolic analyst's work creates a different form of literacy using computer networks and databases. To a large degree, this symbolic-analytic form of digital remixing requires people to "manipulate information, sorting, filtering, synthesizing, and rearranging chunks of data in response to particular assignments or problems" (2004, p. 201). In this view of literacy work, writing within digitally networked environments, such as websites and databases, is more "a process of arrangement and connection rather than simply one of isolated creative utterance." Meaning within a text doesn't come from an individual's mind but from what bits are collected and recombined from other databases and interfaces of text. Different contexts will require different choices of recombination and syntheses of information.

In contrast, then, to the *Onion's* parody of Google's plan for omnipotent power, Johnson-Eilola states that companies in the knowledge economy do not profit from hoarding all fragments of information. Rather, profit in the information economy requires the *continual recirculation* of textual content within various digital networks. To accomplish this recirculation, companies break information into increasingly smaller fragments to be commodified as raw materials. For example, consider the selling of individual tracks of music, the licensing of individual images from television or movies, or the selling of copyright permissions for use of small chunks of text from proprietary databases. To earn profit, these fragments "must be put into motion in the capitalist system, forced to earn [their] keep by moving incessantly [. . .]." Most digital information is becoming "increasingly fragmented and broken apart so that they will fit into the increasingly small micro channels of capitalist circulation" enabled by the modular structures of digital technology (Johnson-Eilola, 2004, p. 203).

But companies must also recombine fragments to offer new products of information databases and transformed content that can now be recirculated as commodities within technological networks. When information of all kinds can be "fragmented into smaller bits," various fragments can be "reassembled and repurposed into new forms over and over again [. . .] each slippage and recombination now generating surplus value to be captured as profit" (Johnson-Eilola, 2004, p. 204).

Intellectual Property vs. Creativity of Literacy in Digital Networks

In regard to these cycles of fragmentation and recombination, the *Onion* portrait of power- and profit-hungry Google execs serves to reveal another truth of the modular information economy. As fragments of information in the form of digital samplings (whether they be text, multimedia, or computer code) have become the major currency of the information age, we are seeing a greater push by corporations to license and control these fragments as *copyrighted intellectual property.* So in the *Onion* parody, the Google execs will maintain rights over the codes for all human DNA, possibly the ultimate example of vital modular fragments in our lives. With these rights, they would police the license to users' remixes of these (thankfully fictional!) digitized DNA samplings.

> **Definition**
>
> *Intellectual Property*
> The protection by U.S. copyright law to prevent the copying of anyone's works or ideas "once they are fixed in a tangible means of expression"
>
> —*Aoki, Boyle, & Jenkins, 2007, p. 31*

When we examine the tension between copyrights and the creativity of multimedia fostered by the accessibility of digital samplings, we lead literacy studies into the murky realm of law and technology.

According to lawyers Keith Aoki, James Boyle, and Jennifer Jenkins (who created the informational comic book essay, *Tales of the Public Domain* from which we have excerpted in the definition

From *Bound By Law * 2006 Keith Aoki, James Boyle, Jennifer Jenkins; available online at http://www.law.duke.edu/cspd/ comics/

box), copyright laws protect creative works within any "tangible medium of expression." Those mediums range from print and film to choreography, audio recording, architecture, and more. Up till 40 years ago, a work was only protected by copyright for a term limit of 14 years, or 28 years if the author still lived. Otherwise the work was legally considered part of the public domain, and was available for copying or sampling in multiple forms.

How Changes in Copyright Laws Affect Creativity in Digital Media

Two major changes in the copyright laws since then have created a serious power imbalance between large corporations and computer users who want to publicly distribute (and possibly support themselves by)

Duke Center for Study of Public Domain.

*From Bound By Law * 2006 Keith Aoki, James Boyle, Jennifer Jenkins; available online at http://www.law.duke.edu/cspd/comics/*

their creations of digital media from samplings and remixes. As for the first change in copyright laws, over the past 40 years as more advanced technologies for sampling and reproducing media and information have flourished, Congress has regularly ruled to extend the term limits for copyright protection. As of 2000, the copyright laws now regulate the use of fragments of any creative work up to 80 years old.

As for the second change in copyright laws, the Digital Millenium Copyright Act ruled that any digital copy of a work, in other words any download no matter how small, also comes under copyright regulations and licensing. Lawrence Lessig, a scholar of copyright law and advocate for free samplings from digital culture, maintains that copyright laws have now shifted from their original purpose of the regulation of publishing to a regulation of copying. And when copying samples or fragments, as opposed to whole works, is legally regulated, Lessig and others contend we lose a greater range of independent creativity, and perhaps social freedoms, that digital technologies can enable.

To better see the implications of these changes in copyright law, lets use Lessig's example of Mickey Mouse in his first Disney animated short "Steamboat Willie," produced in 1928. As Lessig points out, Walt Disney at the beginning of his career "stole" the concept for the short from the silent comedian and film director Buster Keaton's 1928 film, "Steamboat Bill." "It was a parody, a take-off. No waiting 14 years [the original copy right term limit]—just take it, rip it, mix and burn, as he did to produce the Disney empire." Lessig reminds us that Disney's genius was to take the previous works of others, such as the fairy tales of the Brothers Grimm, and remake them in new forms. But today the lawyers and the digital technology of the Disney Corporation keeps a watchful eye on the licensing and profiting from any fragment of Disney's works. Nobody can freely distribute remixes of Mickey as Disney did with Buster Keaton's character. In fact, some refer to the latest copyright term extension law as the Mickey Mouse Act because "every time Mickey is about to pass through the public domain, copyright term [limits] are extended" once more.

This imbalance of copyright and creativity in the digital age isn't just about uses of fragments in digital media. For instance, a documentary filmmaker filmed a scene backstage in an opera house where *The Simpsons* was playing on the TV in the background for 4½ seconds of the film. Fox media corporation demanded ten thousand dollars for the right to include Homer Simpson's image. Pay up or delete the image.

Fair Use vs. the Cost of Legal Suits over Copyright

The authors of *Tales in the Public Domain* point out that in many instances, these uses of fragments are not violating copyright laws but instead come under the provisions of *fair use* of copyrighted materials. Fair use refers to uses of materials for particular purposes: in reporting of news, for use in classes, to make parodies,

> **Key Idea**
> *Fair Use*
> The legal permission to use copyrighted materials for:
> - News reports
> - Use in teaching
> - Research
> - Quoting for scholarship
> - Criticism
> - Parody

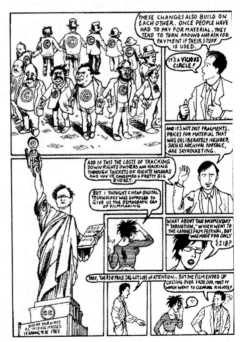

Duke Center for Study of Public Domain.

*From Bound By Law * 2006 Keith Aoki, James Boyle, Jennifer Jenkins; available online at http://www.law.duke.edu/cspd/comics/*

for criticism, to quote for scholarly purposes, and for research. Fair use also refers to using a very small portion of the original work, often less than 5%. But when the copyright owner challenges the user of the fragments, it's the user who must prove fair use in courts of law. Consequently, the threat of costly legal suits when the copyright holders are large corporations often intimidates users. As Aoki and his colleagues (2007) demonstrate, the new laws and digital technology have produced a "permissions culture premised on the belief that copyright gives its owners the right to demand payment on every type of usage no matter its length, or its purpose, or the context in which it is set" (p. 70). In their comic book essay, they depict the permissions culture as a vicious circle. Incidentally, that's Lessig playing the role of the statute of liberty in the lower left panel of the image on page 199.

How Do We Return to a Balance of Creators' Rights and Public Domain?

Up to 40 years ago, Aoki and his colleagues (2007) explain, copyright law served to maintain a balance between the rights of creators to control and get paid for their work on the one hand, and the necessity of maintaining a large public domain of "raw materials" available for creators to use in their works on the other hand.

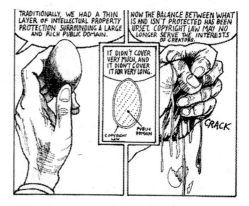

So while digital technologies have opened up new approaches to literacy within new kinds of social networks, the permissions culture that has arisen with the technology tends to prohibit the full potentials of these literacies within these new media. As Aoki, Boyle, and Jenkins (2007) see it:

Duke Center for Study of Public Domain.

From Bound By Law * 2006 Keith Aoki, James Boyle, Jennifer Jenkins; available online at http://www.law.duke.edu/cspd/comics/

Copyright is not an end in itself. It is a tool to promote the creation and distribution of knowledge and culture. What could be a better manifestation of this goal than a world in which there are few barriers to entry, where a blog can break a major political scandal, a $218 digital film can go to the Cannes Film Festival, a podcast can reach tens of thousands of listeners, a mash-up can savagely criticize the government's response to a hurricane, where recording and mixing technology better than anything Phil Spector ever had may come bundled free with your laptop? (p. 70)

In response to the imbalance of the permissions culture and the increasing revisions of copyright laws that support it, scholars of copyright law call for a return to sustainable cultural development. This approach is based on principles of environmental stability. For environmental sustainability, development must be balanced with preservation of nature. For cultural sustainability and more democratic development of ideas in the knowledge economy, Aoki, Boyle, and Jenkins (2007) maintain, "we need to have a similar balance between what is owned and what is free for everyone to use." To these ends, Negativiland, a collective of artists working in digital multimedia, call for two major changes in copyright practices. First, we should change the laws to recognize the unregulated use of fragments for the purposes of transformation, to create something different. The Negativiland collective contends that we can make distinctions between bootlegging and the creative use of fragments. Bootlegging should be recognized as the outright stealing of another's wholle work for the same purposes as the original, in contrast to the transformational use of fragments. And second, that the burden of legal proof that copyright has been violated should fall on the copyright owners, not on the user of the fragments.

The Politics of Writing as Design

Digital multimedia design, such as that created by processes of remixing fragments, has also been labeled *new media*. But could we also see other kinds of material designs,

Pam Geisel, http://
www.forquiltssake.com

Thomas Kjaer

such as quilting and graffiti as new media as well? And to what extent is new media really *new*?

What's at stake in our definitions of these different media of design? In 20 to 40 years from now, will new media be considered no longer new? And what's at stake for people in different social classes and other identity formations when they have to balance accumulating literacies of print culture and emerging literacies of technological design?

How Should We Define New Media?

Media scholars and educators tend to define *new media* by the digital environment in which the media is produced and distributed. In sharp contrast, Anne (Wysocki et al. 2004), a rhetoric scholar, artist, and graphic designer, asserts that we should define new media texts not by the technology with which they are created, but by the composer/designer's choices of media for communication. From Wysocki's view, it's the composer/designer's awareness of his or her chosen medium's "materiality" that matters most (p. 15). Wysocki's use of the word *materiality* refers to the physical production of a text, whether it's drawn with crayon, pen, and ink, or digitally manipulated with software; whether its produced on paper, cardboard, silk, or streamed through the Internet. Her use of the term *materiality* also calls attention to the craft and physical labor involved in composition and design. It may even be the materiality of the speaking human voice as it is recorded contrasted with the labor that goes into the printed page.

> **Definition**
>
> **Defining New Media**
> Common Understanding: media created with digital technologies
> Wysocki's Definition: Texts created by composers/designers who have consciously considered the materiality of the text's medium and the medium's possible effects on the interaction between composer/designer and audience.

Each instance of these choices of medium will embody different values that will be conveyed to the audience, whether the audience consciously recognizes those values or not. Just consider the difference between handing in a business report written with multicolored crayons in a hand-sewn book of parchment compared to digitally processed and printed pages of block-formatted text. Clearly, this example also shows how a composer/designer's choice of medium also relates to social context and audience expectations. Wysocki wants to highlight the importance of making the medium of communication visible. Her definition alerts us to the values and social contexts embodied in the composer/designer's choices of materials to create a particular set of interactions with readers/viewers.

From this perspective, Wysocki might claim the cultural practices of quilting and subway graffiti as new media, even though these practices and material forms date back before digital technologies. In the folk traditions of quilting, quilters often chose very carefully their scraps of cloth material for their designs. They selected scraps from a family's, or community's, old clothing, bedspreads, curtains, and so on that then stand as collective memories for the family and community—in a sense, a fabric time capsule. Moreover, the materiality of the scraps themselves carries social significance as well in conveying rural values of thrift and making do with what's available.

Similarly, the subway graffiti writers' choice of aerosol spray cans as the medium and the subway cars as their canvas conveys much about their social context and situation. For better and worse, the choice of subway cars as a social canvas suggests the graffiti artists' desire to express a public statement of outsider identity and marginal status within the dominant culture. People from all parts of the city will see their work; it is not meant as private expression. Possibly graffiti writers first chose spray cans as the medium because it allowed them to create designs more quickly in sometimes dangerous situations, and later they developed styles of design they discovered in the effects of that medium. But the medium of the spray paint also came to symbolize the socioeconomic situation of the graffiti writers and artists, as well as their values of resistance to corporate-owned mainstream forms of expression.

In contrast to these examples, Wysocki would not automatically categorize digital text that includes images or websites that incorporate sound as "new media." To count as new media, Wysocki would insist that the composer/designers have made conscious, deliberate choices about how they want to communicate with their particular audiences through their medium, modes, and design.

The Social Significance of Literacy as Design and Medium

So why should this approach to designing and teaching new media matter to us, and to the future of literacy? First, Wysocki's insistence on this definition of new media highlights issues of control and choice involved

Artifact Analysis Activity: When Might New Media Not Be so New?
In a small group, choose a digital object, composition, or design. In choosing this digitally created artifact, make sure it meets Manovich's criteria for digital media discussed earlier in the chapter.

Once you have chosen your digital artifact, explore its properties, its materiality (as Wysocki identifies the term), and discuss these questions to report back to the class:

- What aspects of the artifact does the digital technology make uniquely possible?

- How would you relate this artifact to Wysocki's claims about the composer/designer's choices of materiality in new media?

- What is not new about it? Are they any ways that versions of this artifact have been done before (as with our discussion of quilting and grafitti)?

- If you could imagine an earlier artifact that influenced this digitally created one, where did that earlier artifact come from? What did people try to do with it?

- What communities and cultures does it have social meanings for now, in the information economy and digital age?

in different modes of communication. Which modes for producing meaning do different parts of society privilege for their communications within different social contexts? Here we see the power dynamics underlying choices of visual versus verbal forms, oral/aural versus print texts, to mention a few tensions of media choices we can trace through the historic and current practices of literacies. Second, as the changes in digital technologies foster more attention on communication through design and multimedia, Wysocki believes these concerns of choice and control should play a role in the teaching of design and composition as an ethical cultural practice.

In terms of the cultural and political aspects of literacy, the emergence of digital technologies makes much more visible a wider range of choices in design and medium. This range of choice makes us more conscious of the limitations of choice and control with the printed page (such as this one). Indeed, the focus on medium and design makes us recognize again that writing is also a visual communication. The meaning in our writing of alphabetic text will be affected by how readers/viewers perceive our choice of font, where we place text on the page, or if we use some other medium, such as paint, digital screens, or embossed stone. Wysocki contends that if we think the medium of the conventional printed 8½-by-11 page contributes no meaning to the content of a text, that is because the choice of this medium has been for us—we can no longer see the medium as a choice.

This view of choice and control in media asks us to consider the larger consequences of these less visible choices of design that have been made for us by institutions:

> How might the straight lines of type we have inherited on page after page of books articulate to other kinds of lines, assembly lines and lines of canned products in supermarkets and lines of desks in classrooms? How might these various lines work together to accustom us to standardization, repetition, and other processes that support industrial forms of production? (Wysocki, 2004, p. 14)

Lines of design show who or what is valued and can implicitly serve to persuade people how they should value themselves. Cultural geographers, and some of our working-class students for that matter, have pointed out how cities and working-class neighborhoods are often designed as uniform grids. In contrast, the roads and sidewalks of suburban and upper-class neighborhoods wind and curve. When housing developers build these curves, their design suggests a class distinction, in ways that we discussed in Chapter Four, meant to contrast with the uniformity that urban planners' designs often implicitly impose on the lower class. In the opening credits of *The Sopranos*, we witness this exact journey of design and social class. Tony Soprano drives from the grids of row houses and urban blocks of his working-class Jersey childhood and current location of his shady business to finally arrive on the winding streets of his wealthy McMansion, the architectural design of which suggests another kind of upper-class conformity.

Social Power and Choice of Design in Literacy Contexts

Yet these distinctions of social class and design also depend on contexts; curved lines don't always convey social or economic power. The necessity to achieve a balance between uniformity and creative choice in print texts can also be about distinction. For instance, consider the delicate balance one must maintain in designing résumés. One must have the social background to know to do something different in terms of page layout and font design that will stand out from the pack but will not be so bold as to advertise a lack of social refinement. As is often the case with men's expensive suits, the greater the position of power, the more subtle will be the choices of design and medium in business communications to convey social distinction. And as people's use of digital technologies makes design a larger part of their literacy practices, mistakes in unwritten rules and expectations of design in digital media will play as much a role in judging people and their social class as penmanship and writing style have in the past.

In these instances of design and text, one can show distinction by striking the right balance between design and text for a given social context. In contrast, Scott McCloud (1994) illustrates how the traditions of high art in both literature and pictorial media demand a total separation of words and images.

The panels on page 207 come from *Understanding Comics: The Invisible Art*, McCloud's historical and theoretical exploration of comics as an art form. The book in itself presents a perfect example of Wysocki's definition of new media, since McCloud clearly chose his medium of comics as the form to address the issues of control and power in the social devaluing of comics as an art form. As a medium that most often incorporates images with words, comics, regardless of their content, have historically been lumped with the other "crass and commercial" culture McCloud depicts here. Yet it is his artistic selection and integration of words and images, along with comics' depiction of time through sequential images (as with the panels of the boy aging as he reads), that makes his argument more emotionally and logically persuasive than just printed words.

McCloud's point about the separation of words and images to historically distinguish high from low art can also be applied to the creation of cultural capital in academia as well. Your textbooks may integrate images with words, but most academic books, particularly in the liberal arts, meant for graduate students and other college teachers rarely contain pictures. Wysocki asks how the "visual appearance of most academic texts of the previous century [. . .] have encouraged us to value (or devalue or repress) the visual in the circulation of academic and other 'serious' writing?" (2004, p. 14).

Understanding Comics by Scott McCloud © 1993, 1994 Scott McCloud. Reprinted by Permission of HarperCollins Publishers

In the Digital Mainstream and on the Margins of Print Culture

Wysocki draws our attention to the social consequences of these tensions between new media and more established forms of literacy. Cindy Selfe's portrait of David Damon, an African American web designer and college student, shows up close the effects of these tensions on an individual. As we discussed in Chapter Five, Deborah Brandt interviewed Americans about their literacy histories in order to examine the social consequences of literacy in 20th-century America. Cindy Selfe and Gail Hawisher (2004) employed a similar method, interviewing Americans from various ages and backgrounds about their digital literacies ranging from 1978 to 2003. David Damon, who came from a poor family, got into a prominent technical university through an athletic scholarship. He only had marginal experiences with computers before his last year of high school when he took a computer literacy course. This experience inspired him to major in computer programming, but he soon switched to scientific and technical communication, which better suited his love of language and general communication skills.

Within this digitally rich environment of the university, David quickly began learning skills in web design. Like most technology-focused students of the early to mid-1990s, David did not learn web design in his classes. Rather, he learned from copying other people's web pages to examine and alter their source codes for his web pages' design. In this respect, David was participating in another aspect of the remix culture, at the level of software code, which digital technologies have encouraged. Soon David began designing and maintaining pages for some of the campus's Black fraternities and later for Black fraternities at other colleges.

The Politics of Identity Formation and Digital Design

David's use of digital literacy technologies for particular social purposes fosters his and the web sites' users' sense of identity within these often marginalized groups. Selfe analyzes David's means of identity formation in the context of globalization and the creation of online communities. Drawing on the work of Manuel Castells, a scholar of global issues of power in the information age, Selfe points out that technologies of the Internet have largely benefited multinational interests in the service of globalization, as we also suggested in Chapter Five. When these interests harness digital technologies to the ends of globalization, the technologies can break down the borders of "conventional central authorities" such as nation-states and political alliances. Power becomes more diffused within "global network's . . . of information and images." (Selfe, 2004 p. 53). Castells contends that the digital information age's diffusion of traditional authority and power can leave people alienated. But it also provides technological possibilities for other forms of identity formation within online communications. It is this new form of identity formation aided by digital design that Selfe sees in David's use of web design to build social and economic networks within the African American fraternities.

Yet while David prospered financially and psychologically from his web design work using the campus resources, he struggled with the university's expectations for more conventional writing in his college major, particularly when it came to papers and essay tests. Selfe points out that the university acted as a literacy sponsor, investing in the hardware and software that enable digitally based new media. But print literacy still holds greater authority within academic settings, especially when it comes to assessment of students' knowledge. In Chapter Three, we considered the cultural power of what Marcia Farr calls essayist literacy, the conventional style of writing in school. Now in the context of emerging new media, the social status and meanings that Farr associated with essayist literacy have passed on to print literacy in general. Selfe characterizes print literacy by its linear propositional logic, use of argumentation, and standard forms of English in contrast to multimedia texts in the popular and commercial realms of everyday life.

"During such periods of rapid change," Selfe writes, individuals are often expected to learn, value, and practice both past and present forms of literacy simultaneously and in different spheres of their lives" (Selfe, 2004, p. 50). From different contexts, the universities are participating in two different kinds of literacy sponsorship. They are increasingly funding and providing the digital tools for the emerging work in new media called for in the world of commerce, yet still enforcing the legitimacy and cultural power of print literacy as the means for mainstream achievement. Selfe suggests that since David's teachers had been "raised and educated in a print culture," they were "unsure of how to value and address new media literacies" and so failed to "link their instruction goals to his developing strengths" with multimedia. Despite David's facility with digital literacies, his story does not offer an easy ending. In the end, David could not successfully negotiate these tensions; he left school and continued his online work.

Reading the Design of Electronic Gaming Literacies

Stan's Dad: Stan, you've been on your computer all weekend, shouldn't you go out and socialize with your friends?

Stan: I am socializing, r-tard! I am logged onto an MMORPG with people from all over the world and getting xp with my party using team-speak.

[pause]

Stan's Dad: (under his breath, with lack of conviction) I'm not an r-tard.

(South Park, *"Make Love, Not Warcraft,"* 2006)

Cindy Selfe's analysis of David Damon's situation suggests another, larger cultural group focused on literacies of design in digital spaces that has mostly been ignored by the worlds of education, business, and those who live solely by the assumptions of print culture. According to the research conducted by John Beck and Mitchell Wade, the authors of *Got Game: How the Gamer Generation Is Reshaping Business Forever* (2004), 92% of Americans from ages 2 to 17 regularly play video games.

The common criticisms of videogames point to many of the games' violent images and aggressive narratives. Yet if we were to total the sales of video games made for both console systems and computers, for all the sales of bloody bad-boy games like *Grand Theft Auto* and *Mortal Kombat,* companies sell just as much *Super Mario Brothers, Sims,* and various strategy games like *Civilization* and *Age of Empires.* Still, we cannot deny that the images and interactive narratives in the majority of the bestselling games do communicate a persuasive message of stark competition and domination. Moreover, we agree with critics who see connections between the designs of many violent games and the ways the U.S. military has visually represented our last wars in the Middle East. Critics have also emphasized the similarity of design between these games and the military's computer simulations for warfare training. These simulations are persuasive experiences of literacy in the information age. However, even though the dangers of video games are a deep commonplace, it might be worth thinking about what other experiences of literacy they afford, since that is *not* so much part of the popular conversation. As James Gee has demonstrated in his theories of learning through video games, which we will soon discuss, much of that time spent playing electronic games builds a keen sense of spatial design tied to problem solving over long-term goals. The best games, Gee asserts, are well designed spaces for learning that offer multiple solutions to problems and challenge players to learn, to adapt, to use metacognitive thinking. They must think in complex ways about the design of the game's world if they are to win. For these kinds of games, Gee claims:

> They situate meaning in a multimodal space through embodied experiences to solve problems and reflect on the intricacies of the design of imagined worlds and the design of both real and imagined social relationships and identities in the modern world (2003, p. 48)

Despite the depth of Gee's thinking here, we don't have to look far in the realm of popular culture to see how the larger assumptions of print culture in education and the business world have mostly dismissed these emerging literacy patterns. In a 2006 episode of *South Park*, "Make Love, Not Warcraft," the boys obsessively play the online multiplayer role-playing game *World of Warcraft*. As a show that parodies popular culture, the episode plays up several criticisms made against electronic gaming within the popular media. The boys ignore their families and their schoolwork. They forsake the wonders of nature in the outside world for the digitally designed forests of the online game. And in the style of a good *South Park* gross-out, as the scope of their lives narrows down to just the necessary key strokes to defeat their virtual enemy, a stereotypical adult geek of a player who "has no life," the boys' physical bodies deteriorate into portly pimply blobs of flesh that do nothing but mash buttons and excrete bodily fluids.

How Does Gaming Literacy Differ from Print Literacy?

Seen from Gee's perspective, however, the writers of the *South Park* episode also capture Gee's main claims for digital games as designs to learn new literacy forms. To better perceive how the *South Park* gaming experience might embody these higher ends of learning that Gee addresses, let's begin with a "thought experiment" from Steven Johnson who also argues for the cognitive value of video games. Johnson asks his readers to flip the historical positions of books and video games—books have only come into existence after centuries of electronic gaming. In this alternate world he imagines, public critics might attack books in this way:

> *Reading books chronically understimulates the senses.* Unlike the long tradition of gameplaying—which engages the child in a vivid, three-dimensional world filled with moving images and musical soundscapes, navigated and controlled with complex muscular movements—books are simply a barren of words on the page. Only a small portion of the brain devoted to processing written language is activated during reading, while games engage the full range of the sensory and motor cortices.
>
> *Books are tragically isolating.* While games have for many years engaged the young in complex social relationships with their peers, building and exploring worlds together, books force the child to sequester him or himself in a quiet space, shut off from interaction with other children. These new "libraries" that have arisen in recent years to facilitate reading activities are a frightening sight: dozens of young children, normally so vivacious and socially interactive, sitting along in cubicles, reading silently, oblivious to their peers [...]
>
> But perhaps the most dangerous property of these books is the fact that they follow a fixed linear path. You can't control their narratives in any fashion—you simply sit back and have the story dictated to you. For those of us raised on interactive narratives, this property may seem astonishing. Why would anyone want to embark on an adventure utterly choreographed by another person? But today's generation embarks on such adventures millions of times a day. This risks instilling a general passivity in our children, making them feel as though they are powerless to change their circumstances. Reading is not an active,

Key Idea
*Video games compared to Books
(an admittedly game-centric perspective)*

- Electronic games engage multiple senses compared to solely vision in reading.

- The act of playing encourages social relationships compared to the act of reading, which may not lead to social engagement.

- Playing requires making choices of design compared to reading, where the narrative is fixed and the reader can only change the design outside the text.

Activity: Interface Analysis of a Video Game

Individually or in small groups, choose a video game, whether for computers or consoles depending on your access, to explore (in other words, play, mess with) its interface presented to the gamer. Take notes on:

- What do you see on various screens when you begin to play within the world of the game?

- What design of a game narrative can you find? And what do you need to do to begin to understand the details of that narrative?

- How are the spaces of the game designed, and how do you navigate them?

- What interactive features contribute to the experience of playing the game?

- What kinds of knowledge and ways of accessing knowledge does the game tend to require?

Report back to the class about your experiences with the game's interface and discuss how they relate to the concepts of learning and literacy addressed in this section of the chapter.

participatory process; it's a submissive one. The book readers of the younger generation are learning to "follow the plot" instead of learning to lead. (Johnson, 2005, pp. 19–20)

Of course, Johnson doesn't devalue books, but he uses this flipped script to show how we shouldn't assume a direct comparison between electronic gaming and books of fiction. This alternative view also shows what can be the strengths of gaming literacy despite some people's concerns over many games' simplistic plots and violent action. Video games can exercise other parts of our cognitive capacities, promoting social problem solving and pushing players to continually adapt and reconsider options of spatial designs.

How Players Can Learn from Well-Designed Video Games

James Gee argues that these features, and more, of the best-designed electronic games suggest why we should look to them for models of motivated learning of complex ideas. He writes, "wouldn't it be great if kids were willing to put this much time on task on such challenging material in school and enjoy it so much?" (2003, p. 5). In this respect, Gee sees analogies of strong video game learning to the best of science learning in schools. Gee proposes that educators draw upon these principles for other domains of learning off the video screen. If Gee's research and suggestions for education look toward the future, the authors of *Got Game* claim with their survey and interview research that the future is already here—that a generation of gamers is already changing the literacy behaviors in the business world. Their research asserts that electronic games help train future corporate workers for the structured social problem solving necessary for the high competition of business in the knowledge economy.

In the *South Park* episode, a silent ultra-powerful rogue player is killing off all the other players' virtual characters in the *World of Warcraft*, despite the game's social code that "players cannot kill other players unless they agree to a duel." Nobody can stop him in the game, including the "admins," the administrators at the Blizzard Company headquarters who police the *Warcraft* game as online characters, because this player has grown so powerful by doing nothing but playing online virtually 24 hours a day. The executives at Blizzard worry in the style of old horror flicks, "How can you kill that which has no life?" Indeed, they fear that "this could very well lead to the end of the world . . . of *Warcraft*." Whenever we see the actual out-of-shape rogue player, carpal tunnel bandage on wrist, crumbs falling on his ratty t-shirt and exposed belly, he is silent, but for the clicking of the keys, staring mesmerized into the screen. After being killed by this player 14 times, Cartman, Stan, Kyle, and Kenny resolve to destroy this enemy that keeps them from pursing their quest for Stone Haven in the *Warcraft* world.

Probing and Hypothesizing Gee and other scholars of electronic games have shown how video games tend to reward nonlinear movement that can lead to multiple solutions, unlike the linear structure of print culture in schools. He offers the example of when a player is learning how to play the role of Lara Croft in the *Tomb Raider* games. Players

> **Key Idea**
> *Four Major Strengths of Socio-Cognitive Learning Through Well-Designed Electronic Games*
>
> - probing and hypothesizing
> - internal and external designs
> - innovation and redesigning
> - identity and learning

must pay attention to Lara's professor when he explains to her how to move through the world of the game, but they must also willfully disobey her professor if they want to find treasures and clues hidden in the design of the game. Gee describes this kind of nonlinear experimentation as a continual recursive process of probing and hypothesizing within the design of each game. To be successful, players need to discern patterns in the design of the virtual world and develop strategies. With each level of a well-designed game, players need to build off these strategies but also figure out how to adapt them to each level's new design spaces. The research of the *Got Game* authors showed that gamers used these behaviors of probing and hypothesizing as their key strategy for problem solving in business situations. For better and worse, gamers working in business tend to see trial-and-error experimenting as the best approach to a problem. In the game, if you die, you just try again.

At the level of satire, we see the *South Park* boys follow through on this process. When the boys cannot defeat the rogue enemy on their own, they convene a meeting of the neighborhood kids at which Cartman argues for a new strategy of collective action.

Cartman: We've learned that the four of us can't fight him alone, but if we all log in TOGETHER, we might have a chance.

Clyde: I'm just going to stop playing.

Cartman: When Hitler rose to power, there were a lot of people who just stopped playing. You know who those people were? The French. Are you French, Clyde?

Clyde: No.

Cartman: Voulez vouz couchez avec moi, Clyde?

Clyde: [goaded into agreement] Alright, Alright, I'll do it.

When one kid remarks that he only plays the *Hello Kitty* game, Cartman patiently advises him with derision to "go buy *World of Warcraft* and join the online sensation before we all murder you."

Internal and External Designs   Gee theorizes two realms of design involved in electronic gaming. First, there is the internal design of the game's content and space, and second, there is the external design created by the social practices of the players as they form affinity groups. As groups form online and elsewhere to further probe and consider other designs for particular games, they develop distributed knowledge across social networks of people, texts, and technology. *The Got Game* authors found that gamers in business thrived on structured social events, problem solving that required team cooperation, as opposed to unstructured social activities where goals and teams were not specified. In several scenes of the *South Park* episode, various maps of the worlds within *World of Warcraft* hang in the background, suggesting the kinds of design sense the boys must develop as an affinity group to hypothesize other solutions to their problem.

Gee also points out that sometimes the alternative designs for particular games created by affinity groups of players can influence the game company's designers to change the internal design or offer other possible designs within the game. In these situations, if players can take on the identities of co-designers, they can gain greater power as learners. In the *South Park* episode, the Blizzard executives need the boys' rethinking of the possibilities of the game, however ludicrous that solution is, to save the world . . . of *Warcraft*. Gee sees this role of gamers as co-designers as the best model for learning. But we must also recognize that the gaming companies' motivation for sharing this role is primarily economic since it involves the gamer even more in their products. In this regard, how much affinity groups are likely to have control of internal design, whether it is a video game or a classroom lesson plan, will likely depend on the relative social power of the group compared to that of the original designers, be they gaming designers or educators.

Innovation and Redesigning   When the entire neighborhood of South Park kids cannot defeat the rogue, everyone gives up until Cartman comes up with a new plan for the boys.

> **Cartman:** Guys! When things look bad, you can't just give up on the world . . . of Warcraft. [. . .] That's why we just need to log in and stay in the forest, killing boars.
>
> **Stan:** Boars?
>
> **Cartman:** There's lots of computer-generated boars in *Warcraft* that die with just one blow.
>
> **Stan:** Dude, boars are only worth 2 experience points apiece. You know how many we would have to kill to get up 30 levels?
>
> **Cartman:** Yes, 65 million, 340 thousand, 285, which should take us 7 weeks, 5 days, 13 hours and 20 minutes, giving ourselves 3 hours a night to sleep. What do you say, guys? You could just hang outside in the sun all day bouncing a ball around or (with hushed tone) you can sit at your computers doing something that matters.

Here in the realm of satire, we see Gee's view of the metacognitive power of electronic gaming. At their best, video games can push gamers to "innovate in the domain and produce novel or unpredictable meanings" (2003, p. 40). From Gee's perspective, when Cartman and the boys develop this solution based on unexpected aspects of the design of the *Warcraft* world, they go beyond reading the domain to participating fully in it to produce ("write") new meanings in it. Gee frames these actions of gamers as active learning where learners become, in a sense, designers—something that rarely occurs in formal schooling. Similarly, the *Got Game* authors stress that gamers as businesspeople often excel at analyzing computer models of economic and business scenarios, navigating and reinventing the spaces of their design.

Identity and Learning   Although not all genres of electronic games call for players to take on virtual identities, as in *World of Warcraft* for instance, Gee argues how this aspect of games with virtual worlds offers a more embodied experience of learning. In some instances, this embodied learning can sometimes transcend the limitations of the individual learner. Gee identifies three identities in virtual world gaming and learning:

1. real-world identity (the player and his or her multiple identity positions)

2. virtual identity (the character in game)

3. projective identity (how the real-world identity and virtual identity interact)

The *South Park* episode parodies this relationship of real and virtual identity when Randy, Stan's dad, also joins the "online sensation" and begins playing *Warcraft* while at work. When a co-worker asks how somebody wins the game, Randy replies that it's more than a game: "In the outside world, I'm a simple geologist, but in here, I'm Falcorn, defender of the alliance. . . ." Gee contends that virtual identities within the games can create a more embodied learning. Players must learn through the experiences of the character they helped to design at the beginning of the game when they selected from options of various traits and attributes for their character. In the virtual world of the game, each new piece of information invites players' "embodied action (action actually carried out or simulated in the mind). And the nature of that invitation changes as you experience new situations and engage in new actions" (Gee, 2003, p. 85). Gee asserts that players learn most from the nexus of projective identity where they build bridges between their real-world identities and the virtual identity of their online characters. Strangely enough, the narrative of the *South Park* episode also plays on this building of bridges between real-world and virtual identities. The Blizzard company designers realize that the boys will require help to finish off the rogue enemy, so they draw out the long-buried "sword of 1,000 truths," in the form of a 1-gig flash drive stored in a desk drawer. When they cannot find one of the boys, "a great knight by the name of 'Loves to Smooch,'" they reluctantly have to entrust the sword to Stan's dad to give to Stan through his online character.

> **Warcraft designer:** We can't trust the sword of 1,000 truths to a Newb!
>
> **Randy:** [with a warrior's conviction] Sounds to me to like you have no choice! [As he heroically raises the flash drive over his head, we hear a chorus of monks in the background.]

Just after Randy's virtual character manages to give the sword to Stan's character, the rogue deals Randy a death blow. In a mythic revenge parody, Stan stabs the rogue, and then cradles his father as he dies.

> **Stan:** You killed my father!
>
> **Randy:** [as his virtual character dies in the arms of Stan's character] I've never been able to say this before, but I love you, Son.
>
> **Stan:** I know you do, Dad.
>
> **Randy:** [as he virtually dies a hero's death, he moans his death rattle into his headset] Rarrrhhhh!

Although the *South Park* writers clearly intend these maudlin lines as humor, they also show Randy and Stan transcending through their projective identities what they couldn't do in their real-world identities. Randy gets his moment of valor in front of his son (virtually anyway), and the heightened, yet fake, moment of death and revenge allows Stan and his dad to finally connect.

Learning by Trying on Virtual Identities

So how does this view of projective identity promoted by virtual-world games relate to learning and literacy? Gee offers an extended example of children learning science through experimentation and playing the role of various kinds of scientists. As they are not actually scientists, they are taking on the virtual identity of a scientist—practicing the language, habits of thinking, and perspectives of actual scientists. Gee also contends that children, or learners of any age, will not engage in deep learning if they cannot find ways to integrate their real-world identities with the virtual ones expected in the classroom. So if a child does not associate his identity with technical thinking, he will have a harder time embodying this virtual identity of scientist.

Because of these differences between real-world identities and the trying-on of virtual identities, Gee advocates for learners' choices about the design of the virtual identities teachers want them to temporarily embody. Whereas video games can allow players choices for character traits, abilities, and so on, teachers should provide learners with options about the kinds of scientists' roles they will take on. Gee tells of one fourth-grade classroom where children decided what kinds of roles in science they wanted to try out. In the context of a unit on fast-growing plants, learners made choices such as whether to create new experiments or to reconsider older ones, to study texts more before experimenting or afterward.

When learners learn through the interface of their projective identities, they will "learn new values and new ways of being in the world based on the powerful juxtaposition of their real-world identities and the virtual identity at stake in the learning" (Gee, 2003, p. 66). They will realize new capacities to take on aspects of the virtual identity. Gee's theories about virtual identity and learning that emerge from digital technology can help us better understand learning of multiple kinds of literacies, whether or not they are digitally based.

One Final Scenario and Activity

In Chapter One, we asserted that researchers of literacy can find all five sites of literacy—mind, culture, class, work, and technology—within any acts of literacy, such as the enforcement of standardized testing. If we look closely at the issue of how public school districts choose to fund new technologies of literacy, we can see the assumptions connected to all five sites of literacy again resurface in various group's motives for or against funding digital literacies. Consider the situation of a poor school district that has just received a major government- and business-funded grant for promoting the literacies of middle school children destined for the 21st-century knowledge economy.

You might immediately assume that the teachers would want to put the funding toward buying digital technology. But often teachers in underfunded schools have different literacy priorities than computers and software, particularly when the computers do not come with the necessary infrastructure of technical support and ongoing training necessary to make them a sustainable part of students' learning. It's likely that the school district's administrators and the legislators who negotiated the funding would have different assumptions about literacy and technology than the teachers. And what about the interests of different cultural groups of parents and children in the district? Would it make a difference if they are mostly new immigrants of various races, ethnicity, and class status that are not part of the dominant mainstream culture?

Activity: Debating Literacy Needs and Funding

As a class, split into five groups, each one representing one of the five sites of literacy. In your groups:

1. List what assumptions about literacy and education your site would emphasize.

2. Based on these assumptions, what group involved in these budgetary decisions do you imagine you would be most likely to represent? You might consider teachers, administrators, legislators, parents (of what cultural and class backgrounds?), children (of what cultural or class backgrounds?), local businesses, workplace educators, or literacy scholars in education, to name a few possible groups who could be involved in these decisions.

3. Imagine these five chosen groups would take part in a public meeting to hear each group's views on how to best spend the money to meet the grant's goals of literacy.

4. Once you have chosen which of these groups (or another of your choosing) would most likely represent the assumptions of your site of literacy, discuss and list:
   - the factors this group might consider addressing in the meeting.
   - the stories about literacy, or the lack of it, they would tell to make a more persuasive case for how to spend the grant.
   - the other groups that might oppose their recommendations. How might they answer those opposing groups?

5. Finally, discuss the different groups' positions as a class.
   - How do they differ? Where do they hold some common ground?
   - When you look at all of them at the same time, what does that analysis suggest about the stakes involved in our assumptions about literacy education for the future?

ACTIVITIES AND PROJECTS

1. **Web Analysis and Historical Comparison: Reading Stages of Literacy Technology.**

   1. Choose an educational or commercial website that focuses on some aspect of technology and literacy, such as sites focused on media literacy or computer literacies. Analyze the language and claims for these questions:
      - What representations of technology and literacy do they foster?
      - What elements of the stages of literacy technology can you see in the design, emphasis, and claims of the site?
      - What definitions for the future of literacy are being promoted?
   2. Now, compare your analysis to a textbook focused on some aspect of literacy from at least 20 years ago, and consider:
      - What different ideas of literacy become evident in the comparison?
   3. Finally, as you develop your paper about this analysis and comparison, consider how you might also include some discussion of the *visual representations* of literacy that you found in the website and earlier textbook.
      - How can you also include visual examples in your paper (saved images from the website and scanned images from the book) and represent the differences between them with your *own visuals* within the paper?

2. **Blog Project: Tracing the Geneology of Blogging.**

   1. Choose and join a group blog that you can then examine in some detail. In making your choice, look for a group blog where you would like to enter into some of the conversation or arguments (depending on the nature of the blog site). In other words, it should relate to a topic for which you have interest. While you don't have to choose a blog used by academics, this choice might assure that the conversations and links in people's postings might be more substantial. Still, the choice of blog is yours.
   2. Once you have spent some time reading around the site, begin to systematically trace the links you find in people's postings. Be sure to keep notes of these links and where they take you. As much as possible, you want to search out the social networks that

the group blog holds together. These networks might be tied to other blogs or to other websites related to themes and concerns of the group bloggers.

Look for patterns of linking: What kinds of links are most often made? Any thoughts on why?

3. As you work on tracing these links and examining people's postings, you also want to start posting and responding to the bloggers as well.

Take notes on what happens to your contributions to the blog. If others interact with your contributions, what do those interactions suggest about where you might fit into the social networks that you have traced?

4. As you begin to develop your written analysis of these social networks, consider how you can design a web version of this project that imitates the style of the group blog that you have traced. (This could simply be a Word document for the web that provides the links of key social networks within the text of your analysis or it could more elaborately imitate web design of blogs.)

5. Finally, in your project, include some reflection on your design for the links of social networks in your analysis. In what ways was this focus different from traditional print papers? Did it give you a different understanding of your project?

(Note: you might also consider posting your blog analysis to the group blog afterward and see what happens then)

3. **Design Project: Designing a Visual Argument.** Anne Wysocki and Cynthia Selfe (2004) have developed several activities to explore the theories of design we have discussed in this chapter. We present here a version of these activities. This project can be done individually or in pairs.

Choosing Your Argument and Generating Appropriate Images

1. Choose one of the main arguments researchers and scholars make in this chapter about literacy and technologies today. Consider how you would represent the claims in this argument visually:

   a. List any visual images that come to mind when you think about these claims.

b. After you have listed as many images as you can decide which ones seem most compelling to you. Write briefly about why.

c. What colors do you associate with these images? Write about why.

d. What associations do you think others would have with the images and colors you chose?

e. What might you do with the images you listed in activity #2 to help other people make similar associations as you do? And who could you imagine would be the audience for this composition of imagery?

2. Now consider what claims about literacy from any of the other chapters—be it mind, culture, class, or work—would complicate or compliment this argument about literacy and technology you are redesigning into a visual mode.

3. Choose one of these claims and generate a list of visual associations (steps a though e) for this claim as well.

4. Once you have chosen your images, search the web to capture copies of these images to use in your design, which can be on paper or on the computer screen.

Designing and Arranging the Visual Argument

5. Now consider how can you arrange these images visually to help this chosen audience see the relationship between this claim about literacy (and either mind, culture, class, or work) and the argument about literacy and technology.

Consider:

- *visual coherence:* how the visual elements are tied together using patterns possibly relating to color or shape, where images are placed in frame, and themes the images suggest.

- *visual emphasis:* how particular visual elements are emphasized (by for instance, size, placement in frame, style of line and angles) and why.

- *visual organization:* pattern of arrangement of visual elements to help show their relationship and associations to better convey to readers/viewers the intended viewpoint of the composer/designer.

6. Once you have finished your draft of the visual argument, reflect in writing about the process and the product so far:
   - What did using visual elements enable you to do differently from when working with solely print text?
   - How would you account for your greater or lesser sense of comfort working in a nonverbal mode?
   - How can you relate that sense of comfort or ease to ideas discussed in this chapter or previous ones?
7. In class, set up an exhibition of all the drafts of visual argument designs. Next to each argument design, set up space for readers/viewers to write down their interpretation of the composition.
8. Discuss in small groups how your readers/viewers interpreted your visual argument. Now reflect in writing again: How do you want to revise your design to better persuade your audience? Other images? Different arrangement(s) in the composition? Changing size or styles within the design?
9. If time allows, revise your design, and then hold another class exhibition.

   Reflect in writing: Discussing specific examples from your design, how was the process of revision different when in a visual medium compared to revising print text?

4. **Free-Culture Manifesto.** Legal scholars Lawrence Lessig and the lawyers of the Duke Center for the Public Domain contend that the permissions culture of excessive intellectual property rights leads to less freedom to circulate and build on others' cultural ideas.

   Much of Lessig's language in public speeches and the writings of artists' collectives like the Negativiland website read like manifestos pressing for political action. For this project, you will research more of these writers' claims and design your own manifesto to address intellectual property issues.

   1. First use a search engine to find these websites:
      1. Lawrence Lessig's speeches and writings
      2. Duke Center for the Public Domain (where you can read the entirety of *Tales of the Public Domain* and possibly other scholarly comic books)
      3. Cultural Commons
      4. Other links you find related to these sites

2. As you read their materials, look for common themes and concerns you would want to include in your manifesto.
3. Look to the Project Appendix for guidelines on writing a manifesto. You might also do a web search on manifestos and read past historical examples to help imitate the style and phrasings that often go with this genre.
4. Once you know what points you want to emphasize in your manifesto, begin searching the web for images to integrate into your writing that can further persuade your readers to take up your perspective toward the issues of intellectual property and the permissions culture.
5. Be sure to also consider the design of your text and images. What kind of fonts, margins, headings, and ways of incorporating your chosen images will most communicate your points to readers?

5. **Interview and Social Analysis: Navigating the Deep Structure of a Video Game and Its Affinity Group.** Recall the video game interface activity earlier in the chapter. Your observations and discussions may have helped you see some differences between learning in video games compared to print culture. Nevertheless, all scholarly research into video game learning and culture suggests it takes many hours of play with particular games to fully experience the kinds of embodied learning that Gee and others describe.

1. To help you better understand that experience of video game learning from an insider's perspective (short of many hours of play), you will interview someone who regularly plays one of the more popular games.
   Look closely at the interview questions template in the Project Appendix and focus on adapting questions about insider knowledge: what you would need to know to fully enter the learning in the world of the game and its affinity groups.
2. To help develop context for your analysis of that interview, you will also research a website(s) for gamers to look for common assumptions of this larger "affinity group" of gamers.
   - Where do you see common assumptions between the gamer's knowledge from your interview and the concerns gamers discuss on the websites?

- What can they tell you about the design of the game and its world?
- How do these insider understandings compare to Gee's claims in this chapter?

FOR FURTHER READING

Bucy, Erik P., & Newhagen, John (Eds. 2004). *Media access: Social and psychological dimensions of new technology use.* Mahwah, NJ: Lawrence Earlbaum Press.

Creative Commons Website (alternatives to copyright law). http://creativecommons.org/.

Gee, James. (2003). *What video games tell us about learning and literacy.* New York: Palgrave Macmillan.

Kress, Gunther, & Van Leeuwen Theo. (2001). *Multimodal discourse: The modes and media of contemporary communication.* London: Arnold Press.

Manovich, Lev. (2001). *The language of new media.* Cambridge, MA: MIT Press.

Selfe, Cynthia L., & Hawisher, Gail E. (2004). *Literate lives in the information age: Narratives of literacy from the United States.* Mahwah, NJ: Lawrence Earlbaum Press.

Wysocki, Anne, Johndan Johnson-Eilola, Johndan, Selfe, Cynthia L., & Sirc, Geoffrey. (2004). *Writing new media: Theories and applications for expanding the teaching of composition.* Logan: Utah State University Press.

Project Appendix

Guidelines for
Literacy Projects

1. Participant-Observation Research
of a Field Site

Ethnographers believe one of the best ways to get insider perspectives on literacy in a culture, workplace, or institution is to conduct field research through firsthand participant-observation. This research method can help you understand the social meanings and cultural values people associate with the reading and writing of all kinds of texts (including visual and oral texts) connected to a particular subculture, work setting, context of people's social class, or people's use of particular literacy technologies. Understanding insider perspectives will also help you analyze cultural values in light of larger social contexts. Although we have designed some of the approaches to these research methods, we also acknowledge the influence of Elizabeth Chiseri Strater and Bonnie Sunstein, whose book *FieldWorking* has advanced the use of field research in undergraduate classes.

1. Choose a Field Site

Choose a field site where you can do participant-observation of a clearly identifiable group for which you already have regular easy access, and where some of the group's interactions involve print or visual texts. Though it often helps if you are already a member of this group because you can more easily take a participatory role as well, being an insider is not a requirement. What kind of group you choose will depend on the site of literacy you are researching, whether it is culture, social class, work, or technology. Use the details of the site's chapter to help you decide on a group for your participant observations.

2. Conduct Observations and Take Field Notes

Do two or more observations at your field site of the group and take notes (4+ pages). More than two observations will give you much better data for finding common patterns in the group's literacy behaviors as well as individual variations within these patterns. Observations should usually be at least 30 to 60 minutes, but this depends on your field site.

As you participate in and observe the interactions of the group, write down anything you notice relating to *literacy events* and the *five main elements of literacy* (*text, context, function, participants,* and *motivations*) as discussed in Chapter Three. If you are doing participant-observation in a field site dealing with work, social class, or technology issues, you can also take notes when you observe behaviors related to the concepts from that particular chapter. Although the goal is to ultimately analyze the meanings of literacy practices within the group, it helps to start gathering and noting some general patterns of behavior to later examine for your cultural analysis. Assume that any patterns of behavior might have connections to the group's literacy practices and cultural values. So in addition to taking notes on what you observe about the five elements of literacy, take notes on

> *talk:* what is said, who says it, when, and in what contexts. Which communications are openly stated and which are unspoken? What patterns of language use can you see?
>
> *behaviors:* How do people act and react to each other? Do members act out any "rituals" of expected behavior? What values

might be associated with these behaviors? What might they be saying to each other through their dress, manner, and so on?

power relations: How might people be showing solidarity and/or status through talk and behaviors? How might talk and behaviors relate to different social roles within the group and culture; do they relate to gender or social class or other social positions?

location: How do people relate to the setting(s) they are in? What does it suggest about the values and attitudes of the culture and the individuals in it? How does the setting influence behaviors and talk?

You should have at least two pages of notes for each observation. Since you probably won't know what you are looking for, use abbreviations and any other note-taking strategies to help you quickly capture what you see and hear. If you can't write during the observation, give yourself time immediately afterward to write notes from memory.

3. Write Response Notes

For each of your observations, write a set of response notes (2 pages each) reflecting on each set of your observation notes to help you identify patterns and make sense out of your experience of participant-observation. You should write about any of the following that you can identify from your observation notes:

- Patterns of behavior you witnessed
- Any contradictions in behavior
- What you think are the reasons for the behavior
- Ideas for what to focus on in your next observation
- Questions about what you don't understand

Ideally, at this point you should also interview an insider in the culture to test your hunches about the patterns of behavior and possible meanings related to literacy practices. If you will be conducting interviews along with this field research, see the interviewing project later in the appendix.

4. Analyze Your Field Notes for Cultural Themes

Discuss your "data" in a small group and look for themes related to these literacy practices. The theme or thesis of your field research paper should come from your research and analysis of your data, not something you decide beforehand.

Take out all of your field notes and, using the following questions, mark or highlight notes that refer to these areas. You are looking for patterns to help code your notes.

1. What common patterns of behaviors have you noticed? How might they relate:
   a. To the group's
      - *social structure:* Who has authority? What is the hierarchy of the group?
      - *social networks:* Who communicates most—with whom, when, and why? Who's connected to whom? In what ways and for what purposes?
   b. To different people's use of the space?
   c. To spoken and unspoken meanings of language there?
2. What tensions have you noticed? These might be uncommon behaviors or behaviors that seem different from the cultural norm of the group, community, or institution. If there seem to be no tensions, what factors might account for that?

Based upon this analysis of your data, what might be a theme or thesis to help organize your draft? If stuck, write about the *kinds of knowledge you think are necessary to be considered an insider.* Do some people display that knowledge to show others their solidarity or status within the group? Describe some examples from your observations.

5. Develop Your Draft

You will want to examine common patterns of group literacy practices and how they relate to other behavior, talk, and so on to build a focused argument about the social meanings and cultural values of literacy *as group members might understand it within this cultural context.* To demonstrate and support your claims, describe examples from your field notes and integrate appropriate quotes from your observations.

6. *Option of Secondary Sources*

Drawing on secondary sources, such as the research we summarize in this book or popular sources such as websites or magazines, can help demonstrate how your study relates to a larger social context by either:

- comparing and contrasting similar research studies to your local situation,
- offering evidence to support and confirm your interpretations and descriptions, or
- using other research to develop a conceptual framework, a theory, for your analysis.

Although the number of secondary sources will depend on the nature of your field research, more secondary support of your research will likely strengthen your authority and credibility for your interpretations in the paper.

2. Ethnographic Interviewing

Ethnographic interviewing can help give you more of an insider's perspective on whatever site of literacy you are researching. When you are looking at literacy and mind, for example, it can help you see what assumptions literacy educators tend to hold about the role of literacy in abstract thinking. When you are looking at literacy and culture, it can help you see how the cultural identities people claim for themselves affect the kinds of literacy behaviors they practice in different parts of their lives. When you look at literacy and class, ethnographic interviewing can help you understand how social stratification and expected literacy practices within different class cultures affect people at the level of the individual. When you look at literacy and work, it can give you a more complex view of the power dynamics involved in collaborative processes of writing. Finally, when you look at literacy and technology, ethnographic interviewing can help you better trace people's actual social uses of the literacy technologies within particular contexts.

Interview analysis can also be used to support other kinds of research, such as participant-observation, web or media analysis, and secondary sources on a specific site of literacy.

1. Choose an Interview Consultant

Your choice for whom to interview will depend on which site of literacy you will focus on for the project. For most of the chapters, we have offered some guidelines to help you choose an appropriate "consultant" to interview for that particular site of literacy research. Once you have made your choice, keep in mind that you are asking a favor of this person, and you should allow him or her to choose the times and settings for the interviews.

2. Develop Interview Questions

We have provided a template of interview questions based on James Spradley's work that you can adapt for your purposes. Looking over these questions should help you generate other questions more related to your knowledge of your interviewee and the specific site of literacy that you are researching. We also strongly recommend that you adapt the questions to the communication style of the person you are interviewing, so that your interviewee will feel more comfortable talking with you.

Questions to test your hunches about what you might have observed

(such as particular literacy behaviors, rituals, social structures, power relations)

- Can you describe a time when . . . ?
- Can you give me an example of . . . ?
- When would you say . . . ? To whom?
- How would you respond if . . . ?
- I noticed that _____ was doing _____. Can you tell me what that was about?

Questions to find out people's perspective about things they do related to literacy

- Tell me what you would do during a typical _____.
- Who would you do it with? Talk with? For what purposes?
- Tell me about the different places involved in _____ activity.
- Whom do you associate with/hang around with the most? Why?

Questions to investigate social roles within a group

- If I wanted to be accepted as a member (insider) of the group, what would I need to know? How to act? How to talk? In different places and times? What to watch out for?
- How would you describe your role in the group?
- What makes you part of the group?
- Do you think there is more than one group here?
- If I were new here, what would I *not* notice? What would label me an outsider?
- What would I need to learn that wouldn't necessarily be taught?

Attitudes and values

- How do you feel about being part of this activity?
- What do you like about this group or place? Tell me of a time you particularly enjoyed.
- What do you dislike? Specific examples?
- How do you cope with the problems you find in the group or place?
- What would you want to change about the group or its unspoken social rules?

  As you develop your interview questions, it's useful to recognize the difference between

■ *Open and closed questions*

An open question leaves open the chance for interviewees to narrate their experiences and knowledge in ways that can give you rich data. A closed question closes down further conversation on that particular question. "What reading was important to you during your teen years?" is an open question because it leaves room for the interviewee to narrate events and experiences. In contrast, the question, "When did you first design a PowerPoint presentation?" is a closed question because it has only one possible answer. In general, you want to use mostly open questions because you want to understand the culture or institution from the worldview of those involved in it.

- *Personal and cultural questions*

  If you want to know something about a group, be sure to include the group in the question, as in "What do all employees do on break?" compared to "What do you do on break?" What this person does on break may be very different from the cultural norm of the majority of workers.

3. Interview Your Consultant

When you conduct your interviews, expect to spend 2–4 hours actively interviewing. In general, you should have 20 or more questions, and you should take a conversational approach to the interview, allowing for digressions in the talk that may reveal your interviewee's larger worldview. Be willing to ask follow-up questions that aren't on your list; they often are more productive than what you might have planned to ask. To accomplish this kind of interview takes some time. You should allot 1 to 2 hours for the first interview. You can break up the first interview into two or three smaller time slots if that works better for your consultant and you.

Be sure to carefully record the interviewee's responses *in the language he or she used* as fully as possible. You will want to do one or two shorter follow-up interviews to check out the hunches that emerge when reading over your interview notes and writing your response notes.

4. Write Response Notes

To help build your analysis for your interview paper, we strongly suggest that you keep response/analysis notes for each interview.

After each interview, allow time to write yourself some notes:

- What surprised you?

- What views seemed to confirm and/or contradict your earlier assumptions about this person's literacy experiences in relation to this site of literacy?

- What do you notice about power relations within the interview or previous experiences the consultant discussed with you?

- What do you notice about the language choices your consultant uses?
- What new insights seem to emerge from your interview data?
- What concepts or ideas from the chapter(s) or class discussions can help you to detect patterns in the perspectives from your consultant?

5. Analyze Patterns and Cultural Themes

To help you analyze cultural patterns and themes from your interviews relating to literacy issues, share and examine your various notes in and out of class. In general, this is a process of looking, highlighting, marking, annotating, and looking again, and again. You want to make connections and contrasts with concepts and/or other research from the chapters.

6. Draft Your Interview Paper

In general, assume that you will select one to three particularly interesting aspects from your interviews and analysis notes to develop for your paper.

Although there will be variations of style and structure in everyone's papers, first drafts should include:

- an introduction (which can start with a moment from interviews, a problem drawn from the research, etc.),
- a thesis indicating the analysis your paper will develop in relation to research in this site of literacy studies,
- a discussion of social or cultural patterns of literacy concerns drawn from your interview data, both quoted and/or paraphrased, that supports and develops your main claims in the paper, and
- conclusions that also suggest further research questions raised by your analysis of these specific literacy situations.

7. An Approach to Revising Your Draft

A good way to develop the themes in your revision of the draft is to find further connections between the personal and cultural aspects of a person's experiences with various kinds of literacy.

a. Go through your draft and/or interview notes and highlight each section or point that indicates your interviewee's personal choices, preferences, or actions regarding his or her different literacies, talk, behaviors.

b. Now consider what cultural or social influences may have played a role in these personal choices, preferences, or actions. Depending on your focus for the interview paper, you might consider neighborhood, friends, school, church or other institutions, and/or workplace(s) or social activities the person values.
Write yourself some notes about these possible influences on his or her personal choices and actions.

c. Now write notes on how these settings or groups intersect with particular identity formations, such as (for example) social class, gender, race or ethnicity, region, and/or age.
You may also find that some of these identity formations overlap or conflict with each other in regard to the person's choices and/or actions.

d. Finally, keeping the local cultural or social group(s) and the larger social context of identity formations in mind, ask:
   1. In what ways does this person identify, accommodate, negotiate, and/or resist these groups and larger social identities?
   2. What can these moments suggest about the "social meanings" of these literacy practices in relation to these local and larger social contexts?
   3. What follow-up interview questions for your final draft could help explore and develop these intersections between the personal, cultural, and social meanings of literacy practices?

3. Writing a Memoir Essay Related to a Site of Literacy

Writing a memoir essay can help you consider the significance of literacy events in your life as you narrate moments or events in your life related to a particular site of literacy—whether it be mind, culture, class, work, or technology—to reflect on its meaning in shaping your perspectives. In a memoir, a writer sets out to revisit moments of his or her life to reflect on causes and effects of these moments. Readers of memoir essays do not necessarily read for a "main idea" or an obvious thesis. They read to learn something about the nature of experience by looking at the world through the eyes of another.

In a memoir, you are both a participant writing about *yourself as a character in the event*(s) and an *observer today* reflecting on your actions, beliefs, and values from that time or moment. Writing about yourself as a character from a past perspective demands that you try to capture how you thought, felt, and reacted at that time. As an observer of yourself as a character, you are a more distanced commentator and interpreter of a past self's actions and perspective. A memoir strives for a balance of the two perspectives of historic character and reflective observer.

For this project, narrate a story about an event or moment (or a series of connected events or moments) from your experiences related to the site of literacy featured in a particular chapter. As you write, reflect on what that story (or stories) suggests about your evolving values and perspectives in relation to literacy.

4. Writing a Dialogue on Issues of Literacy

In our first chapter, we examined how the issues involved in standardized testing initiatives like No Child Left Behind could be seen from multiple sites of literacy. One way to consider the implications for multiple perspectives within any of the five sites is to stage a dialogue between different perspectives on a particular aspect of literacy in our world. In his book *Forms of Wondering* (1990), William Covino creates a series of dialogue assignments using the form of dialogues written in ancient Greece and Rome. With Covino's permission, we have reproduced and adapted his dialogue and Play on Word projects here.

Your dialogue must follow these guidelines:

Characters

1. Create at least three or five voices (depending on your class assignment) that represent either:
   - different positions on the issues of literacy in a particular chapter (these positions might come from scholars cited in the chapter and/or various societal views about this site of literacy), or

- different aspects of your own identity that relate to literacy as defined in a particular chapter and/or your different uses of literacy in various settings (such as school, online groups, community organizations).

2. Write a full description (3–4 sentences) of each character/voice at the beginning of the dialogue.

Rules of the Dialogue

3. Each character speaks at least twice, for at least 100 words at each turn.

4. No one "wins"; that is, no one view finally seems more intelligent, persuasive, or inclusive than the others.

How Can Characters Listen and Reconsider?

Often what we call a dialogue in our popular culture becomes a shouting match, as on many talk show debates. In these instances, people only focus on voicing their own position. They do not take time to listen and seriously consider how another's perspective might make them rethink aspects of their own.

As you develop and revise your dialogue, think about how your characters can listen and learn from each other's viewpoints. Look for how they might voice connections, as well as differences, between their experiences and examples. How might those connections help them see and verbally acknowledge some aspect of another view than the one with which they entered the dialogue?

Dialogue Variation: A Two-Act Play on a Word

The title of your play is the word whose definition you will explore. The word you choose should:

- relate to a particular chapter's multiple views of literacy in that site, and

- be open to different definitions of the word's possible meanings.

  1. Choose five different definitions of the same word and create a character to represent each definition. Each character's characteristics (physical appearance, age, sex, background, culture, income, job, manner of speaking) should relate to the definition of this word that he or she represents.

2. Create a realistic scene in which the characters come into contact with one another, and their conflicting definitions create a *problem*. Your play needn't solve the problem, but should indicate what a possible solution to the problem might be.

3. In Act Two, create a different scene that allows for a different problem involving the same characters. Acts One and Two may be independent of each other—Act Two need not be a continuation of Act One.

4. Begin the play by describing each character and the definition each represents. At the beginning of each act, describe the scene in which the act takes place; visualize it, and give some details about the scenery, props, lighting, and so on. If any of the characters are visible at the opening of the act, describe what they are doing and in what manner they are doing it.

5. Writing a Group Manifesto

A manifesto is a document—most often authored by a political group—that boldly declares a set of aims and principles in calling for change. Usually, a manifesto is written for a wide public audience—it's written in strong, straightforward language so that it can be easily understood by many people. Manifestos are most often highly political in their motives and intended effects, and aim to raise public awareness of a pressing situation. The ultimate goal of the manifesto is to move people to action, but a more immediate goal might be to provoke a wider public to learn more about the situation and the group whose mission is to initiate change.

With others in your group, think of a current policy, practice, or predicament involving literacy and create a manifesto in which you describe the current situation and call for change. Your manifesto should have the following components:

- A declaration of the context that gives rise to the manifesto (current situation) and necessitates change,

- A list of critiques, principles, or demands, and

- A statement describing the effects of the changes you're calling for (how the world will be a better place) and/or an exhortation for others to join in the effort.

6. Writing an Advocacy Letter

Nancy Mack, David's colleague at Wright State (and the most innovative writing teacher we know), has developed a repertoire of writing assignments she uses for various situations depending on whether she wants students to engage in critique, inquiry, affirmation, or action. One of Nancy's "action" assignments is the "Advocacy Letter," the purpose of which is "to advocate a specific change that is more ethical than current practice."

As Nancy describes it, the advocacy letter

- Gives a detailed description of the desired change,
- Considers the costs and related effects of the change, and
- Explains long- or short-term benefits.

Working in a group or alone, begin by identifying a local situation (in your school or community) related to literacy policy and practices that you think should change. Your audience can be a person, organization, institutional office, business, or government office. Then, draft a letter in which you suggest a change to the practice or policy you have identified. Be sure to elaborate a rationale for the change and, as indicated, note the costs, benefits, and related possible effects of the change you're recommending.

Bibliography

Chapter One

Brandt, Deborah. (2004, May). Drafting U.S. literacy. *College English, 66*(5).

Cushman, Ellen, Rose, Mike, Kroll, Barry, & Kintgen, Eugene. (2001). *Literacy: A critical sourcebook.* Boston: Bedford-St. Martin's.

Elliot, Scott. (2004, May). Nonhuman factors. *Dayton Daily News, 23*, Sunday City Edition. With Mark Fisher.

Hirsch, E. D. (1988). *Cultural literacy: What every American needs to know.* New York: Vintage.

Overview: Four Pillars of NCLB. (2004, July 1). U.S. Department of Education. Available online at http://www.ed.gov/nclb/overview/intro/4pillars.html.

Pattison, Robert. (1984). *On literacy: The politics of the word from Homer to the age of rock.* New York: Oxford.

President Bush discusses No Child Left Behind and "Reading First." (2004, May 12). White House Press Release. Available online at http://www.whitehouse.gov/news/releases/2004/05/20040512-8.html.

Scribner, Sylvia. (1984, November). Literacy in three metaphors. The development of literacy in the American schools. *American Journal of Education, 93*(1), 6–21.

Chapter Two

10,000 Maniacs. (1990). Cherry tree. *In My Tribe.* Elektra.

Born Yesterday. (1950). Dir. Martin Cukor. Film. Columbia.

Cunningham, Anne, & Stanovich, Keith. (2003, Nov./Dec.). Reading can make you smarter. *Principal: What Principals Need to Know About Reading, 83*(2), 34–39.

Goody, Jack. (1977). What's in a list? In *The Domestication of the Savage Mind.* (pp. 74–111). Cambridge: Cambridge University Press.

Goody, Jack, & Watt, Ian. (1968). The consequences of literacy. In *Literacy in traditional societies* (pp. 27–68). Cambridge: Cambridge University Press.

National Commission on Educational Excellence. (1983). *A Nation at Risk: The imperative on educational reform.* Washington, DC: U.S. Government Printing Office. 1983.

Ong, Walter. (1986). Writing is a technology that restructures thought. In Gerd Baumann (Ed.), *The Written Word: Literacy in Transition.* Oxford: Clarendon Press.

_____. (2002). *Orality and literacy: The technologizing of the word.* London: Routledge.

Plato. Phaedrus. Trans. Benjamin Jowett. Available online at http://www.fordham.edu/halsall/ancient/plato-phaedrus.txt.

Scribner, Sylvia, & Cole, Michael. (1981). *The psychology of literacy.* Cambridge, MA: Harvard University Press.

Stanley and Iris. (1990). Dir. Martin Ritt. Film. MGM.

Chapter Three

Farr, Marcia. (1993). Essayist literacy and other verbal performances. *Written Communication, 1*(10), 4–38.

Heath, Shirley Brice. (1983). *Ways with words: Life, language, and learning in communities and classrooms.* Cambridge, UK: Cambridge University Press.

_____. (2001). Protean shapes in literacy events: Ever-shifting oral and literate traditions. In Eugene R. Kintgen, Barry M. Kroll, & Mike Rose (Eds.), *Literacy: A Critical Sourcebook.* Bedford: St. Martins.

Jenkins, Henry. (1992). *Textual poachers: Television fans and participatory culture.* New York: Routledge.

Mahiri, Jabari. (1998). *Shooting for excellence: African American and youth culture in new century schools.* Urbana, IL: National Council of Teachers of English Press.

Quinones, Sam. (1997, December). Narcocorridos—polka beat, gangsta rap lyrics, top the charts in Mexico's northwest. *Jinn Magazine.* Retrieved August 1, 2007, from http://www.pacificnews.org/jinn/.

Safe. (2004, April 20). *The Shield.* Sony Pictures.

Shuman, Amy. (1986). *Storytelling rights: The uses of oral and written texts by adolescents.* Cambridge, UK: Cambridge University Press.

Street, Brian. (1993). Introduction: The new literacy studies. In *Cross-Cultural Approaches to Literacy.* Cambridge, UK: Cambridge University Press.

Szwed, John. (2001). Ethnography of literacy. in Eugene R. Kintgen, Barry M. Kroll, & Mike Rose (Eds.), *Literacy: A critical sourcebook.* Bedford: St Martins.

Chapter Four

Anyon, Jean. (1980, Fall). Social class and the hidden curriculum of work. *Journal of Education, 162*(1).

Area man constantly mentioning he doesn't own a television. (2003, June 25). *The Onion: America's Finest News Source, 39,* p. 24.

Black, Laurel Johnson. (1995). Stupid rich bastards. In Dews, C. L. Barney, & Carolyn Leste Law (Eds.), *This fine place so far from home: Voices of academics from the working class.* Philadelphia: Temple University Press.

Bourdieu, Pierre. (1987). *Distinction: A social critique of the judgment of taste.* Boston: Harvard University Press.

College. (1999, February 7). *The Sopranos.* Dir. Allen Coulter. Written by David Chase and Jim Manos, Jr. HBO.

Cushman, Ellen. (1998). *The struggle and the tools: Oral and literate strategies in an inner-city community.* New York: SUNY Press.

Freire, Paulo. (1973). *Pedagogy of the oppressed.* Trans. Myra Bergman Ramos. Seabury Press.

Friere, Paulo. (2006). The banking concept of education. In Linda Adler-Kassner (Ed.), *Considering literacy: Reading and writing the educational experience.* New York: Pearson Longman.

Fussel, Paul. (1992). *Class: A guide through the American status system.* Touchstone.

Gardaphe, Fred. (2002). Fresh garbage: The gangster as suburban trickster. In *A Sitdown with the Sopranos: Watching Italian American Culture on T.V.'s Most Talked About Series.* New York: Palgrave McMillan.

Gee, James Paul. (1996). *Social linguistics and literacies: Ideology in discourses* (2nd ed.). New York: Routledge/Falmer.

Gee, James Paul. (2001). Literacy, discourse, and linguistics: Introduction and what is literacy? *Literacy, a Critical Source Book.* New York: Bedford/St. Martins.

Gee, James Paul. (2001). Teenagers in new times: A new literacy studies perspective. [Electronic Version]. *Journal of Adolescent and Adult Literacy, 43*(5).

Gee, James Paul. (2004). *Situated language and learning: A critique of traditional schooling.* New Jersey: Routledge.

Hirsch, E. D. (1988). *Cultural literacy: What every American needs to know.* Vintage.

Hirsch, E. D., Kett, Joseph F., & Trefil, James. (1988). *The dictionary of cultural literacy.* Houghton Mifflin.

Lareau, Annette. (2003). *Unequal childhoods: Class, race, and family life.* Berkeley: University of California Press.

Lindquist, Julie. (2002). *A place to stand: Politics and persuasion in a working-class bar.* New York: Oxford University Press.

Rat Pack. (2004, March 14). *The Sopranos.* Dir. Alan Taylor. Written by David Chase and David Weiner. HBO.

Rose, Mike. (2006). I just wanna be average. In Linda Adler-Kassner (Ed.), *Considering literacy: Reading and writing the educational experience.* New York: Pearson Longman.

Seitz, David. (2004). *Who can afford critical consciousness? Practicing a pedagogy of Humility.* Cresskill, NJ: Hampton Press.

Stuckey, J. Elspeth. (1991). *The violence of literacy.* Portsmouth, NH: Heinemann/ Boynton-Cook.
U.S. Department of Education. (2004, October 1). Prepared remarks for Secretary Paige before the Kiwanis International Leadership Council Meeting. Press Release. Available online at http://www.ed.gov/news/speeches/2004/10/10012004.html.

Chapter Five

Bellifore, Mary Ellen, Defoe, Tracy A., Folinsbee, Sue, Hunter, Judy, & Jackson, Nancy. (2004). *Reading work: Literacies in the new workplace.* Mawah NJ: Lawrence Earlbaum Press.
Boiarsky, Carolyn, & Liggett, Sarah. (1998). Technical and political literacy: Training and communicating in the nuclear power industry. In Mary Sue Garay & Stephen A. Bernhardt (Eds.), *Expanding literacies: English teaching and the new workplace.* Albany, NY: SUNY Press.
Brandt, Deborah. (1998). Sponsors of Literacy. College Composition and Communication, 2(48), 165–185. Literacy sponsorship CCC or CE?
_____. (2005). Writing for a living: Literacy and the knowledge economy. *Written Communication, 22*(2), 166–197.
Cross, Geoffrey. (2000). *Forming the collective mind: A contextual exploration of large scale collaborative writing in industry.* Cresskill, NJ: Hampton Press.
Darrah, Charles. (1997). Complicating the concept of skill requirements: Scenes from a workplace. In Glynda Hull (Ed.), *Changing work, changing workers: Critical perspectives on language, literacy, and skills.* Albany, NY: SUNY Press.
Folinsbee, Sue. (2004). Paperwork as the lifeblood of quality. In M. Bellifore, T. Defoe, S. Folinsbee, & J. Hunter (Eds.), *Reading work: Literacies in the new workplace.* Mahwah, NJ: Lawrence Earlbaum Press.
Gee, James, Hull, Glynda, & Lankshear, Colin. (1996). *The new work order: Behind the language of the new capitalism.* Boulder, CO: Westview Press.
Gung Ho. (1986). Film. Paramount Pictures.
Hull, Glynda. (Ed.). (1997). *Changing work, changing workers: Critical perspectives on language, literacy, and skills.* Albany, NY: SUNY Press.
Hunter, Judy. (2004). Working life and literacies at the Urban Hotel. In M. Bellifore, T. Defoe, S. Folinsbee, & J. Hunter (Eds.), *Reading work: Literacies in the new workplace.* Mahwah, NJ: Lawrence Earlbaum Press.
Office Space. (1999). Film. Twentieth Century Fox.
The Secret of My Success. (1987). Film. Rastar Pictures and Universal Pictures.

Chapter Six

Aoki, Keith, Boyle, James, & Jenkins, Jennifer. (2007, August 16). *Tales of the public domain: Bound by law.* Comic book. Available online at http://www.law.duke.edu/cspd/comics/.
Baron, Dennis. (2001). Pencils to pixels: The stages of literacy technologies. In Eugene R. Kintgen, Barry M. Kroll, & Mike Rose (Eds.), *Literacy: A Critical Sourcebook.* Bedford: St Martins.
Beck, John, & Wade, Mitchell. (2004). *Got game: How the gamer generation is reshaping business forever.* Boston, MA: Harvard Business School Press.
Boisvert, Anne Marie. (2007, August 16). On bricolage: Assembling culture with whatever comes to hand. *HorizonZero Issue 08: REMIX.* Available online at http://www.horizonzero.ca/textsite/remix.
Clanchy, Michael. (1993). *From memory to written record: England 1066–1307.* London: Blackwell Publishing.
Cope, Bill, & Kalantzis, Mary. (Eds.). (2000). *Multiliteracies: Literacy learning and the design of social futures.* London: Routledge.
Crystal, David. (1987). *The Cambridge encyclopedia of language.* Cambridge: Cambridge University Press.
Eternal Sunshine of the Spotless Mind. (2004). Film. Anonymous Content and Focus Pictures.
Gee, James. (2003). *What video games tell us about learning and literacy.* New York: Palgrave Macmillan.
Google announces plan to destroy all information it can't index. (2005). *The Onion, 41,* p. 35. Retrieved August 16, 2007, from http://www.theonion.com.

244 *Bibliography*

Johnson-Eilola, Johndan. (2004). The database and the essay: Understanding composition as articulation. In Anne Wysocki, Johndan Johnson-Eilola, Cynthia L. Selfe, & Geoffrey Sirc (Eds.), *Writing new media: Theories and applications for expanding the teaching of composition.* Logan, UT: Utah State University Press.

Johnson, Steven. (2005). *Everything bad is good for you: How today's popular culture is actually making us smarter.* New York: Riverhead Books.

Lessig, Lawrence. (2002). Free Culture. Keynote talk at OSCON, 2002. Retrieved August 16, 2007, from http://randomfoo.net/oscon/2002/lessig/.

Make Love not Warcraft. (2006, October 4). *South Park.* Comedy Central.

Manovich, Lev. (2001). *The language of new media.* Cambridge, MA: MIT Press.

Manovich, Lev. (2006, November 16). Remix and remixability. *NewMediaFIX.* Retrieved August 16, 2007, from http://newmediafix.net/daily/?p=204.

McCloud, Scott. (1994). *Understanding comics: The invisible art.* New York: Harper.

Negativland's tenents of free appropriation. Retrieved August 16, 2007, from http://www.negativland.com/riaa/tenets.html.

Selfe, Cynthia. (2004). Toward new media texts: Taking up the challenges of visual literacy. In Anne Wysocki, Johndan Johnson-Eilola, Cynthia L. Selfe, & Geoffrey Sirc (Eds.), *Writing new media: Theories and applications for expanding the teaching of composition.* Logan, UT: Utah State University Press.

Tribble, Ivan. (2005, July 28). Bloggers need not apply. *Chronicle of Higher Education.*

Trunk, Penelope. (2006, April 16). Blogs essential to a good career. *Boston Globe.*

The upside of anger. (2005). Film. Media 8 Entertainment and New Line Cinema.

Van Dijk, Jan. (2004). Divides in succession: Possession, skills, and use of new media for societal participation. In Erik P. Bucy & John Newhagen (Eds.), *Media access: Social and psychological dimensions of new technology use.* Mahwah, NJ: Lawrence Earlbaum Press.

Wikiality. (2006, July 30). *The Colbert Report.* Comedy Central. Retrieved August 16, 2007, from http://www.comedycentral.com.

Wysocki, Anne. (2004). Opening new media to writing: Openings and justifications. In Anne Wysocki, Johndan Johnson-Eilola, Cynthia L. Selfe, & Geoffrey Sirc (Eds.), *Writing new media: Theories and applications for expanding the teaching of composition.* Logan, UT: Utah State University Press.

Wysocki, Anne, Johnson-Eilola, Johndan, Selfe, Cynthia L., & Sirc, Geoffrey. (2004). *Writing new media: Theories and applications for expanding the teaching of composition.* Logan: Utah State University Press.

Credits

Index